LIFE AND LETTERS OF
JOEL BARLOW

LIFE AND LETTERS OF
JOEL BARLOW

Poet, Statesman, Philosopher

By Charles Burr Todd

DA CAPO PRESS · NEW YORK · 1970

A Da Capo Press Reprint Edition

This Da Capo Press edition of the *Life and Letters of Joel Barlow* is an unabridged republication of the first edition published in New York and London in 1886.

Library of Congress Catalog Card Number 70-106988

SBN 306-71875-8

Published by Da Capo Press
A Division of Plenum Publishing Corporation
227 West 17th Street, New York, N.Y. 10011
All Rights Reserved

Manufactured in the United States of America

LIFE AND LETTERS OF
JOEL BARLOW

JOEL BARLOW.

J. Barlow

LIFE AND LETTERS

OF

JOEL BARLOW, LL.D.

POET, STATESMAN, PHILOSOPHER

WITH EXTRACTS FROM HIS WORKS AND HITHERTO
UNPUBLISHED POEMS

BY

CHARLES BURR TODD

"*The author of the Columbiad and the Hasty-Pudding was a man of might
in his day, and will not pass out of literature or history.*"—STEDMAN.

NEW YORK & LONDON
G. P. PUTNAM'S SONS
The Knickerbocker Press
1886

INTRODUCTORY NOTE.

THE great men of the post-Revolutionary age were not, as a rule, versatile. Their development was largely in one direction—statesmanship. Jefferson, it is true, shone both as a statesman and philosopher; so did Franklin: but it would be difficult to carry the parallel farther. There was one, however, among this group of worthies who excelled in at least three great departments of human effort—in statesmanship, letters, and philosophy—and whose practical talents were perhaps greater than those of any of his cotemporaries. That man was Joel Barlow, the subject of these pages. His verse first gave American poetry a standing abroad. His prose writing contributed largely to the triumph of Republicanism in 1800. He was the first American cosmopolite, and twice made use of his position to avert from his country a threatened foreign war. He was the godfather of the steamboat and canal, and sponsor with Jefferson of our present magnificent system of internal improvements, while had he been permitted to carry out his grand idea of a national university it is safe to say that American art, letters, science, and mechanics would now be on a much more advanced and satisfactory footing.

His biography has never been written. This is not strange, for it is only recently that the story of any of the great Republican leaders has been fairly and honestly told. In Barlow's case there were special difficulties in the way. He was cut off suddenly, in a foreign land, before what he regarded as his crowning work was completed. He left no children to gather up and preserve his literary remains, and after a short time material for a biography could be collected only after long and tiresome research; then after it was collected, properly to present so many-sided a career involved grave literary difficulties.

The writer admits that the present work is the fruit of his interest in his subject—an interest arising rather from propinquity than from any particular sympathy with the poet's political or religious views.

Born and reared almost in sight of Barlow's birth-place, the writer early became interested in his history, and with the knowledge of so much that was really noble and useful in his career, came the desire to present it fairly and honestly to his countrymen. After he had been engaged on the work for several years, the death of Prof. Lemuel G. Olmsted, a grandnephew of the poet, placed at his disposal the vast mass of Barlow's literary remains, which that gentleman had accumulated by fifty years of painstaking labor. These letters and papers, after having been carefully sifted, have been freely used, and form the bulk of the volume. In preparing the work the aim of the writer has been to give details rather than generalizations; to present his subject as he lived rather than ideally, and to this end he has told his story, wherever practicable, by the letters and writings of his subject.

The author regrets that he cannot acknowledge all the favors received in the prosecution of his labors. He is especially indebted to the Astor Library; to Professor F. B. Dexter, of Yale College; to Miss Ada J. Todd, of the Bridgeport High-School, for the translation of the French letters, and to S. L. M. Barlow, Esq., of New York, the present owner of the Olmsted collection, by whom it was freely placed at the author's disposal, together with his own private collection of Barlowana.

C. B. T.

New York, *December*, 1885.

JOEL BARLOW.

CHAPTER I.

1754–1778.

In Fairfield County, in south-western Connecticut, near
the New York border, lies the quiet rural town of Redding,—a town founded by one of the most distinguished
jurists of the Massachusetts Colony—John Read—and
settled by the choicest of that "sifted wheat" for which,
to the sowing of New England, three kingdoms were
winnowed. The place is rich in all that could fashion or
stimulate poetic fancy.

It is situated on the lower slope of the beautiful hill-
country of Connecticut. Its salient features are three
great parallel ridges running north and south and separated by deep valleys, the channels of watercourses.
Westward, the tumbled masses of the Taghkanics, hill beyond hill, rise from the deep valley of the Saugatuck. In
summer, all the accessories of the pastoral—green fields,
furrowed hills, thick wood, deep glen, and foaming cas-
cades—were to be found here; nor were historic scenes
and points of interest wanting to lend them dignity. On
the westernmost of these ridges, barely eight miles from
the granite pillar separating New York from Connecticut,
in a long-roofed farmhouse, Joel Barlow was born. The
Barlows were what is known in Connecticut as " good
stock," that is, they were respectable landholders, paid
their tithes promptly, and gave no one occasion to speak

ill of them. Samuel Barlow, the poet's father, was de-
scended from John Barlow, of Fairfield, who first appears
in that town about 1668. Samuel removed to Redding
about 1740, and on the death of his first wife married, in
1744, Esther, daughter of Nathaniel Hull, a member of a
family which gave to the American navy one of its
brightest ornaments. Her fourth son was Joel, the poet,
born March 24, 1754. The boy owed his bias toward a
liberal career, it is said, primarily, to an unconquerable
passion for rhyming, which manifested itself while he was
among his books, and secondarily, to the Rev. Nathaniel
Bartlett, pastor of the village church which his parents
attended. Fully to make our meaning clear it will be
necessary to notice briefly the state of society in his
native town at this period ; this was highly oligarchical, as
throughout New England at that time ; a few " first families " were the ruling element in both church and state.
Social privileges and distinctions were rigidly observed.
The pews were " dignified," and assigned to families according to their tax-lists and social position—the patri-
cians beneath the pulpit, the plebeians nearer the door;
while the Burrs, Reeds, Sanfords, Hulls, Herons, and
other first families exacted a homage from the common-
alty the same in kind if not in degree with that paid the
English squire by his dependents. The central figure in
such a parish was the clergyman ; he was priest, teacher,
oracle, monitor in manners and morals. Happy was it
when the man was not dwarfed by the office. In the
case of Parson Bartlett this was not the case. Wise with
such learning as the Yale College of that day could furnish, eloquent, unaffectedly and simply pious, possessed
of rare tact, he presided over the church in Redding for
fifty years, including the stormy days of the Revolution,
with such dignity and moderation that no breath of
calumny or whisper of complaint arose, and he only
yielded up his trust at the command of death. To his
parochial duties the clergyman added those of the ped-

agogue, maintaining a " select school," which attained a
high degree of excellence, insomuch that it secured a foreign constituency. Parson Bartlett, like most educated
men of his day, was ardently looking forward to the advent
of a national poet, and certain pencillings of verse by the
lad which fell into his hands awakened in his breast the
liveliest interest in their author. He at once declared
that the boy's talent should be fostered and stimulated
by a liberal training and contact with other minds. The
parents interposed no objection—in such a case the minister's word was law—and the lad was soon conning his
Alphas, Betas, Kappas, under the direction of Parson
Bartlett himself. His progress seems to have been
rapid, for in a year's time his preceptor declared he could
take him no farther, and began looking for a school in
which he might be fitted for matriculation.

There was at this time a school at Hanover, N. H., recently instituted on a charity foundation, chiefly to train
young men for the ministry, or as missionaries to the
Indians, and here the lad was placed, no doubt because
of the leanness of his father's purse. Boys educated at
this school generally matriculated at Dartmouth College,
and at the Commencement of 1774 we find Barlow en-
rolled in the freshman class of that institution. The
death of his father, soon after, placed quite a little patrimony at his disposal, and he determined to avail himself
of the superior advantages of Yale. These, judged by
modern standards, were ridiculously small. Two small
buildings and a chapel were all that the pretty campus
could then boast. The college butler was still an institution, and the students were still gathered in the Commons Hall, under the eye of tutors. A few young members of the faculty, by strenuous efforts, had just succeeded
in admitting English composition and oratory to a curriculum which had before embraced only the dead languages, mathematics, philosophy, and polemic divinity.
Poetry, belles-lettres, and the modern languages were

largely ignored, the commencement poem having only
come in with the graduation of such favorites of the
Muse as Trumbull and Dwight. To offset this, however,
there was Dr. Daggett at the head of affairs, and such men
among the professors and tutors as Timothy Dwight,
Abraham Baldwin, and Joseph Buckminster. The latter
was the young poet's favorite, and, as we shall have occasion to note, exerted a greater influence over his mind
than the remainder of the faculty combined. The class
which he entered, that of 1778, was remarkable for the
calibre of its members. It is evident that he who excelled in mental rivalry with Oliver Wolcott, Noah
Webster, Zephaniah Swift, Uriah Tracy, and Josiah
Meigs possessed undoubted talent, and the necessary
application to bring it into play.

Of the poet's college course, though covering a pregnant and exciting period, we have only meagre details.
The American Revolution opened during his first year
in the cloisters, yet of the many letters that must have
been written to his friends from college we have but one
containing any reference to this subject. July 6, 1775,
he wrote his mother, " The students are sensibly affected
with the unhappy situation of public affairs, which is a
great hinderance to their studies, and for that reason there
has been talk of dismissing college ; but whether they
will is uncertain." The college was not dismissed, however, except for a brief period in 1777, when the pupils
were scattered, the junior class (Barlow's) being sent to
Glastonbury, Conn., in charge of tutor Buckminster, but
in deference to the unhappy condition of the country
no public commencement was held during the war. Barlow himself did not enter the army, although four of his
brothers did, one dying in the service, and another,
Aaron, rising to the rank of colonel ; but during the long
summer vacations he more than once joined his brothers
in the field, and twice at least saw active service—once in
the sharp engagement at Long Island, and again at

White Plains. This period was one of almost as great activity in the affairs of the college as of the country: the transition from the narrow, pedantic training of the old regime to the broader, fuller curriculum of Trumbull and Dwight was being effected, and it is evident, from the nature of the poet, that he must have taken a deep interest in the success of the innovations. Two other traits of character marked this period in his career—a deep devotion to the Muses, and a fitting appreciation of the charms of the lovely young women whose beauty illumined the somewhat sombre atmosphere of the little university town. Scraps of the poetry written at this time were collected and sacredly preserved by Mrs. Barlow after their marriage, and remain to pleasantly indicate these efforts of budding genius. There were amorous epistles in verse, sentimental addresses in the Coryn and Phyllis style, scraps of song and madrigal.*

One of these ladies had the honor of ensnaring the poet's heart, insomuch that they were engaged to be married before his college career ended. Her name was Ruth Baldwin. She was not so high in worldly station as the poet might fairly have aspired to: it was whispered over more than one tea-table, that the President's

---

* Some of these were melodious, though manifest imitations—the following, for instance, "To a Young Lady":

> "Go, Rose, my Chloe's bosom grace!
>   How happy should I prove,
> Might I supply that envied place
>   With never fading love;
> There, Phœnix-like, beneath her eye,
> Involved in fragrance, burn and die.

> " Know, hapless flower, that thou shalt find
>   More fragrant roses there;
> I see thy withering head reclined
>   With envy and despair:
> One common fate we both must prove—
> You die with envy, I with love."

daughter had set her cap for him. Michael Baldwin, her father, had begun life as the village blacksmith in Guilford, and a few years before had removed to New Haven with two objects in view—the enlargement of his business, and the education of his children. The family was, however, a remarkably intellectual one. There were three sons—Abraham, Dudley, and Henry—and three daughters—Ruth, Clara, and Lucy. All three of the sons graduated at Yale College and became eminent. Abraham was a man of undoubted talent, and in the hands of a republican purveyor of history would have figured as one of the leading characters of his day. He filled the office of Senator from Georgia for several terms with great ability. He aided Milledge in founding Georgia University and drew up its charter, and the task of drafting the famous Constitution of 1787 was committed to him, his success in that work earning him the soubriquet of " the Father of the Constitution." Dudley studied law and settled at Greenfield, Conn., and acquired great reputation as a lawyer. Henry also studied law, settled in Pittsburg, and became an associate justice of the Supreme Court of the United States. Ruth to great personal beauty added a piquancy of manner and amiability of character that afterward made her an object of adoration in the polite circles of Europe. She inspired in the poet's breast a remarkable passion, one that survived all the mutations of a most adventurous career, and glowed as fervently at fifty as at twenty-five. The elder brother of this lady, Abraham Baldwin, was a tutor in the college during a part of Barlow's term, and often invited the poet to his home, where the attachment was formed.

Barlow's standing at college is satisfactorily shown by the fact that the coveted honor of delivering the commencement poem was awarded him. The term "commencement poem" is, however, a misnomer, the poem having been delivered at the last examination of the senior year, which occurred in 1778, on the 23d of July.

During the war, as has been remarked, no public com-
mencements were held, the graduating exercises being
limited to the conferring of degrees. There was, however, a public exhibition in the college chapel at the closing examination of the senior year, and it was on this
occasion that the poem was delivered and its author first
introduced to the public. The programme for that day,
as printed in the newspapers of the next week, introduced other members of the poet's class who later became known to fame; it read as follows:—

A Cliosophic Oration in Latin, by Sir Meigs.

A Poetical Composition in English, by Sir Barlow.

*A Dialogue in English, by Sir Chaplin, Sir Ely, and Sir
Miller.*

A Cliosophic Oration in English, by Sir Webster.

*A Disputation in English, by Sir Swift, Sir Wolcott, and
Sir Smith.*

A Valedictory Oration in English, by Sir Tracy.

An Anthem.

This programme was carried out in the presence of the
President, fellows, students, and a large body of invited
guests. The poem followed the salutatory, and from contemporary notices seems to have been one of the features of the occasion. With rare good judgment, the
poet had chosen a theme of the deepest interest to his
audience, the return of peace and the glorious future it
presaged for Columbia. For the poem the reader is referred to Dr. Smith's work. It would be regarded as a
respectable effort for commencement day even now, but in
the paucity of poets which then existed, it was received
with the highest marks of favor. The newspapers printed
it with commendatory notices: it soon appeared in pamphlet form, and finally reached the summit of a fugitive

poem's career by being embalmed in Dr. Smith's collection of American Poems, published at Litchfield, Conn., in 1793.

A few days later the associations of four stirring years were sundered, and the young men departed to win fame and fortune in a wider arena. A bright future awaited some of them. It was perhaps the strongest class that Yale had ever graduated. Most of its members made a respectable figure in society, and there were several who achieved national fame. Sir Webster became the great lexicographer, Noah Webster ; Sir Swift — Zephaniah Swift—Chief Justice of Connecticut and Member of Congress; Sir Tracy—Uriah Tracy—the famous jurist and statesman ; Sir Meigs — Josiah Meigs — President of Georgia University and a well known educator, and Sir Wolcott—Oliver Wolcott—Washington's Secretary of the Treasury after Hamilton, and later, Governor of Connecticut. These brave young spirits emerged from the cloisters, parchments in hand, and little else wherewith to begin the battle of life. With the exception of Wolcott, they were without money or friends. Our hero's patrimony had been expended in his education, and although, by the death of his mother in 1775, he had fallen heir to a small sum, he was sensible that his bread in the near future depended on his own exertions. Marriage, and a home too, were promised him as soon as he could command a settled position in life. His desires all centred in a literary career. His commencement poem was only the *initium*, the nucleus of a great patriotic epic which had already taken shape in his mind, and to which he longed to devote the best powers of mind and body. But the gaunt wolf—poverty—which has dogged the steps of almost every man of genius, confronted him. Literature, so poorly rewarded in our day, was far less remunerative then. The most sanguine could see no prospect of bread-winning in it. The poet's fancies, if indulged at all, must be pursued in connection with some avocation that would afford support and the necessary leisure. Divinity and a tutorship in the college were the only two professions which seemed at all conducive to this end. Barlow's friends recommended the former, as being, all things considered, the most lucrative, congenial, and least exacting: none of his friends urged this with more vehemence than his former tutor, the Rev. Joseph Buckminster, now settled over the North Church in Portsmouth, N. H., as successor to Dr. Stiles, and who seems to have formed a very high opinion of the capacities of his pupil. Barlow, however, shrunk from the sacred calling; he doubted his fitness for its grave responsibilities. But a tutorship in the college he ardently desired; he expected it, since it was the custom of the corporation to thus honor students who had won distinction in the course, and he spent two years at New Haven in post-graduate studies, waiting for the honor which never came, supporting himself in the mean time by fitting a class of boys for college. The failure undoubtedly engendered a bitterness toward his Alma Mater which time never wholly effaced. His chief correspondents during this crucial period were Mr. Buckminster, Noah Webster—who on leaving college had taken a school at Glastonbury, Conn.—and Miss Baldwin. The letters from Mr. Buckminster were the most important and interesting. This gentleman, who will be remembered as one of the most eloquent and liberal divines of his day, and the father of Joseph Stevens Buckminster, of Boston, a leader in the Unitarian movement of the succeeding generation, on leaving his tutorship at Yale had accepted, as before remarked, a call to the old North Church at Portsmouth, N. H., a connection which terminated only with his death thirty-three years later. Certain letters addressed by him to Barlow at this time materially encouraged the poet to continue his literary efforts, and were largely responsible for his later successes. We present them seriatim.

CHAPTER II.

1778–1780.

"PORTSMOUTH, *Oct.* 5, 1778.

"I RECEIVED under cover from our worthy friend, Mr. Baldwin, two of your poems upon the Prospect of Peace, with an intimation that you desired they might be conveyed in that way. I am very much obliged to you for them, but not so much as I should have been had they been accompanied with a letter from you. I am sure you are not so little acquainted with my disposition, or my particular tenderness for your class and for you, as to think that a letter would not have been particularly agreeable. The long acquaintance I have had with your class, the many favors I have received from them, the particular tenderness and respect with which most of them have treated me, joined to the peculiar share of genius and merit with which, as a class, they were distinguished, have begotten and cherished such feelings in me as time can never totally remove, and as I never shall feel for any other members of society. . . . Your poem does you honor in this part of the country, and every person that has seen it speaks very highly of it. It is particularly agreeable to me, perhaps because my vanity would assume part of the merit, as it grew up, in a sort, under my auspices. But I am so little of a poet that I think the smallest share only is thus due to me. I advise you to encourage and cultivate your turn for poetry. I should think myself particularly honored if you will favor me with a view of some of your fugitive lucubrations. . . ."

He wrote again, March 9, 1779:—"I am exceedingly pleased with your letter, and the rather, as it intimated

that your mind is not idle, but that you are at least med-
itating something above the common level. Efforts of
genius are ever to be commended, and it is in that way
that we are to expect any improvement in those things
which ennoble human nature. Your sentiments respecting divinity give me some reason to hope that you will
make that your study. I certainly hope to see you in
the sacred desk. . . . I ever encouraged freedom of inquiry in your class, and though it sometimes occasioned
me a little difficulty, I never repented it. In the sacred
history you will find a variety of subjects which will assure a field for your poetic genius, and that which you
mention is by far the most interesting and affecting; but
I fear you poets are so fond of fiction, that in writing upon
this you would introduce rather too much of it to suit
the solemnity of the subject, or please the serious and
devout heart. The history of Joseph has never had justice done it in poetry that I have seen; of Cain and Abel,
in which a little machinery and fiction would do very
well ; of Daniel, and a variety of others. If you will be
kind enough to send along some of your poetic lucubrations, I shall esteem it a particular mark of friendship."

The poet's reply has not been preserved. The correspondence continued, and, in a succeeding letter, Mr.
Buckminster returned to the subject as follows :—

" I am glad you have not given up the design of attempting something in poetry, and your " Vision of Columbus "
I fancy must be interesting and improving. You will be
kind enough to give me the plan at some time or other.
I wish you might obtain a place where you might attend
principally to this poem till it was finished, and happy
should I be to recommend a family in this part of the
country which would be agreeable to you ; but the times
have reduced our best characters to moderate means of
subsistence, and those that are now rising are but mush-
room gentry, and knowing but little of learning themselves, they are but little anxious that their children

should know more. I believe, my dear friend, unless
something unexpected opens, you must follow the advice
I gave you, perhaps twelve months past, and with the
help of a few sermons support yourself in application to
your proposed poem for a time. But let me hear still further from you upon this matter, and I will endeavor to
digest my thoughts upon this subject." And again, Dec.
26, 1779: " I have not yet had much time to turn my attention to your plan for the poem styled, ' The Vision of
Columbus,' but will soon, and give you my thoughts
upon it with my wonted freedom. The few lines that
you have subjoined increase my desire of your having leisure to complete your wishes, for I think they give us reason to believe that you will answer all reasonable expectations. . . . I believe I could procure something of a subscription for you here among several gentlemen of liberality if you desired it ; and if there is any prospect of your
being able to pursue your plan write to me particularly,
and you may be assured of all possible assistance." And
again, Jan. 11, 1780: "The marks of sincerity and confidence that I discover in it (the letter) give me peculiar
pleasure, and I shall be very happy if I can be instrumental in promoting your interests at this frightful distance. I find you feel as young men usually do upon receiving the honors of college, and going out into *the
world*, as it is termed. Were I to say all I think of your
abilities, you would, perhaps, judge it flattery, and your
fondness for the quiet scenes of literature will perhaps
be productive of something that will hereafter do you
honor and benefit mankind. . . . I think a number of
years may be as profitably spent at college after a person
has received its honors as before, and especially at Yale
with its present governors. Your President is a most
worthy man ; he is a living library, a fund of good humor
and sociability, and you may always obtain from him
something new and useful. Mr. Baldwin is as improving
a companion as you will ever find.

"If you will allow me to advise, you will be contented with your present circumstances, and pay a general attention to all branches of education: you may pay a more particular attention to that which best suits your humor and inclination. This seems to be poetry, and you modestly intimate a scruple whether you have anything more than an inclination.

"I believe you are the only person that has this scruple who has seen the 'Prospect of Peace.' . . . But you must remember that neither our country nor our countrymen are sufficiently refined, enriched, and improved to give a sufficient support to works of genius merely, and had you the genius of a Pope or a Milton, nay, as much superior as you wish, you might starve upon the pittance that a few persons capable of relishing your productions would give. Persons that give themselves up to the Muses must have a patron, and if you have a ———— either in your own pocket or elsewhere, you may make this desideratum for yourself. The question then arises, which of the learned professions is the most favorable to the Muses? I don't hesitate to pronounce, it is the ministry. The study of the law is dry, far from insuring refined or ennobling sentiments or feelings; that of physic we should think would inspire tender and sympathetic feelings, but experience contradicts our theory. Divinity contains the most sublime subjects, the most elevated thoughts and exalted ideas, and in the Bible we shall find poetry that has never been equalled by mere man, and forces from us the confession that it is the breathing of a God. . . . The work of the ministry will afford you the fairest opportunity of indulging your poetic genius, and you will find connected with its study the noblest subjects to excite it."

The following July he wrote in reference to the plan of the "Vision of Columbus" which Barlow had submitted to him :

"I forget whether I have written since you were kind

enough to favor me with your plan for the 'Vision of Columbus'; if I have, I was not prepared to make any considerable observations upon it. I have in some of my leisure hours, which are very few, turned my attention to it. I have read it, with the sample you were kind enough to transcribe, to several gentlemen, to procure their sentiments: they all approve and applaud, wish to see it executed, and encourage pretty raised expectations. For my own part, I am exceedingly pleased with it, and long for the execution with all the avidity that my attachment to you, to Yalensia, and the fine arts can inspire. You will perhaps find in your progress that the plan may in some parts be abridged and others will want enlargement; some of the articles may be too trivial to need a particular description, and will only be hinted at or their places supplied with some others. In the contents of the second book, as they stand in your letter, you have supposed the reformation in religion to be the effect of the discovery of America. Though it might be the means of reviving learning, and perhaps awakening an attention to the rights of mankind, yet I think the reformation in religion must be ascribed to a different cause; but perhaps it may be justified by the license of the poets. I have no kind of hesitancy as to your poetic ability to execute your plan so far as that can go, but it requires an amazing, universal knowledge to treat of the great variety of articles that you propose. A man must be not only a poet and man of letters, but a lawyer, politician, physician, divine, chemist, natural historian, and an adept in all the fine arts. Your knowledge in all these branches is as great as any person of your age and advantages, but you must depend, I presume, in some of those branches upon those who have turned their particular attention to them. You will need to be careful in your choice. Another article that you will need particularly to attend to is the choice of those in whose judgment and criticism you can confide. You must be open to

all, and the more observations you have made, whether in
a way of praise or blame, the better; but you will not let
them influence you greatly, for you will find the tastes
of mankind as different as their faces. There was never
yet a sentence written but what somebody thought
might be altered to advantage, and in your large design
what touches upon any person's profession every one
will think he has a right to judge. It will be of advantage to you to have a select number in whom you can
confide to assist you, but do not confide so much in any
as to give up entirely your own opinion, unless in some
article where they have had greatly the advantage. Be
open to conviction; keep your eyes, your ears, and your
heart open; note what is well said by those in the lower
walks of life, and be unmoved by what is ill said, though
the person be ever so distinguished."

The poem on which all these fears and hopes were
based was the " Vision of Columbus," the first important
poem distinctively American in subject and authorship
ever projected, and which had so far taken form in the
author's mind that in the summer of 1779 an elaborate
draft of it was drawn up at Northampton, Mass., whither
business of an unknown nature had taken him. This
draft was as follows :

"THE VISION OF COLUMBUS.

" A plan for a poem on the subject of America at large,
designed to exhibit the importance of this country in
every point of view as the noblest and most elevated part
of the earth, and reserved to be (the) last and greatest
theatre for the improvement of mankind in every article
in which they are capable of improvement. The poem
will be rather of the philosophic than epic kind. The
machinery is simple, and it is hoped will be natural. As
an angel is employed in unfolding these scenes to
Columbus, nothing ought to be mentioned but what is

important to the happiness of mankind, of whom these superior beings are always considered as the guardians. The circumstances of Columbus after his last return from America are well known to be (to have been) very melancholy. Queen Isabella, his only benefactress, is dead. The King refuses to fulfil the contract upon which the discoveries were undertaken. The unfortunate, after a life of toil and disappointment for the good of mankind, is deserted by his friends and insulted by his enemies. In this situation the poem opens.

"*Book* 1st.—Condition of Columbus. Night. Columbus' lamentation. Appearance and speech of the angel. His message to Columbus (is) to repay his toils by representing the importance of them. They ascend a mountain that looks westward over the Atlantic. The continent of America draws into vision. General appearance of America. Description of the Andes and other mountains through the continent. Seas and coasts, rivers, lakes, forests, valleys, soil, fruits, flowers, air, predominancy of cold, animals.

"*Book* 2d.—Manners of the natives. A philosophical account of their constitution. Cause of the dissimilarity of nations. Wars of the natives. Hunting. Food and clothing. Education of their children. Arts of the natives. Their civilization — religion. The Esquimaux. Mexico. Peru. Story of Mango Capac.

"*Book* 3d.—New face of things throughout America occasioned by the toils of Columbus in the introduction of Europeans. Effect of this in Europe. It enlarges the human mind and throws mankind into a different system of political interests. Its effect in the revival of learning in Europe, freedom of inquiry, civil liberty, reformation in religion, and happiness of mankind. Meantime the southern continent fades into obscurity with the rest of the world and the vision is confined to the northern continent.

"*Book* 4th.—Arts of utility and domestic life. Buildings, towns, manufactures, clothing, iron, sulphur, salt-petre, medical inventions. Mercurial inoculation. Husbandry. Commerce.

"*Book* 5*th.*—Wars down as far as the present day, with some particular descriptions.

"*Book* 6*th.*—Political arts. Police of every particular colony. General confederation. Independence. Foreign negotiation which introduces some reflections upon civil government in general and the progress of society.

"*Book* 7*th.*—Liberal arts. Gardening, architecture, painting, fine writing. Mineral, mechanical, electrical and astronomical. Philosophy. Moral philosophy and religion.

"*Book* 8*th.*—Invocation for the unfolding of a more general and important scene. The particular articles which in the preceding books are traced as far down as the present day, are here thrown into a general view and carried into futurity. General view of science. Its use in exalting reason to its proper dignity over the passions. Female sex. Their importance in a moral view. Misery occasioned to mankind for want of attention to them. Their future progress in the advancement of science and happiness.

"*Book* 9*th.*—Philosophy of the human mind. Nature of God. Connection and necessary happiness of the intelligent universe. This happiness interrupted with respect to man. Promotion of this happiness a complete system of religion, as it is the end of all revelation and the complete duty of man. Deism, superstition. Future progress of society. Happy effect of an open communication of all nations, as it will promote an assimilation of manners, a liberality of sentiment, a union of interests, and a union of language. This will make the acquisition of knowledge more easy, policy more mild and extensive, wars less frequent, the earth more populous and cultivated and human nature more glorious.

"NORTHAMPTON,
    "*Aug.*, 1779."

We shall presently follow this plan to its fruition. While it is being formulated, the reader will remember, the author is at Yale College, pursuing post-graduate studies, writing poetry, taking tea with young and old ladies, ripening his acquaintance with Miss Baldwin, at whose father's house he boarded, and eking out slender finances by tutoring the scions of wealthy families in the city. Sundry letters to his college chum, Noah Webster, and to Miss Baldwin during her frequent absences, give pleasant glimpses of his life and thoughts during this period. On the first letter to Webster the latter has endorsed: "I was keeping school in Glastonbury (Ct.), the first school I undertook after leaving college." The letter is dated Jan. 30, 1779. "You and I," he wrote, "are not the first in the world who have broken loose from college without friends and without fortune to push us into public notice. Let us show the world a few more examples of men standing upon their own merit and rising in spite of obstacles. I have too much confidence in your merits, both as to greatness of genius and goodness of heart, to suppose that your actions are not to be conspicuous; and I hope you have too much confidence in my friendship to suppose that I don't speak from the heart. We are now citizens of the world in pursuit of different interests, no longer in circumstances of warming the soul and refining the sensibility by those nameless incidents that attend college connection. Let us lay flattery wholly aside, and improve our friendship and refine our tastes by a serious correspondence. I am yet at a loss for an employment for life, and unhappy in this state of suspense. The American Republic is a fine theatre for the display of merit of every kind. If ever virtue is to be rewarded it is in America. Literary accomplishments will not be so much noticed till some time after the settlement of peace, and the people become more refined. More blustering characters must bear sway at present, and the hardy veterans must retire from the field before the philosopher can retire to the closet. I don't feel as if I ever should enter upon either of the learned professions for a livelihood. I move at present in as regular a sphere as if I was governed by Sir Isaac Newton's laws; my circuit is from new college to old, and from old to Mr. Baldwin's for study, school-keeping and eating, all which movements are regularly pointed out by my inclinations, my poverty, and my appetite. I have, however, some irregular movements. I spend every evening in ladies' company; this I call an eccentricity in my orbit. I wish I could say something upon politics, which I think is necessary for every man. I think, however, the civil dissensions you mention are a necessary evil in a republic. I am at a loss whether they are really for the disadvantage of the community or not. They enlighten the common people and make them better judges of public characters. This will make candidates for public honors more cautious and more faithful. The author of 'Common Sense,' it seems, has felt too secure and important. Had he been cautioned a year ago that America was as independent in sentiment as he would represent her in his policy, he would probably have continued in office and deserved the honors we were willing to bestow upon him. His removal will make room for others, and his example will be their caution. Respecting your request, I have but few copies of the 'Prospect of Peace' left. I will, however, send you three or four the first chance I get."

Webster's reply called out another letter on the same general subject.

"Yours of the 17th I received by post. It breathes kindness like yourself and considerably reinspires my ambition. It won't require the accuracy of a meteorological instrument to give an account of my feelings since your good genius first led me into thoughts of my present plans. Hopes and fears succeed one another very frequently, though the former are generally very weak, and I cannot but think your friendship for me induces you to be too sanguine in your expectations. My obligation to you is as extensive as your good wishes can be, and if ever I succeed in this way, I shall always consider you as the foundation of all my good fortune. At present, I must own, my prospects are clouded. Mr. Perkins treats me like a gentleman and a man of sense. He expressed his diffidence with respect to the generosity of people, and appeared to be very frank and friendly. I received a letter from him to-day with my papers that I had left with him. He has now entirely given up the matter and advises me to go into business for a living, and make poetry only an amusement for leisure hours, as the most that can be expected from our countrymen in this age is ' Be ye warmed and be ye filled.' These leisure hours will never come to me after I am buried in business for life. I am now willing to devote the heat of youthful imagination to these objects; if that cannot be done, I shall give it up forever. I am determined to make every effort within the reach of modesty this fall. Mr. Lockwood and Mr. Atwater are as zealously my friends as I could wish. They have seen your letters, and they will engage the President in my favor, as he has always been friendly to me. You are sensible that the matter is delicate,* and you must be careful of saying too much or driving too fast. I shall tarry at New Haven till I hear from you, which must be by next post. . . ."

The reader is by no means to infer, however, that grand designs alone occupied the poet during this period. His was a versatile mind, and glided without friction from the discussing polemics and theology with grave professors to the gossip and merry badinage of belles and beaux. Letters of the period show him to have been a favorite in society. His letters to his lady-love, many of which lie before the writer, prove him to have been an ardent, tender, impassioned lover,—qualities, we may remark,

---

* Of the tutorship.

which distinguished him to the end of life. The reader may be curious to know how a lover thought and wrote in 1779, and so, deprecating criticism, we include a few extracts. They will be given to an appreciative audience, for only the scholarly and refined will be interested in this story of a poet's trials and triumphs.

On one occasion the lady is visiting in North Guilford, and the swain affects to be jealous.

" Do, Ruthy, tell me sincerely," he urged, " don't some of those mountain swains invite you to ramble in their green retreats, entertain you with fine stories about Arcadian nymphs and rural innocence? Don't you never rest half raised in silent attention on a bed of gold, to hear some gentle Alexis tell how Apollo became a shepherd, and led the same course of life that they do? how he became angry with Jupiter because he raised thunder-storms to vail the face of the sun? how he went and killed the Cyclops because they made thunderbolts for Jupiter? how these Cyclops were Vulcan's journeymen, and that, enraged at Apollo, Vulcan went limping up to heaven and complained to Jupiter? Jupiter immediately kicks Apollo out, and leaving the chariot of the sun he went to keeping sheep on earth. He taught the shepherds all these fine Arcadian schemes, taught them to relish the sweets of rural innocence, and introduced the golden age. I tell you, Ruthy, you must be on your guard; these stories will be told with all the persuasive arts of eloquence and music, so you will be induced to imitate the example of Apollo, quit the chariot of your beauty as he did that of the sun and turn your attention to the humble pursuit of rustic sports. But you must remember, *ma amie*, that your old friend Apollo was a poet as well as shepherd, and in winter time the most likely place to find him will be at college, so I advise you to return to New Haven as soon as you receive this letter. . . ."

The following are interesting for their local and personal gossip. July 26, 1779, he wrote to Miss Baldwin from Middletown :

"I have a happy moment this morning to devote to you, and I can do it with all the eagerness of a Persian when he addresses the rising sun, and I wish I could do it in as visible a manner. The bearer, Miss Fowler, will tell you what a fine family dance we had last night at Capt. Starr's. I came from New Haven yesterday ; am now with Meigs, who sends love to you. I am going to Hartford this morning ; shall return to New Haven next week, either after my things or else to stay at New Haven for the winter. My prospects are as uncertain as ever. . . ."

And the same day, from Hartford: "Saturday I came as far as Wethersfield, and drank tea at Col. Beldrige's with Mr. Lockwood and his sister, then rode into Hartford to Mrs. Whitman's, where I am intending to stay till Tuesday morning: this is Monday afternoon : Betsey Stiles is coming here to drink tea. Mr. Lockwood and Betsey say they will certainly come and see you pretty soon, and I wish you would come up here with them. I wish you to spend as much time in this town as you can : you may depend on being treated well. Besides the company here, Sammy Lyman, of Litchfield, will be at Mr. Ellsworth's all summer. I dined with him and Webster yesterday and to-day."

From Redding, where Putnam's division of the Continental army had just gone into winter quarters, he wrote in October, 1779:

"I had the happiness, when I came into Redding, of meeting both your brothers at Gen. Parsons'. Dudley went off Sunday morning. Abraham* preached, to the great approbation of Mr. Bartlett's little flock. I spent that day with him, and Monday morning he came to mingle souls along with me at my brother's. We drank,

---

* Now a chaplain in the army.

and dined, and talked politics with my brother till after noon. Then, to speak in the Arcadian style, we retired to a wild autumnal grove back of the home lot. In this grove the ground is so accustomed to rise to see people pass in the road at some distance, that it now overlooks the country round, and the valleys have so long acknowledged its eminence that geographers won't call it a hill. The leaves kept constantly falling from the trees to give us as good a prospect as possible. To a fancy as lively as yours this situation won't appear romantic. But our romance was of a more serious kind : we received no aid from the situation, except being out of hearing of other folks. We built castles much higher than the hill, and wanted nothing to support them but a little of the mammon of this world—the pursuit of which for any other reason than to make virtuous people happy I most heartily despise. I spent the day with infinite satisfaction, and now I part with the dear man as the body parts with the soul. I tarried at General Wolcott's six days ; they are all alive in Litchfield. I am not determined what I shall do this winter, or where I shall live."

CHAPTER III.

1780–1783.

THE uncertainty as to his prospects, indicated in the
last letter, continued into the summer of 1780. Toward
the end of this summer he was commissioned a chaplain
in Poor's Brigade of the Massachusetts line, and in September joined the brigade, then engaged in guarding the
passes of the Hudson. Motives both of patriotism and
self-interest prompted him to this step, the army being
then sadly in need of able and properly qualified chap-
lains. He evidently took the step with reluctance, and
chiefly from the solicitations of friends. Some of these
are indicated in a series of letters from Abraham Baldwin, then a chaplain in Putnam's division, and which
also contain pleasant descriptions of camp-scenes and an
interesting allusion to the "Vision of Columbus." The
first is dated in May, 1779, at Redding, where the division had wintered. "To-day," wrote the future senator,
"we have been over to General Putnam's to a splendid
entertainment, which, if I should use you as they frequently do the public, I should describe to you at large
as to guests, covers, toasts, and music, but shall only tell
you in all that it was very agreeable, such as you might
expect from a collection of careless, friendly, sensible
gentlemen whose plan of life precludes any great multi-
plicity of interests and vexations, and permits them to
enjoy each other. Major Putnam was fitting for a journey through New Haven. I have stolen a few minutes
to write you by him. . . . I doubt not you have frequently thought of me since my sudden elopement, how
I made out, how enjoyed myself, etc. The plan and
scene of action you are but too well acquainted with.

My particular situation is in a very agreeable family, who treat me with every mark of friendship and respect. The General will not fail in inclination to make me happy here, and it is in his power. We are about three miles from the brigade and visit them once a day. I have a retired study to myself when I please, a very clever set of company in the house, whom I can enjoy at any time. . . . . There have been two general reviews, parade, salutations, firing, etc. Yesterday a very grand one. What will be the plan for the summer campaign is not at all known in this quarter. The generals have just received letters from generals Washington and Greene, which I have read. They say nothing determinate. It was before conjectured the movement would be to the northward. Guards and baggage were called in for that purpose, but the word now is to wait further orders. They will get into tents in a few days,—rather suppose the encampment will be below here, in Wilton. Perhaps there will not be a move from here for some time. If so, I will write you when college collects. That seems yet to be my only home; but if a person sees clever things one way, that is no reason why he should never look another." The letter ends : " *There are several commissions vacant in this brigade ; the General asked me to recommend some good fellows to him. If you know of any, write me. It will be determined soon.*"

In March, 1780, he thus returned to the attack, with an allusion to the poem, writing from the camps on the Hudson : " You tell me that you are very choice in your company, and talk very little with anything clothed in flesh-and-blood and grosser than spirits—that you can raise ghosts, apparitions and folks dead for centuries, and everything in that way but the devil. All I have to say is, remember Salem, beware of the ghost of Cotton Mather or any of his descendants. . . . I doubt not your plan gives you an elegant and refined pleasure in the pursuit of it. That part of the profit is certain and is no inconsiderable one to a person determined to enjoy himself. I fear your circumstances will oblige you to hurry matters more than you would choose. Hoard it if possible. It is to live forever : therefore follow nature and let it have a long youth. Can't you lay some plan for business which will support you and yet allow you to prosecute this? The plan is for you to come and be chaplain for our other brigade, for I have them both to preach to. Bishop Ellis is not here, and it is a chance if he joins again. Depend upon it, there is not a situation in the army that would be more agreeable to your turn. You would be happy in it ; you could get matter and work it up, and do just as you pleased. If you won't believe me, come and see. I will engage to make you happy, a little while at least.

" You ask me for family and state anecdotes to weave into your ' Vision.' I have come across several, which, if properly volatilized, sublimated, etc., in your poetical alembic, I doubt not might make a pretty little relish between some of the dishes of your entertainment. There is the story of the second unfortunate colony, which came to Virginia under Mr. John White in 1587, and was never after heard of. There were no traces of their being destroyed ; by some inscriptions found ten or twelve years after, it was supposed they moved off, and has given ground to the conjecture that they may have given rise to a set of inhabitants which will yet be discovered in the western parts. The character of Captain John Smith I will recommend to your attention. It was uncommon before he came to America. In the war between the Germans and Turks he was taken prisoner, carried into Turkey, and subjected to an interesting variety of fortunes. But in the first settlement of America he was a capital character. Without him it scarcely seems that a settlement would have been effected. You will find much said of him in Hakluyt's ' Voyages and

Discoveries,' a respectable clergyman in the reign of Elizabeth, who is very particular upon those times."

After instancing the story of Pocahontas, Colonel Beverly's " History of Virginia," and Thomas Hariot's treatise on Raleigh's dominions, the letter proceeds: "I have got acquainted this winter with Mr. Kemble, father to General Gage's lady, who before Whig and Tory times was a principal character here, and have had the fingering of his books. He is a native of Smyrna, but is now a Tory of New Jersey. Be that as it may, I have got much satisfaction from him. He tells me the best account he has ever seen of this continent is in the *New American Magazine* for the years 1758–59. It also contains the travels of Mr. Thomas Gage through the greater part of South America, finished about the year 1740. You may perhaps find them among some of our curious geniuses. President Stiles can tell you about it. . . ." Barlow seems to have listened to the proposition, for, May 2d, his friend wrote that he had set the necessary wheels in motion to secure his appointment. " I know it would be highly agreeable to the officers of the brigade," he says, " for they feel a pride in showing out in those ways. Here is Stark's Brigade in our neighborhood which I often visit, and as worthy a one as any in the army. It is composed of Webb's, Jackson's, Angel's, and Sherburn's regiments. They have never had a chaplain. The difficulty in the way there is, S—— himself is a goose-head, and you would not be happy in his family. The regiments are not of the line of any state, are therefore continually diminishing, and in no way to be recruited. The General, I believe, will not return to them again. There is a committee of Congress coming here, whom they expect to take the matters of this brigade. If they get a clever fellow for a general and are put upon a good footing, it will be as clever a post as there is in the army."

July 2d he wrote again, his letter containing an interesting reference to Colonel Humphreys, the poet.

" I am very sorry you have been obliged to wait in suspense when everything was fixed to your mind, and you left the only person to put in motion. We conversed with the commandant and a number of the officers of the brigade ; they all expressed themselves well pleased ; the commandant said you should have an appointment whenever you pleased. Parson Hitchcock, who belongs to one of their brigades, said it would be best for you to make them a visit first, the sooner the better, and take your appointment when you pleased. Hitchcock is a very clever fellow, and interested himself to have you come. His brigade and yours always lie together; he wants a good man to be company for him. We wrote you this immediately after our arrival here from New Haven. The purport was to have you take a letter from the President to introduce you to Hitchcock, which would not be bad to have him show to the officers of the brigade, and with that come on as soon as was convenient. Come as soon as you can, Joel, prepared to preach or not, as you like best, you know I shall be glad to see you. Our friend Humphreys is appointed aid to His Excellency.* Show us a better man."

These arrangements were successful, and two months later the poet received his appointment as chaplain in Poor's Brigade of the Massachusetts Line. His life in the army, covering a period of three years, was one of the most interesting epochs in his career. We shall describe it, first, generally, and then more particularly by means of a series of interesting letters written his wife and other friends. The duties of the continental chaplain do not seem to have been onerous. Abraham Baldwin writes his sister Ruth in 1781, that he has as much leisure and feels as cleverly as ever. " I read French, write, and

---

* General Washington.

make visits from morning till night, and then sleep from
night till morning," he continues. Preaching one sermon
on a Sunday—attending a funeral or a wedding, he
might have added—made up the sum of his duties. To
Barlow, however, the period was one of intense intellectual
effort. In addition to his professional duties he was hard
at work on his poem, and in conjunction with his friends
Humphreys and Dwight, both of whom were in the army
at this time, the former as aid, the latter as chaplain, he
wrote a series of stirring lyrics, designed to stimulate and
encourage the ranks, and improve their *esprit* as well as
morals. Not sufficient importance has been given the
minnesingers of the Revolution by our historians. Their
number was much greater than has been supposed. Mr.
Moore, in his " Songs and Ballads of the Revolution," has
preserved ninety-two of their fugitive pieces; but they
by no means include all: " The Ballad of Nathan Hale,"
Dr. Hopkinson's " Battle of the Kegs," and the scathing
satires of Philip Freneau remain to prove the effective-
ness of these warriors of the pen. But the majority were
produced for the occasion, and after being repeated from
mouth to mouth perished with those who used them.
This fate seems to have overtaken the productions of
our triumvirate, scarcely one of their fugitive pieces having been preserved.*

---

* One was discovered among the earlier efforts of the poet, preserved by
his wife. It has no date, but was evidently written to celebrate Burgoyne's
defeat. The following are the opening stanzas and chorus:

> " While scenes of transport every heart inspire,
> The Muse, too, triumphs in her kindling fire.
> Blest in their bliss, she lifts a bolder wing,
> Aids every wish and tunes the harp to sing;
> To their glad concert wakes the accordant strain
> And mingles with the music of the plain.

> " ' Joy to the Bands,' her voice arose,
> ' Who chained that veteran host of foes;
> Who bade Britannia's glory fade
> And placed the wreath on fair Columbia's head.'

Having now a settled position the poet thought he might safely marry : the lady blushingly consented, but the father was obdurate.   He had never had as high an opinion of the rhyming lover as his daughter and sons, and now refused consent to the marriage on the ground that the candidate's prospects would scarcely warrant it. No arguments that the lover urged could change his purpose, and the latter resolved on bolder measures.   In January, 1781, while the army lay in winter quarters, he paid a visit to New Haven, and on the 26th the couple were privately married, the marriage having been kept a secret from all for nearly a year, though there is among the letters evidence that the young wife was restive and ill at ease under the weight of her secret.   When it was finally discovered, the husband wrote a manly letter to the wronged father, containing as ingenious a defense of an indefensible action as was ever penned.   And so, to

---

CHORUS.

" ' Hail the day and mark it well :
Then the scourge of Freedom fell,
Then your dawning glory shone,—
Mark it, Freeman ! 'tis your own.

" ' Now recount your toils with pleasure,
View the strife and sum the treasure ;
Run the battles o'er again,
Sound the charge and sweep the plain ;
Here behold the foe pursuing—
How he drives his headlong way,
Whelming towns and realms in ruin,
Sure to seize the distant prey.
False and faithless tribes adore him,
Join the shout and yield him room.
Now, Albania, fall before him—
Now, Rebellion, learn your doom.' "

The concluding stanza is as follows :

" Then every glad blessing thy country can lend
When her foes and her slaughters shall cease,
Shall arise to the Hero who bade her ascend
To conquest, to glory, and peace."

the burdens of his office and his ambition while in the army our hero added a husband's fears and anxieties.

In the letter to his sister before quoted, Abraham Baldwin pokes fun in his quiet way at these distractions. "Poor Joel has been over here looking for opportunities to send to you these ten days. He hears of one, hurries home and writes his letter—when he returns the man is gone! A few days after, I sent to him for his letters, but he must wait to write a new cover, and when they come the opportunity is lost again; this has happened about every other day this week past. I have now sent after them again, and hope, in mercy to the unhappy man destined at last to be the bearer of such multiplied and mighty materials, they will come soon, and not saddle the poor man with a weight of copies more burdensome than though he carried the original himself with the love, sighs, dreams, heart, and meat all together. The packet, even if it comes now, I believe will be like Dick's patched jacket, eighteen thicknesses." These letters we shall next consider and transcribe somewhat in full, both from the pleasant glimpses they give of the minutiæ of the camp, and as tending to interest the reader thus early in the fortunes of the young people. The first is dated "Near Paramus, Sept. 11, 1780."

"I have just returned from making a visitation to my brigade. Brother Bram (Abraham) and I have been the grand rounds to-day through all the encampment, which is about four miles in length, in a fine open country between Hackensack and Paramus. We have visited all our friends, which are very numerous, and have had a happy day with them. I was detained at Redding some days and did not arrive at camp till Saturday night. I lodged in a tent on a bed of bark that wet night; next day found Abram; we agreed to live together in houses as long as the army kept together. Monday, the army marched from that place to this, a few miles. Here, with getting wet and my fatigue, and by eating too much fruit,

I got cleverly sick and really felt quite ill for two or three days, when I began to see that that was nothing to the purpose.   On Thursday evening I began to open my mouth, which is none of the smallest, and out of it there went a noise which the brigade received as the duty of my office.   On Sunday, or rather on the Sabbath, I gave them a preachment, and will you believe, Ruthy, I was flattered afterward by some of the most sensible hearers with the great merit of the performance.   I know you will ask me how I made out; I really did well, far beyond my expectations, and I find it all a joke, as much as Cassius did, to be in awe of such a thing as myself.   I now feel hearty and well, and begin to grow fat and talk Dutch. Yesterday the funeral of General Poor was attended with great solemnity and military parade.   All the officers of the army—perhaps five hundred in number—with a regiment of infantry and a regiment of dragoons, marched in procession, with a large band of music playing the funeral march.   In the first rank the deceased general's horse was led with his usual trappings, his saddle and holsters, and boots fitted in the stirrups with no rider.   In this situation the horse was a perfect picture of bereavement, and the most striking object that could be imagined; then followed the corpse with his sword and pistols hanging on the coffin, then the particular mourners, the two regiments, the officers, beginning with the juniors, while His Excellency closed the procession, which was about a mile long and extremely slow.   Parson Evans gave us an oration at the grave, and these were the last honors paid an exceeding worthy character.   I then was introduced to several gentlemen of the first merit, and was treated with particular attention by General Greene, who, I find, is reckoned the second character on the continent.   After all my bad feelings I have certainly done right in coming with the army.   My duty is extremely easy and is not disagreeable; they certainly treat me with attention. Colonel Bailey, our commandant, is a good, easy, sensible man. In short, Ruthy, I will say but one word farther about myself separate from you, and that is this following, viz.: that I sit here half asleep at a Dutchman's table, with brother Abram snoring by my side."

CAMP NEAR HACKENSACK, *Monday.*

"Yesterday I had another preachment, which kept me awake awhile—whether it had the same effect upon others I am not certain. I expect Mr. Lockwood along in a few days, when, if I don't have a good long letter, I shall flog somebody. Perhaps I shall think he has thrown the letter away if he don't bring me one, in order to carry out his plans with you. By the way, tell Dudley between him and me Lockwood will undoubtedly join the army. Tell me about your commencement-time, whether you were happy, because I contemplated you all that morning flashing away in a dance so gay and so busy that you scarcely rayed a thought so far as New Jersey, but after you returned home, you sweet girl, I know you thought of me. . . . Enjoy what friends you can pick up, but put little confidence in the generality of them ; and as for the work, let it slide, for it never does *good folks* but very little good. . . . Abraham's little general is come, and he and I will separate, though not very distant."

Sept. 23, 1780.

"This is Saturday afternoon. I have fixed my magazine for to-morrow, and my thoughts are at liberty to dwell upon their favorite object, the centre of all my happiness. We have to-day made a move back from Hackensack to an old encampment here near the river, where I have taken lodgings in an old Dutchman's bedroom, as snug as a poker, and have as good a study as ever lived. Since Abram has gone into the General's mess I have come in with my commandant, as hearty and as clever as you could wish. The worst difficulty is, the

Sabbath days come rather too thick: there will be one upon my heels now before I finish this letter. . . . On Tuesday Mr. Lockwood gave me your dear good letter and told me a thousand clever stories about you, as he knew it would make me feel happy to hear your praises; he made us a good visit and is gone on. The way is open for him to join the army and he will leave college this fall, but the corporation are so cunning that Dudley can have no advantage of it. . . .

"My dear, it is now Monday morning. I have left that blank in the line for Sunday, when I had no feelings worth communicating, except a few anxious thoughts about the preachment, which I made in a great Dutch barn. This is the third sermon I have given them and I feel pretty well about it. We are going this day to see a grand parade of the whole army, which will be worth my attention. We have fourteen brigades lying upon this ground in a pleasant country, and they don't make a bad figure. I shall see Bram and shall probably find a conveyance for this paper, if I can find nonsense enough to fill it. . . . . The two great articles of your attention will be to make yourself agreeable to others and agreeable to yourself, or in other words to *improve* and be *happy*. I have no doubt but you will attend to these. The only way to be happy is to think you are so—you have many of the materials and will undoubtedly find more. With regard to improvement, only aim at the two grand objects of dignity and ease, and let them be carried to perfection and traced into all their consequences; they will comprehend all the graces of *manner* that you need attend to. We must be careful that *stiffness* is not assumed for *dignity* nor a trifling littleness for ease; but dignity and ease united and softened into a lady's character are a great ornament, and I know no place where they make a happier concert than they do sometimes in my Ruthy. . . . It is now Monday evening, my love. Billy Little came in and broke me off in the forenoon to go to the parade, which was indeed grand. He sends love to his sister. Abram sends his boy this minute for my commands to New Haven, and I finish my letter in a flutter. I must tell you one word: here is a pair of folks requesting to be joined in matrimony this evening. I have been advising them to suspend the matter a few days, as it is but one day since they ever saw each other; but they will take no denial. They are here in my study and I must link them, but I'll warrant you I'll not kiss the bride. Oh, Ruthy! do laugh at me."

ORANGETOWN, *Oct. 2.*

" I had written so far when General Pattison and Mr. Hutchins called, and I have been since to attend the execution of Major André, Adjutant-General of the British army, hanged as a spy. A politer gentleman, or a greater character of his age, perhaps is not alive. He was twenty-eight years old. He was dressed completely and suffered with calmness and cheerfulness. With an appearance of philosophy and heroism, he observed that he was buoyed above the fear of death by the consciousness that every action of his life had been honorable; that in a few minutes he should be out of all pleasure or pain. Whether he has altered his mind, or whether he has any mind, is now best known to himself. My heart is thrown into a flutter, my dear, at the sight. My situation in the army grows more and more agreeable. I am as hearty and as healthy as I can be in your absence. I gave them a preachment yesterday for the fourth time—a flaming political sermon, occasioned by the treachery of Arnold. I had a number of gentlemen from the other brigades, and I am told it did me great honor. My vanity will show you that I write just as I think. I had a billet last week from General Greene to dine with him. There were a number of gentlemen, etc. . . . ."

NOTOWAY, *Oct.* 10.

" My feelings with regard to myself are very easy. I grow fat and handsome as well as you. . . . I am *here* sitting in this window in just such a Dutch bedroom as I had before. I have the knack of turning Dutch folks out of their bedrooms—but they love to oblige the *Domine.* Tell my wife, Nancy, that I shall soon get so Dutchified that I never will have a Yankee wife. I have never seen an English woman since I crossed the river. . . .

" A beautiful morning, my dear. I am just called up to a fine breakfast of butter and honey, which we generally have with our tea. But I gladly leave it to steal an interview with my Ruthy, or rather a *view*, which is greatly obscured by a distance of one hundred and twenty miles."

NOTOWAY, *Oct.* 18.

" I grow more fleshy and more happy, or I should be more happy if I could make you happy. My prospects for my poem are better now than ever. I shall have more leisure than I expected, and in winter shall have scarcely any interruption if I choose to pursue the plan. I intend to take winter quarters in the vicinity of camp, wherever it may be, and set Quamminy to work like a sprite all winter.

" I will tell you more about it when I see you. Yesterday the Rev. Mr. Claremont * had a billet from General Washington to dine. How do you think I felt when the greatest man on earth placed me at his right hand, with Lord Stirling at his left, at table ? I graced the table with a good grace, and felt perfectly easy and happy. There were many gentlemen there. You must allow me a little vanity in these descriptions because the scenes are new. Since the preaching of my sermon upon the treason of Arnold and the glory of America, several gentlemen who did not hear it, and some who did, have

---

* One of Barlow's aliases.

been to read it. They talk of printing it. Colonel Humphreys has made me promise to loan him the plan and the first book of my poem to read at headquarters. He and many other friends pay me particular attention. . . . My dear, it is now Sunday evening. I have been preaching to the Connecticut folks to-day, exchanging with Abram. I shall stay in camp but one more Sunday evening, and the next after, whose arms do you think will be open to receive me? Our Colonel Bailey says I must go and preach in his own town of Hanover in the Bay State this winter. I wonder whether I shall. We have news from the northward that Colonel Brown, classmate of Colonel Humphreys, is killed in a skirmish on the Mohawk River; his party, however, gained a considerable victory. The loss of Brown is much lamented: he was a promising character, and as worthy an officer as any of his rank."

LITCHFIELD, *Dec.* 19, 1780.

"I have been these four days in Litchfield, enjoying some of the best friends I have in the world. . . . This is a blank of three days. It is Friday morning. I have preached at Redding and this place since I saw you, and shall have to do it again if I stay here another Sunday. I am uncertain whether I shall make myself happy at camp this winter on account of accommodations. If I cannot, I am determined to return either to this town or to Hartford. If this is the case, I am determined that you shall be with me or near me The people are uncommonly sociable and friendly, and you would spend as happy a winter here as at Hartford."

During this absence from camp he visited New London, and offered his fair correspondent these observations on the town: "I have spent a good evening with the Miss Thomsons and am now at liberty to make as many philosophical remarks upon the people of New London as I please. They attend more to commerce than any

town in this state. This branch of business polishes
the mind to a certain extent, yet, as it leads the whole
body of the people into a constant pursuit of gain in one
particular way, it leads the mind to a particular narrow-
ness of thought, which always prevents any eccentric exertions of giving, and superinduces an illiberal turn of
mind. This is exemplified in Holland. A Dutchman's
brain is said to be too fat for the play of genius or refine-
ment of taste. This is truly the case here. The price
of insurance and the property of a good sailing-vessel are
the usual topics, and sailors are the greatest pedants in
the world. . . ."

The next summer was largely spent with the army, but
in the mass of letters we find none of general interest except the following description of life in the camp:

CAMP *not* ON GALLOWS HILL.
October 16, 1781.

" I wish I could tell you how we live here ; it would be a
curious description to one who never saw it. What do
you think of my not having sat two minutes by a fire this
fall ? What do you think of a thin *tow tabernacle* that
trembles at every breath of air, spread out upon the cold
ground, affording a free passage for moons and stars and
suns and dews and rains and winds, where I can lie and
count the stars all night ? It was by this contrivance that
the old shepherds at Babylon became the greatest astron-
omers in the world. I want nothing but Father Atwater's
celestial globe, and a little of his patience, and a few warm
blankets (of which I bought one to-day in addition to one
I had before), to enable me to call all the constellations by
name, and become an accurate star-gazer. One thing is
apt to obstruct my nightly visions : John has been fixing a crotch at each end of my bed, about six feet high,
on which he has laid a pole. This pole supports a
small tent, which depends on each side of the bed to the
ground. This he calls curtains, hence it is evident that I

have two thicknesses of linen cloth between me and heaven. This will not only keep off the dew, but it will prevent my counting the stars—at least, without some difficulty. And lastly, what do you think of Ben Welles' sitting here reading poetry while I write to Ruthy. We all live grandly and feel well. To-morrow brings the memorable 17th of October. We have invited about 80 officers to dine, among whom is General Heath and a number of grandees. Letters are received this day from General Washington, informing us that Lord Cornwallis is closely besieged; that he has left several of his outposts, and has retired to his inner works. The General says it is probable his Lordship's resistance will be very obstinate; that he commands six thousand regular troops, and that he will not resign so respectable a force without being pushed to the last necessity. The events of this month I think the most capital that ever America saw. We long to have them known."

The succeeding winter was spent almost entirely in Redding, at the house of his brother, Col. Aaron Barlow.* He was hard at work on his poem. Frequent references to it occur in his letters, but the most interesting is in a letter from Abraham Baldwin to his sister Ruth, dated Greenfield, Jan. 23, 1782.

"On my way hither," he writes, " I made a long and happy visit to our friend (Barlow), and must tell you, as you are somewhat interested, that I never was more pleased with him in my life. He is certainly one of the worthiest and best lads in the world. He never did that which will be to the world a greater proof of it than this winter. He has not written less than sixteen hundred lines within these eight weeks, and as good as ever was. I believe from my soul he will get the palm from every one of our geniuses. The burden of the work he will go

---

* The house is still standing and inhabited, a brown, long-roofed structure on the banks of the Saugatuck, in West Redding.

through with this winter, so that I imagine it will do to open his subscriptions next summer. He has also written an elegy on Mr. Hosmer,* one of the best in that kind of writing, which I have done him the honor to pronounce not inferior to Gray's, or any of the rest of those who are already consigned to immortality. I tell him to print it immediately. I congratulate you and your brothers on this connection." On Barlow's return to camp the next summer (1782) he found nothing being talked of but a speedy peace, which he is " fully confident will take place." " In that case," he sagely remarks, " furloughs will become fashionable, and I shall go to Philadelphia much earlier than I had expected." His object in visiting that city, then the centre of the publishing interest, was to secure subscriptions for his poem, and probably to secure a publisher. A few days later he writes that he is busy preparing the subscription papers, and getting letters to Philadelphia " which were absolutely necessary, and must be had then or never." At length, on the 24th of October, 1782, he is able to write from camp:

"General Lincoln rides to-morrow morning to Philadelphia, and I go with him under the most favorable auspices. Many circumstances have occurred here since I left you which have assisted my affairs beyond my expectations. The subscription here is likely to be more extensive than I expected. I have more and better letters to carry, and indeed every wish I have formed upon the matter is likely to be more than answered. General Lincoln treats me with the greatest friendship, and promises me a most favorable introduction at Philadelphia."

Before setting out, however, he received and answered a letter from his old friend, Noah Webster, who, during the four years which had elapsed since his graduation, had been employed in school-teaching, first at Glastonbury, and later at Hartford, Conn., and Goshen, N. Y. His

---

* Titus Hosmer, Member of Congress.

genius had also been developing, and in this letter he unfolded a scheme on which he had been long brooding, and which ripened soon after into his "Grammatical Institute of the English Language." This book was an improvement on Dilworth's "New Guide to the English Tongue," then in general use in our schools, and the forerunner of the famous Dictionary. Any one who will take the trouble to examine the "Grammatical Institute," or read Mr. Scudder's description of it in his "Life of Webster," will see that several of the suggestions given in the following letter from Barlow were heeded.

CAMP, *Aug* 31, 1782.

"DEAR WEBSTER :—Your agreeable favor of the 25th is received by Mr. Lockwood. Poh! I am all aground now. I don't mean that Mr. Lockwood received it, I mean that I received it, and I can assure you, my good friend, I am extremely happy in being so kindly remembered by one whom I hold so dear—one to whom I am bound by gratitude as well as by many other tender ties, which it is my ambition to feel and acknowledge. Neither has neglect nor forgetfulness been the occasion of my silence, but I have been most intensely employed. This has obliged me to forego the most agreeable amusement of my life, writing letters of friendship to those who are entitled to my tenderest attention. I most heartily feel for you, my Webster, in everything you feel as a misfortune, though perhaps they are not really such which wear that appearance. Your perseverance will certainly overcome them. You will gain from them experience in the knowledge of human life, and be ready to relish better fortune when it shall appear. We are all a pack of poor dogs. I have half worn out my life in buffeting my destiny, and all I have got for it is the knack of keeping up my spirits, letting the world slide, and hoping for better days. I like your plan about Dilworth ; it will be useful and successful in the world at large if you can make it useful to yourself.

Your attempting it is an expression of that benevolence to your fellow-creatures which I know you to possess: but it is a work of labor, and you ought to make something by it. You know our country is prejudiced in favor of old Dilworth, the nurse of us all, and it will be difficult to turn their attention from it; you know, too, that the printers make large impressions of it and afford it very cheap.

"Now if you make an impression, unless it be very large, you can't afford it so cheap as they do: even if you get nothing for your copy, if it is large the novelty of the book will make it lie upon your hands. If the impression is small, the greatness of your necessary price will be another reason why it will lie upon your hands. I once ventured an impression of Lowth and lost half the cost and all my labor. However, yours is a thing more generally wanted, and the risk may not be so great. I only suggest these facts for your caution. If you contract with your printers upon good terms, or take some other cautious plan, you may make advantage from the design. I wish well to the plan. Dilworth's grammatical plan is much worse than nothing. It holds up a scarecrow in the English language, and lads once lugged into it when young are afraid of all kinds of grammar all their days after. I will help you to what knowledge I can upon the subject you mention. But it appears to me at first thought that the names of places, except a few of the most noted, will not be useful to be spelled out by children. I would prefer filling a few pages with detached pieces of American history, or some other history, or geography. However, this by the bye. It is a happy thought and it comes cheap."

His letters from Philadelphia, describing the journey and his reception there, are interesting. Under date of November 2d, he writes: "On the morning after I wrote you from Peekskill, which was Friday morning, I left camp with my friend General Lincoln and my friend

Mr. Pierce, Paymaster-General. We had a most delightful time of it, except one wet day and one Sunday, each of which we rode forty miles. The whole length of New Jersey is through one of the most delightful countries in the world. The towns of Hackensack, Newark, Elizabethtown, Brunswick, Princeton, and Trenton, extending in a direct line from the Hudson to the Delaware, are beautiful villages, some larger and some smaller than our Wethersfield. We passed along this fine road from King's Ferry to this city, one hundred and thirty miles, without any remarkable occurrence except friendship, merriment, and philosophy, which the General dealt out in large rations, and which I endeavored to return to the best advantage. The worst of it was we got into several very learned disputes, which are yet unsettled, but which we are to adjudge before I return. He is really one of our first characters, and he is as amiable as he is great. You know he is *Secretary at War,* which gives him the superintendence of all the military arrangements of America. But that by the bye. My reception here is quite as favorable as I ever expected. I am treated with civility by the great, with formality by the many, and with friendship by the few. I am rather agreeably disappointed in the general character of the town. There doesn't appear to me that extravagance, that haughtiness, or idleness which I have heard represented. There is a mixture of all nations and all creatures; they serve to correct each other. The polite circles are easy, thoughtless, and agreeable. I don't think there is that affectation by any means which we find in Boston and many places of less report. They have a strange knack of turning day to night, and the contrary. It is common in splendid entertainments not to sit down to dinner till candle-lighting. *Monday evening.*—I have been to the post-office, and, you dear girl, to my great surprise I find no letter, though the post came to-day. . . . The post comes from New Haven to Danbury, there falls in with the

Fishkill post, which is direct; so there is a direct conveyance in six days, or from Tuesday till the next Monday,
from you to me. . . . My business here, I think, will
succeed to my wishes."

In a second letter, dated November 12, he returns to
the subject: "My reception is flattering beyond our
expectations. Not only those gentlemen to whom I had
letters, which were fifteen in number, but many others
of the first and greatest character, offer the matter the
warmest encouragement, and think that they and their
country will be more indebted to me than I to them.
This, you see, depends upon my judgment, which is not
unbiassed by vanity. The possibility that this letter may
be lost or opened prevents my being particular about my
prospects here; but this be assured of, they are good, and
extensive beyond our hopes."

There is no further reference in the letters to this visit
to Philadelphia.

The winter of 1782–83 was spent by the young couple
in their own hired house in Hartford, Barlow employing
himself in the revision of his poem, and in securing a subscription-list large enough to warrant its publication.
Presumably, he also entered on the study of the law,
toward which, rather than to divinity, his thoughts were
now tending. This is the more probable, as his intimate
friend, John Trumbull, the poet, had settled at Hartford,
and was now practising before the courts. Barlow still
retained his chaplaincy, however, and on the 1st of May,
1783, again set out for the camps at Newburgh. One
letter written from there to his wife will complete the
pictures he has given us of life in the army:

CAMP, *May 6th.*

"I have but a moment to give you, by Whitman, the
history of the last eight days. We arrived at camp and
dined at headquarters on Thursday. We find everybody merry and sociable. On Sunday I made a preach-

ment, and yesterday we came down here twelve miles to see Prom.* . . . He has taken the attorney's oath. Major Trescot saw Dudley at Greenfield, well, a few days ago. It is uncertain yet whether I go to Philadelphia. Times are very punctilious about leave of absence. . . . I don't believe the army will disband till August or September. . . ."

Twelve days later he is in Philadelphia with Trumbull, (both presumably having business with the printers), and on May 19th writes a characteristic letter from that city:

"We expect to tarry in this town about eight days, just long enough to show ourselves. I grow black and handsome; Trumbull grows red and fat." Returning, the summer was spent with his brigade, nominally at least, though in that season of inaction it is probable that frequent furloughs were obtained, and after the joyful disbandment in October at Newburgh, he returned to private life.

---

* Abraham Baldwin, who had just been admitted to the bar.

CHAPTER IV.

1783-1788.

HE at once fixed his abode at Hartford, the little capital on the Connecticut, even then the seat of a refined and cultivated society.   His career there was a com-
plex one, exhibiting many phases.   He soon abandoned
the plan of an early publication of his poem, probably
from the shortness of his subscription-list, and also perhaps with a view to a more careful revision.   He studied
law, however, wrote a great deal of poetry, annuals, New-
Year's verses, bon mots, political squibs and satires,
hymns and paraphrases of the Psalms, and with Elisha
Babcock, a substantial printer of the town, established
a weekly newspaper, called *The American Mercury*—a
scholarly, thoroughly respectable sheet, with a mild bias
toward republicanism, or what later came to be thus
designated.   The office copy of this periodical is preserved in the library of Yale College, the first number
bearing date July 12, 1784.   Modern newspaper readers
would regard it much as the archæologist looks on Cypri-
ote antiquities.   Perhaps we cannot better describe it
than by presenting the prospectus, which was as follows:
" Barlow and Babcock have established a new printing-
office near the State House in the city of Hartford.   They
propose publishing a weekly paper, entitled *The American
Mercury*.   As they have a prospect of a very extended
circulation and constituency they will exert their utmost
abilities to furnish a useful and elegant entertainment for
the different classes of their customers.   The paper will
be a sheet of white, demi-imperial, with an elegant new
type, published every Monday morning, and delivered to
subscribers in the city at eight shillings the year, one-

half to be paid on delivery of the first number and the other at the end of the year. To gentlemen at a distance, who send for single papers enclosed and directed, five shillings paid on subscribing and seven at the end of the year. . . . In order to render the publication as useful as possible, the publishers propose occupying the first page with regular extracts from Cook's last voyage (published by authority in London and lately come to hand) until the whole of that valuable and original course of discoveries shall be communicated to their customers, who will thus, in the course of one year's paper, be possessed of the whole of that celebrated work which is now sold at four dollars. There will likewise be inserted in a supplement, if there is not room in the sheet, all the future acts and resolves of the states of Massachusetts and Connecticut. Advertisements will be inserted at a reasonable price."

A series of careful essays on current political and social topics contributed by Barlow to this journal were the progenitors, it is said, of the modern editorial. For nearly a year and a half—from July 12, 1784, to November, 1785—the young poet continued his connection with the paper, relinquishing it at last to turn his attention more particularly to the study of the law. The next spring, in April, 1786, he was admitted to the bar at Fairfield, and read at the time a long dissertation on the principles and practice of law.

He did not, however, succeed as a lawyer. He was averse to practising the arts of the shyster or the pettifogger, and without making use of these it was almost impossible at that time for a young lawyer to rise in his profession. He always, however, entertained the highest respect for the law as a science, and subsequently, in his "Advice to the Privileged Orders," showed that he had not only mastered its principles, but had excellent ideas on the necessity of a reform in its administration.

In literature, however, he was more fortunate, and in these years, otherwise barren of results, there came to him the assurance—so cheering to the heart of the neophyte—of literary success.

The General Association of the Congregational Churches of Connecticut, at their session in 1785, had voted a revision of the Book of Psalmody then in use. This book was the version of Dr. Watts, which had been given to the religious world half a century before. There were several reasons why the American churches desired a new version. Many of the Psalms had been "locally appropriated," that is, applied to the peculiarly isolated condition of the dissenting churches in England, and it was thought desirable that they should be altered and more generally applied.

Furthermore, twelve of the most beautiful Psalms of David had been wholly omitted by Watts in his version, it is said because he was never conscious of a sufficient degree of poetic inspiration to attempt them. It is perhaps the best proof that can be given of our poet's reputation at this time that the work of revising this collection was tendered him. He readily accepted it and at once began his task. He re-wrote the misapplied portions, corrected the antiquated phraseology, and with the aid of his poetical friends supplied the omitted Psalms. One of these—the one hundred and thirty-seventh—from Barlow's pen, has never been equalled, not even by Halleck, who attempted it in 1821. We give examples of both versions, allowing the reader to make his own comparisons.

Original version, from the Bay Psalm Book, 1640, not attempted by Dr. Watts:

> 1. "The rivers on of Babilon
>   There where we did sit down,
> Yea, even there we mourned when
>   We remembered Sion.

2. " Our harp we did hang it amid
    Upon the willow tree,
  Because there them that us away
    Led in captivitee, etc."

BARLOW'S VERSION.

" Along the banks where Babel's current flows
    Our captive bands in deep despondence strayed,
While Zion's fall in sad remembrance rose,
    Her friends, her children, mingled with the dead.

" The tuneless harp that once with joy we strung,
    When praise employed, and mirth inspired the lay,
In mournful silence on the willows hung,
    And growing grief prolonged the tedious day.

" The barbarous tyrants, to increase our woe,
    With taunting smiles a song of Zion claim,
Bid sacred praise in strains melodious flow
    While they blaspheme the great Jehovah's name.

" But how, in heathen climes and lands unknown,
    Shall Israel's sons a song of Zion raise?
O hapless Salem, God's terrestrial throne,
    Thou land of glory, sacred mount of praise.

" If e'er my memory lose thy lovely name,
    If my cold heart neglect my kindred race,
Let dire destruction seize this guilty frame—
    My hand shall perish, and my voice shall cease.

" Yet shall the Lord, who hears when Zion calls,
    O'ertake her foes with terror and dismay ;
His arm avenge her desolated walls,
    And raise her children to eternal day."

Barlow's version was well received by the New England churches, and was in constant use among them until rumors of the poet's lapse from orthodoxy in France became so rife that it was discarded for one prepared by Dr. Dwight. The work, however, did not escape criticism. The changes of expression, the " improvements " on Watts, and the verbal alterations in the text were regarded with suspicion by the more rigid, and the author was declared to have taken unwarrantable liberties with the word of God.

During the poet's residence in Hartford there arose and flourished a somewhat remarkable association or club, which, from his intimate connection with it, deserves an extended notice. It was known far and wide as the "Hartford Wits." Its original members were Dr. Lemuel Hopkins, John Trumbull, Joel Barlow, and David Humphreys. We call it remarkable, because at a day when Boston was as barren of literary talent as she has since been prolific, the little provincial village on the Connecticut boasted at least four poets, each of whom had gained a national reputation, while three of them at least were favorably known on the other side of the Atlantic. The four were equal in age as well as similar in temperament, and the place of their nativity was the same—the hill country of Western Connecticut.

Hopkins was born at Waterbury in 1750, and, after studying medicine, settled in Hartford about 1784, where he spent his life in the practice of his profession. He died in 1801.

Trumbull was born at Watertown, in the same year, 1750; graduated at Yale College in 1767; spent two years as a tutor at Yale; in 1773 entered the office of John Adams as a student of law, and in June, 1781, removed to Hartford, and was now living there in the practice of his profession. His "McFingal," first published in 1782, achieved several editions in this country, and was republished in England.

Humphreys, born at Derby in 1753, has been mentioned in the letters of his friend Barlow as having been appointed aide-de-camp to Washington, a position which he retained until the close of the war. At Yorktown, for gallant conduct, he was voted a sword by Congress. In 1784, when Franklin, Jefferson, and Adams were appointed commissioners to negotiate treaties of commerce with various European powers, he accompanied them as their secretary. He returned to America in 1786, and was now in Hartford as a representative from Derby in the State Legislature, and in other official positions. An old friend and comrade who sometimes met the tuneful circle at their reunions was Dr. Dwight, now a quiet country pastor at Greenfield Hill, near Fairfield. Richard Alsop, Theodore Dwight, Drs. Nathan Cogswell and Elihu Smith, were later added to the club, but this was *après des Rois.* These four congenial spirits formed a union as brilliant as it was powerful : their influence on the politics and society of their age cannot be overestimated. The first effort of the club was a series of satirico-political papers, aimed at the factions whose wranglings then threatened to strangle the infant republic in the very morning of its days. The series comprised twelve numbers, and was modelled somewhat on the plan of the *Rolliad* of the English satirists. The initial number appeared in the *New Haven Gazette and Connecticut Magazine* for October 26, 1786, accompanied by an ingenious introduction, which described the discovery, in a ruined city of the New World, of an epic poem of great antiquity, but complete, which was styled " The Anarchiad : a Poem on the Restoration of Chaos and Substantial Night." The poem detailed the several steps by which the " restoration " had been accomplished, which steps were connected in an ingenious way with the factions which were then distracting the country.

The appreciation of the satires was intense and their popularity unbounded. They were copied into scores of newspapers, became the theme of common conversation, and aided largely in forming the popular feeling that made possible the Federal constitution of 1787. Although no names appeared to these productions, it was well known that Humphreys, Barlow, Hopkins, and Trumbull were the authors, and their reputation rose accordingly. The last paper of the " Anarchiad " appeared in the *Gazette* for September 13, 1787. The club's next venture was the " Echo," a series of lampoons directed more especially against certain social and literary follies then rampant, and particularly against the stilted and magniloquent language then used in speaking of the commonest events.*

---

* As a literary curiosity, take the following account, by a Boston editor, of a thunderstorm that visited his modest capital: " On Tuesday last, about 4 o'clock P.M., came on a smart shower of rain, attended with lightning and thunder no ways remarkable. The clouds soon dissipated, and the appearance of the azure vault left trivial hopes of further needful supplies from the uncorked bottles of heaven. In a few moments the heavens were again overshadowed, and an almost impenetrable gloom mantled the face of the skies. The wind, frequently shifting from one point to another, wafted the clouds in various directions, until at last they united in one common centre and shrouded the visible globe in thick darkness.

" The attendant lightning with the accompanying thunder, brought forth from the treasures that embattled elements to awful conflict, were extremely vivid and amazing loud.

" Those buildings that were defended by electric rods appeared to be wrapped in sheets of livid flame, and a flood of the pure fire rolled its burning torrents down them with alarming violence. The majestic roar of disploding thunders, now bursting with a sudden crash and now wasting the rumbling echo of their sounds in other lands, added indescribable grandeur to the sublime scene.

" The windows of the upper regions appeared as thrown wide open, and the trembling cataract poured impetuous down. More salutary showers and more needed have not been experienced this summer.

" Two beautiful rainbows, the one existing in its native glories, and the other a splendid reflection of primitive colors, closed the magnificent picture, and presented to the contemplative mind the Angel of Mercy, clothed with the brilliance of this irradiated arch and dispensing felicity to assembled worlds.

" It is not unnatural to expect that the thunderstorm would be attended with some damage. We hear a barn belonging to Mr. Wythe, of Cambridge, caught fire from the lightning, which entirely consumed the same, together with several tons of hay, etc."

The club's " echo " is equally delightful :

> " On Tuesday last, great Sol, with piercing eye,
> Pursued his journey through the vaulted sky,
> And in his car effulgent rolled his way,
> Four hours beyond the burning zone of day :
> When, lo! a cloud, o'ershadowing all the plain,
> From countless pores perspired a *liquid rain*,

The winter of 1786–87, however, was spent by our poet in more serious literary labor. He was bringing out his epic, "The Vision of Columbus." In the spring of 1787 it appeared—a small octavo, with a dedication to "His Most Christian Majesty, Louis the Sixteenth, King of France and Navarre." The Preface was dated March 1, 1787. Nearly a score of the opening pages were devoted to a biography, in prose, of Columbus, the hero of the epic. The poem followed, in plan substantially the same as that sketched at Northampton in 1779, and the volume closed with a list of the subscribers, 170 in all, by whose aid it

---

> While from its cracks the lightnings made a peep,
> And chit-chat thunders rocked our fears asleep.
> But soon the vapory fog dispersed in air,
> And left the azure, blue-eyed concave bare.
> Even the last drop of hope, which dripping skies
> Gave for a moment to our straining eyes,
> Like *Boston rum* from heaven's *junk bottles* broke,
> Lost all the corks, and vanished into smoke.
> But swift from worlds unknown, a fresh supply
> Of vapor dimmed the great horizon's eye.
> The crazy clouds, by shifting zephyrs driven,
> Wafted their courses through the high-arched heaven,
> Till, piled aloft in one stupendous heap,
> The seen and unseen worlds grew dark, and nature gan to weep.
> Attendant lightnings streamed their tails afar,
> And social thunders waked ethereal war ;
> From dark, deep pockets brought their treasured store ;
> Embattled elements increased the roar.
> Red, crinkling fires expended all their force,
> And tumbling rumblings staid their headlong course.
> Those guarded frames, by thunder-poles secured,
> Though wrapped in sheets of flame, those sheets endured ;
> O'er their broad roofs the fiery torrents rolled,
> And every shingle seemed of burning gold.
> Majestic thunders, with disploding roar
> And sudden crashing, bounced along the shore,
> Till, lost in other lands, the whispering sound
> Fled from our ears, and fainted on the ground.
> Rain's house on high its window-sashes oped,
> And out the cataract impetuous hopped.
> While the grand scene by far more grand appeared
> With lightnings never seen, and thunders never heard.

had been published. The poem was a success in every
particular. At home it was received with unbounded
applause, and rapidly passed through several editions. It
was re-published in England, then not partial to American productions, and was not unkindly received by the
critics. It also appeared in Paris in a French dress, where
it met with distinguished marks of approval from the
Parisian *raconteurs*, with whom, indeed, everything *Amer-
icain* was then in high favor. For years no literary American was so well-known, so much read, or the subject of so
much eulogy, as Joel Barlow.

More salutary showers have not been known
To wash dame Nature's dirty, homespun gown.
For several weeks the good old Joan's been seen
With filth bespattered, like a lazy quean;
The husbandman, fast travelling to despair,
Laid down his hoe and took his rocking-chair,
While his fat wife, the well and cistern dried,
Her mop grown useless, hung it up and cried.
Two rainbows fair that Iris brought along,
Picked from the choicest of her colored throng :
The first-born, decked in pristine hues of light
In all its native glories, glowing, bright ;
The next, adorned with less refulgent rays,
But borrowing lustre from its brother's blaze,
Shone, a bright reflex of those colors gay,
That decked with light creation's primal day.
When infant Nature lisped her earliest notes,
And *younker Adam* crept in petticoats,
And to the people to reflection given,
"The sons of Boston," the elect of Heaven,
Presented Mercy's angel, smiling fair—
Irradiate splendors frizzled in his hair—
Uncorking demijohns, and pouring down
Heaven's liquid blessings on the gaping town.
N. B.—At Cambridge town, the selfsame day,
A barn was burnt well filled with hay.
Some say the lightning turned it red,
Some say the thunder struck it dead,
Some say it made the cattle stare,
And some it killed an aged mare ;
But we expect the truth to learn,
From Mr. Wythe, who owned the barn."

CHAPTER V.

1788-1795.

IN the midst of these varied pursuits there appeared in the poet's horizon one of those speculative barks,

> " Built i' the eclipse
> And rigged with curses dark,"

which have from time to time sunk beneath the waves of the American political sea, engulfing whole platoons of statesmen in their vortices. On the close of the war the attention of the speculative was attracted to the magnificent public domain of the nation, and syndicates were formed to purchase large blocks of virgin land, survey and map, and sell at an advanced price to settlers. The first and most notable of these were The Ohio Land Company, and its satellite, The Scioto Land Company. The former originated with two New England gentlemen of standing and character, Rufus Putnam and Benjamin Tupper, both of whom had served in the Revolution with distinction. The latter, while exploring the Ohio valley in 1785 as Government geographer, became impressed with the fertility and resources of the country, and returning to New England, early in 1786, sought out Putnam at his home in Rutland, Worcester County, Massachusetts, to confer with him in regard to their purchase and settlement. The result of this conference was an address to the people, and more especially to the officers and soldiers who had served in the late war, and who were, by a recent act of Congress, entitled to receive certain tracts of land in the Ohio country, stating that the subscribers, from personal inspection and from other incontestable evidences, were fully satisfied that the lands in that quarter were of a much better quality than any other known to the New England people ; that the climate, seasons, products, etc., were in fact equal to the most flattering descriptions published of them, and that, determined to become purchasers, they were desirous of forming a general association with those who entertained the same ideas ; and closed by proposing the following plan, viz.: "that an association by the name of The Ohio Company be formed of all such as wish to become purchasers in that country who reside in the Commonwealth of Massachusetts only, or to extend to the inhabitants of other states as shall be agreed on"; and to bring the matter to a focus, all disposed to engage in the enterprise were instructed to meet at designated places in their several counties and elect delegates, who should meet at the Bunch of Grapes Tavern, at Boston, on the 1st of March, 1786, and there perfect the plan of the Association. The meeting was attended by eleven delegates, articles of agreement signed, and officers elected. A year later the delegates met again, and finding that two hundred and fifty shares of one thousand dollars each had been subscribed, deputed one of their number, the Rev. Manasseh Cutler, of Ipswich, to negotiate with Congress for the desired lands. They could not possibly have secured a more adroit and diplomatic agent. Dr. Cutler was a graduate of Yale, a man of wit and genius, who had taken degrees in three learned professions—law, divinity, and medicine—and who was favorably known in the most cultivated circles of Boston, New York, and Philadelphia. On July 5, 1787, Dr. Cutler rode into New York, " by the road," he tells us in his diary, " that enters the Bowery," and put up his horse at the sign of the Plough and Harrow in the Bowery barns. The Continental Congress was then in session, in labor with the Constitution which made a nation of a group of warring and independent sovereignties. Dr. Cutler had many forcible and weighty arguments to urge in favor of his proposition : the wealth of the infant nation, the security for its public debt, lay in its lands. To sell and settle these as fast as possible was therefore an object of financial and patriotic interest. The proposition of The Ohio Company was entirely straightforward and business-like. It proposed to buy one million and a half acres of land on the Ohio, lying about the present city of Marietta, at a specified price, and to pay for it at a specified date. Men of the highest standing in Congress and out of it favored it, among them St. Clair, the president, and Osgood, the head of the Board of Treasury. By the majority, however, it was received with marked disfavor, some professing to see in it a scheme of speculators to get possession of the public lands, and thus advance their price, some arguing that Congress itself should dispose of the lands to actual settlers, while the Southern members opposed it from the sectional feeling, and the known anti-slavery views of Dr. Cutler and his associates. In his journal, under date of July 19th, Dr. Cutler records that "there are a number in Congress decidedly opposed to the terms of negotiation, and some to any contract." The diplomat was discouraged at the strength of the opposition, and for a time inclined to abandon the cause as lost. But at this juncture aid came from an unexpected quarter. There was living in the city at the time a gentleman named William Duer, a man of talents and distinguished service, the Secretary of the Board of Treasury, and a personal friend of Alexander Hamilton. He came to Dr. Cutler with a proposition, which we will describe in the latter's own words, as recorded in his journal under date of July 20th: " Colonel Duer came to me with proposals from a number of the principal characters in the city, to extend our contract and take in another company, but *that it should be kept a profound secret*. He explained the plan they had concocted, and offered me generous conditions if I would accomplish the business for them. The plan struck me

agreeably. Sargent * insisted on my undertaking it, and
both (Duer and Sargent) urged me not to think of giving up the matter so soon.   I was convinced it was best
for me to hold up the idea of giving up a contract with
Congress and making a contract with some of the states,
which I did in the strongest terms, and represented to
the committee and to Duer the difficulties I saw in the
way, and the improbability of closing a bargain when we
were so far apart, and told them I conceived it not worth
while to say anything further to Congress on the matter.
This appeared to have the effect I wished.   The committee were mortified and did not seem to know what to say,
but still urged another attempt.   I left them in this state,
but afterwards explained my views to Duer and Sargent,
who fully approved my plan.   Promised Duer to consider his proposal.   I spent the evening closeted with
Colonel Duer, and agreed to purchase more land, if terms
can be obtained, for another company, which will probably forward the negotiation."

Saturday, July 21st, he adds: " Several members of
Congress called on me early this morning.   They discovered much anxiety about a contract, and assured me
that Congress, on finding that I was determined not to
accept their terms and had proposed leaving the city,
had discovered a much more favorable disposition, and
believed if I renewed my request I might obtain conditions as reasonable as I desired.   I was very indifferent,
and talked of the advantages of a contract with some of
the states.   This I found had the desired effect.   At
length I told them that if Congress would accede to the
terms I had proposed I would extend the purchase to the
10th township from the Ohio and to the Scioto, exclusively, by which Congress would pay nearly four millions
of the national debt.   That our intention was an actual,
an immediate settlement of the most robust and indus-

---

* One of the associates.

trious people in America. In these manœuvres I am much indebted to Colonel Duer and Major Sargent.

" By this ordinance we obtained a grant of near five millions of acres, amounting to three and a half millions of dollars—one and a half million for The Ohio Company *and the remainder for a private speculation, in which many of the principal characters in America are concerned. Without connecting this speculation similar terms and advantages would not have been obtained for The Ohio Company.*"

The shrewd reader will observe at once that as soon as this "plan" of Colonel Duer's, in which "many of the principal characters in America were concerned," was broached and acceded to by Dr. Cutler there was a marvellous change in the attitude of Congress, and that not a paltry million and a half, but nearly five millions acres of land were sold the petitioners, and will be perhaps a little curious as to the nature of this "plan."

The Doctor nowhere gives a hint as to its character, but from other sources we learn that it was substantially as follows :—

1st. To purchase four and one half million acres of Government land, at $1 per acre.* Should the large sum required for its purchase not be readily obtained, it was thought that a loan on the land could be negotiated in Holland; 2d. To sell the lands thus obtained in Europe to capitalists or actual settlers at an advanced price; and, 3d. To employ an agent or agents for the purpose.

In a few months this private speculation appeared, thoroughly organized and equipped, as The Scioto Land Company, with Col. William Duer as president; Richard Platt, treasurer; Andrew Craigie, formerly Apothecary-General of the Revolutionary army, Royal Flint, of New York, Gen. Rufus Putnam, of Connecticut, as trustees, and among its shareholders, "the principal characters in America."

---

* Less 33⅓ per cent. for " bad land," surveying, etc.

An authentic history of the whole affair—except the negotiations with Congress—is given in the transfer from The Ohio Company to The Scioto Company of the residue of the grant, after the former's one million and a half of acres had been taken out.

As tending to throw light on a very obscure portion of our early history, as well as for its important bearing on our hero's fortunes, a pretty full abstract of this instrument is presented.

Its preamble recites that "Whereas, by the resolves of Congress of the 23d and 27th of July last, the Rev. Manasseh Cutler and Major Winthrop Sargent, for themselves and associates, procured the right of preëmption of a certain tract of the western territory of the United States, bounded as follows, viz.: A tract of land bounded by the Ohio, from the mouth of the Scioto River to the intersection of the western boundary of the seventh range of townships then surveying; thence by the said boundary to the northern boundary of the tenth township from the Ohio; thence by a due west line to the Scioto, thence by the Scioto to the beginning; and whereas, in pursuance of the said resolves, the said Manasseh Cutler and Winthrop Sargent have, on the 27th of October instant, entered into a contract with the Honorable the Board of Treasury of the United States, as agents for the Directors of The Ohio Company of Associates, for the purchase of a certain portion of the above described tract of land—(a definition of the boundaries follows),—such as will, with the other lines of the said described tract, include one million and a half of acres of land, exclusive of certain reservations as specified in the said deed. And whereas the residue of the general tract, as described in the Act of Congress of the 23d of July last, remains wholly unappropriated and is subject to the disposal of the said Manasseh Cutler and Winthrop Sargent, who have accordingly entered into a contract for the purchase of the same on the 27th day of October instant with the Honorable the Board of Treasury of the United States, describing in the said contract the boundaries of the said tract in the manner following, to wit: . . . the whole being the tract mentioned in the resolution of Congress of the 23d of July last, except what is contracted for by the said Manasseh Cutler and Winthrop Sargent, as agents for the directors of The Ohio Company and their associates.

" Be it known that it is this day agreed between the said Manasseh Cutler and Winthrop Sargent, for themselves and others their associates, and William Duer, of the State of New York, for himself and others his associates, their heirs and assigns, one equal moiety of the tract last described. Provided always that the respective parties to this writing shall be jointly and equally concerned in the disposal of the same, either in Europe or America, as circumstances will best admit of ; and that they share equally in any profit or loss which may accrue in attempting to negotiate the sale or mortgage of the same, and in paying the purchase money due to the United States.

" And it is hereby agreed upon and understood by the parties, that the property in the residue of the general tract as above described is to be considered as divided into thirty equal parts or shares, of which thirteen shares are the property of William Duer, in which he may admit such associates as he may judge proper, and thirteen shares in like manner the property of the said Manasseh Cutler and Winthrop Sargent. That the other four shares may be disposed of in Europe at the direction of an agent, to be sent there for the purpose of negotiating a sale or loan as above mentioned, and if not so disposed of to be equally divided among the parties to this writing. It is further agreed that the said William Duer be, and he hereby is, fully authorized and empowered to negotiate a loan on, or sale of, the above lands in Holland or such other parts of Europe as may be found expedient, with power of appointing an agent under him in the said negotiation, agreeably to such instructions as he may receive for such purpose. Provided always, and it is hereby understood and agreed on between the parties, that the said William Duer shall from time to time (when so required) make known and communicate to the said Winthrop Sargent and Manasseh Cutler the progress of the said negotiation and the correspondence and instructions relative thereto. And it is also agreed between the said parties that Royal Flint be, and is agreed on by the said parties, as the present agent for undertaking the proposed negotiation, under the superintendence of the said William Duer, and that if, from the death of the said Flint or other circumstances, it may be proper to appoint another agent for the purposes above stated, the person so appointed shall be agreed on by the said Manasseh Cutler and Winthrop Sargent and William Duer. And whereas the whole benefit of the preëmption of the residue of the land as above described may depend on the punctual payment on the part of The Ohio Company of our moiety of the purchase-money of the tract contracted for in their behalf, it is hereby agreed that the said William Duer shall (if it be found necessary) advance, on account of the said contract, one hundred thousand dollars, provided that whatever sum so paid in by the said William Duer shall exceed thirty thousand dollars shall be reimbursed to the said Duer out of the first moneys which the said Sargent and Cutler may receive for subscriptions."

This instrument was signed on the 29th of October, 1787.

Royal Flint does not seem to have acted in the capacity of agent. Brissot, the traveller, and a Major Rochefontaine, in France, with a man named Parker, in England, appear to have made some effort to sell the Company's lands, but without success. Andrew Craigie writes from England to William Duer about the Company's affairs in August, 1787, probably as agent, and adds, " Let silence cover our transactions." In the spring of 1788, however, the trustees decided on more energetic efforts ; they were desirous of sending a responsible, thoroughly efficient agent abroad, and what seems at first sight inexplicable, their choice fell on Joel Barlow. He had then discovered no aptitude for business, and possessed no business experience ; yet a moment's reflection convinces one that the astute managers acted with reason. No American was more popular in England or France at that day, and none better calculated to win confidence—a prime requisite in conducting negotiations such as they were engaged in. That his brother-in-law (Abraham Baldwin) was now a Senator in Congress had perhaps its due weight. Duer, as appears by a letter from Richard Platt to Barlow, was not heartily in favor of the appointment, and, as Barlow afterward charged, was unfriendly to him from the beginning. The poet himself seems to have readily consented. It offered a chance of bettering his fortunes, then at a low ebb, and would give opportunities of travel, while it would not wholly rob him of literary leisure. It is not probable that the full scope of the Company's designs were disclosed to him, while the patriotic considerations advanced —the sale of the Government's land and the promotion of emigration—must have appealed powerfully to one of his ardent, patriotic temperament. However this may be, he accepted the trust. Leaving his wife with her brother Dudley, now a lawyer at Greenfield Hill, he arranged his affairs with the Company, and on the 25th of May, 1788, embarked at New York on a French packet for his new scene of labor. Before sailing, he wrote a letter to Matthew Carey, the Philadelphia publisher,* which furnishes interesting data as to the fortunes of " The Vision of Columbus." The letter is as follows :

" Mr. Hazard showed me a letter, in which you request him to apply to me on the subject of reprinting my poem. As I mentioned to you some time since, I have

---

* Author of the " Vindiciæ Hibernicæ," of which Archbishop Troy, of Dublin, said : " It has done more to vindicate Ireland than all that ever was written or published on the subject."

part of the second edition on hand in sheets, which I wish to dispose of, that I may not lose money by the work—for I expect not to make any. One hundred of the copies I designed for Philadelphia and its neighborhood, by which I mean all the Middle States south of this place. To accommodate us both, I will now send you, by the first vessel, this hundred copies, which if you will receive and account for to Mr. Hazard at three shillings Penn. currency, you have my full consent to publish one impression as numerous as you please, and as soon as you please, besides inserting it in the *Museum*. They have never been sold at less than half a dollar in sheets and a dollar bound, and they will not be sold at less this way. None of the first edition were ever offered for sale south of Philadelphia, and none of the second between New York and Charleston, and I shall send no more to the southward of this except two dozen to Baltimore."

The young envoy bore, besides numerous letters of introduction to noblemen and men of letters abroad, an instrument by which William Duer nominated him agent of The Scioto Company in Europe, "to undertake and conclude such engagements with such bodies or such individuals as he shall judge the most suitable for the interest of the Company in disposing of the territory they have acquired of the United States altogether, or of whatever part of said territory, or to bind it for whatever sum he shall judge suitable." Duer also promised and engaged, for himself, in the name of the Company, to ratify and confirm all engagements that his agent should make in virtue of the powers delegated. This paper was dated May 16, 1788, and was signed by William Duer in the names of the associates of The Scioto Company. He bore also a transfer to himself, from Cutler and Sargent, of one sixtieth part of The Scioto Company's lands, and also one fifty-second part of eight sixtieth parts of the same tract, in case the above mentioned fractional parts were not disposed of in Europe,—he agreeing to bear his proportionate share of the loss, if such should arise, either from the negotiation of the tract in Europe or America, or from a failure to pay the purchase-money to Congress. He also bore a transfer from Duer to him of one sixtieth of the tract, with the same penalties attached, so that he was in effect an associate of the Company, with his fortunes embarked in the enterprise as much as those of any other member.

The name of the packet that bore the young envoy on his mission is not given, but we have in his journal an entertaining description of the vessel with the minutiæ of the voyage. Modern travellers will relish these details of a sea voyage in 1788.

" Our accommodations on board were wretched. The ship was a sixteen-gun frigate, taken from the English during the late war, and is very unfit for a packet. The dining-room is small but tolerable, the cabins which we sleep in are wretched little dark holes, six feet and a half in length, three in breadth, and five in height, without air and intolerably dirty. The inside had been formerly lined with calico instead of paper; this, by being sufficiently tattered and dirtied, has become a commodious receptacle for bedbugs and fleas, which are found here in the greatest plenty and perfection. Indeed, I could not help remarking to a fellow-passenger that the Count de Buffon, when he drew the comparison between the European and American animals, must have had his eye upon the fleas; for taking those on board the ship as a sample of this species of European animals (and they are doubtless either French or English, as the ship has been owned by no other nations), it appears that the European flea is at least heavier by one third of a grain than that of America. This remark I should not venture to make in this serious journal did I not find it confirmed by subsequent observations made on shore. I am now in the fourth loft of the *Hôtel de l'Argle d'or*, in Havre, where the true French flea, as well as bedbug, grows to a most respectable size, and gives great countenance to the philosophy of the above mentioned author. Captain Rolland is extremely parsimonious in his provisions and barbarously inattentive to his passengers. We had, indeed, plenty of live-stock, such as sheep and poultry; he had salted beef and pork, but not good; he had smoked hams, but they were dry, hard, and very salt; I believe not more than half of one ham was eaten on board, though it was brought to the table at least forty times. In the article of cheese he was still more fortunate; his store in this consisted of the half of one which was made of goats' milk; this, he often assured us, was good, and had it at table twice a day the whole passage. I am sure not two ounces of it were consumed. He had plenty of bad Bordeaux wine and some Madeira, but he had no tea, coffee, chocolate, nor loaf-sugar; no beer, cider, nor biscuit. His flour, of which he often boasted that he gave us fresh bread every morning, was originally made in France, but having been badly put up, and that a long time before, it was become intolerably musty. I never ate a single mouthful of this bread the whole passage. The sailors' hard bread, which was baked in France six months ago, was more palatable. Of this I probably consumed two pounds during the voyage. The regulations of the French packets require the captain to furnish the table, for which he receives one half the passage money. This furnishes a strong temptation to him to confine his provisions to cheap articles, or at least to such as suit his own palate, and Rolland is a proper man to make his advantage of these regulations. When we engaged our passage and paid our money, we were told that every article of good living was furnished; we need give ourselves no trouble, but depend on the best possible accommodations. When the ship was nearly ready to sail we found there was no provision made for lodging. The captain told us it would be very unbecoming in him to offer a gentleman a mattress and sheets that had been used by others; it was therefore customary for every passenger to find his own. This position we subscribed to and furnished ourselves with lodging, at the same time secretly praising his sagacity in discovering that, as these articles would be useless to a land traveller, not being worth putting to auction in a foreign country, they would probably be left on board ; by these means a large quantity of useful furniture would soon accumulate, to the great benefit of the captain. Aside from this consideration Rolland's argument would as well apply to every tavern-keeper as to the captain of a packet. Several days after the ship was to have sailed, having waited for a wind, we discovered by mere accident the real state of the captain's stores, and we took a hasty opportunity to purchase a little tea, coffee, and sugar. But fresh flour, biscuit, cheese, beer, vegetables, etc., were omitted. But the worst circumstance about the provisions was the manner of cooking. The table was set at ten o'clock and at four, and the captain had no idea that any person, sick or well, could eat at any other hours or fail to eat at those. His dishes at four o'clock were, first, strong pea-soup, thick with musty bread, garlic, and onions ; second, mutton, fowls, or turkey, roasted in the pot or baked in the oven, stiff with garlic and onions and covered deep in melted butter. No other vegetables, except a few potatoes, which lasted about half the voyage, and these were brought to the table cut to pieces and stewed in butter-and-fat. The breakfasts were the relics of these dishes, sometimes warm and sometimes cold, together with a mutton cutlet stewed in butter, fat, and onions. I rarely sat at table and made no complaint of his dishes, as all food was alike indifferent to me ; but the other passengers, refusing one dish after another, ought to have induced him, sometimes, at least, to consult their appetite respecting the choice of food and the mode of cooking. But nothing of this was ever heard of : if a person would eat with him it was well ; if not, he would praise the meat and eat it himself. I endeavored many times to get some chicken or mutton broth, but the cook could not possibly be taught to make it. Much of my vexation arose from the ignorance or obstinacy of the cook, but I suspect his conduct arose in part from another motive: he might fear that by obliging me he should disoblige his master. . . . On approaching Havre I was presented with the first clear view of the Old World. The first thing that strikes an American eye is a certain air of antiquity, which renders every object venerable. Not a tree on the coast but what seems to have furnished colonies from its branches, as they are generally trimmed and taught to grow in a particular manner to answer some purpose of the owner."

The packet arrived at Havre on the 24th of June. In the diary, kept with considerable particularity for the first four months of his stay abroad, there is little reference to his mission or its results. He went first to Paris, thence to London, where he met Mr. Parker, a former agent, and probably, associate of the Company. He was not long in discovering that the times were very inauspicious for his mission. All Europe was in a ferment. The Turks were battling against the Russians; the Swedes had just begun a war for the recovery of their possessions in Finland; England was engrossed with the trial of Warren Hastings and the conduct of her East Indian affairs, and France was within a year of the Revolution. There was, too, a scarcity of money and a general distrust of new enterprises, especially in England, which had been overrun with agents from her dependencies with all sorts of schemes and speculations to offer. They left London for Brussels on the 7th of September to consult the Messrs. Van Staphorsts, of Amsterdam, on " business about the lands," presumably to negotiate a loan on them. No hint is given as to the result of this mission. From Amsterdam Barlow returned to Paris, and at once seriously addressed himself to the object of his mission. He employed to assist him in the enterprise two agents, an Englishman, named William Playfair, whose chief recommendation was that he spoke and wrote French perfectly, and was well acquainted with the Gallic temperament; and a mercurial Frenchman, named La Chaise de Soissons. In both, as the sequel proved, he showed himself a poor judge of character. To these two agents was delegated largely the work of securing emigrants, while the principal addressed himself to the task of enlisting the nobility and wealthier classes. The prospectus and maps of the lands which had been prepared by the directors of the Company in America seem to have been misleading documents, and with the additions which Playfair and De Soissons undoubtedly gave in translating, almost reached the point of misrepresentations. Volney, in his " View of all Nations," gives what he calls " specimen extracts," as follows :

" A climate wholesome and delightful, frost even in winter almost entirely unknown, and a river called by way of eminence ' The Beautiful,' and abounding in excellent fish of a vast size; noble forests, consisting of trees that spontaneously produce sugar and a plant that yields ready-made candles ; venison in plenty, the pursuit of which is uninterrupted by wolves, foxes, lions, or tigers. A couple of swine will multiply themselves a hundred fold in two or three years without taking any care of them. No taxes to pay, no military services to be performed." These seductive circulars were distributed extensively throughout France, but particularly in Paris. Of their effect Volney gives what we must believe an exaggerated picture : " In France—in Paris," he says, " the imagination was too heated to admit of doubt or suspicion ; and people were too ignorant and uninformed to perceive where the picture was defective and its colors too glaring. The example, too, of the wealthy and reputedly wise confirmed the popular delusion. Nothing was talked of in every social circle but the Paradise that was opened for Frenchmen in the western wilderness, the free and happy life to be led on the banks of the Scioto.

At length Brissot* published his 'Travels' and completed the flattering delusion; buyers became numerous and importunate, chiefly among the better sort of the middle class. Single persons and whole families disposed of their all, flattering themselves with having made excellent bargains."

Barlow was equally successful with the higher orders. It is safe to say, perhaps, that the young poet became one of the lions of the capital. Jefferson, then Minister to France, received him kindly, endorsed his mission, and presented him to the eminent men in letters, divinity, and the nobility who then adorned the French Court. He wrote in his journal of dining on several occasions with the Marquis de Lafayette. At Calais he regrets the absence of the Count de Rochambeau, Governor of the town, because he " is addressed to him by General Washington." His reputation, as well as his connections, admitted him to the choicest circles of French society. The only data we have of his operations in Paris are given in his letters to Colonel Duer and others interested. On the 29th of November, 1789, he writes the former that a contract for the sale of three million acres had been entered into with a French company, the price being six livres the acre. The object of this company, he says, is an immediate settlement by the sale of portions to individuals and by sending cultivators in the name of the Company, and he informs Duer that a colony will be ready to sail in January for Alexandria, Va., at the head of which, he thinks, will be Major General Dupontail and Major Rochefontaine. As the reports which these emigrants might be expected to send back to France would make or mar the enterprise, he entreated that every exertion should be made by the Company to fulfil its promises to them, and suggested that " a person of activity " be sent from their proposed settlement to

---

* " New Travels in America," Paris, 1791. English edition, London, 1794.

Alexandria, "to make all the preparations on the route and at the fort for their reception and journey to the Scioto, and to wait at Alexandria to conduct them thither." It is, he adds, "an immense undertaking to the poor creatures who adventure in it; a situation in which all the passions are alive to the slightest impressions. They who lead the way trust their lives and fortunes to the representations that I make to them. The evidence is slight; it will be strengthened or destroyed in the minds of those who are still to be engaged by the testimony of those who first arrive. If the first one hundred persons should find things easy and agreeable as it is in our power to make them with a little attention, the stream of emigration will be irresistible—20,000 people will be on those lands in eighteen months and our payments will be made in twelve. Do, my friend, exercise your rapid imagination for a moment in writing to those gentlemen—the subject lies with weight on my mind; it is, though small, one of the most essential services that now remain to be done. Whenever you shall know the complication of difficulties I have struggled with in bringing the unwieldy business thus far, you will excuse the warmth of my entreaties, and believe that they are founded on the maturest reflections, as well as on the most ardent desire to serve the interests of the concern." But, alas! what Barlow most desired to have done the Company failed to do. Indeed, before this first shipload of emigrants arrived at Alexandria its affairs had become almost desperate. Circumstances seemed to conspire to render this nicely planned, most promising speculation a failure. The efforts to negotiate a loan failed; consequently, when the date of preëmption arrived the Company was unable to pay the sum fixed, and thus acquire a title to the lands. Other difficulties, too, beset it. The hostility of the Indians, whose camp-fires encircled its purchase, prevented its surveys and clearings from being made, and any considerable stream of settlers from flowing in ; and in France the outbreak of the Revolution, in 1789, precluded its agent from forming new contracts, or indeed from collecting the moneys due on those already made. The body of emigrants referred to sailed late in the December of 1789 and arrived safely at Alexandria, Va., whence they soon set out under the care of an agent of the Company for their homes in the West. They did not go, however, to the lands they had bargained for. The Scioto Company had failed to secure a title to them, though it made desperate efforts. A petition to Congress to extend the time of making payment was denied, ugly rumors of the ulterior designs of the Company having by this time reached that body. In this strait The Scioto Company entered into an agreement with The Ohio Company, by which a tract of some 196,544 acres in the latter's purchase was ceded the former, The Scioto Company agreeing to pay the original price, and to give as security their interest in their original purchase. It was on this purchase on the Ohio, four miles below the mouth of the Kanawha, that the colony of emigrants was planted, their settlement having now blossomed into the flourishing town of Gallipolis. But, as it proved, The Scioto Company was unable to pay even for this small purchase, and as, on its failure to do so, the land reverted to The Ohio Company, the unfortunate Frenchmen again found themselves without a title. In this strait they petitioned Congress for relief, and that body, in 1795, meted out to them tardy justice by granting them 24,000 acres on the Ohio above the mouth of the Scioto, which is still known as the " French grant." This was the end of a most disreputable business. There are documents in existence which would give a much more complete *exposé* of the whole affair, but as no possible good could come of such an exposure it is perhaps better that they should remain unwritten history. Colonel Duer, who figures most prominently in the matter, but who was probably no deeper in the mire than his associates, was heartlessly abandoned by them when the failure of the affair became certain, was bankrupted in fortune and reputation by it, and died broken-hearted soon after its collapse. Much of the odium of the Company's failure was cast on Joel Barlow, who was well known as its agent abroad. That he was innocent of any complicity in its inception, or in the glowing promises to emigrants and capitalists never fulfilled, or in any way responsible for its failure, is not proven by the papers above mentioned. That he established his innocence to the satisfaction of the people of France is evidenced by the esteem and respect in which he continued to be held there. It is also proper to state that Col. Benjamin Walker, who, in the fall of 1790, was sent to France by the trustees to investigate Barlow's proceedings, returned a report completely exonerating him. The poet himself, in various letters to his wife and to Abraham Baldwin, complains that he was practically abandoned by his associates in America almost immediately on reaching his post, and intimates that his conversion to republicanism may have had something to do in influencing their action.

The reader is not to suppose that affairs of the Company solely occupied the poet's attention during this period. There was considerable literary activity, careful study, some travel and intercourse with the most learned and polished minds of Europe. It will be proper to return somewhat in our narrative, and, by means of his journal and letters, present this phase of his career more at length. This journal clearly indicates his practical bent and his very considerable powers of observation. His eyes are always open. He is a true American, too, and compares everything with his own country. His naïve comments are always interesting, often amusing. He describes Havre at length, and naïvely compares the *Maison de la Ville* with the City Hall of New York, to the disadvantage of the latter; he even thinks it would compare favorably with the State House at Philadelphia. Two days after landing he dines with the Swedish consul, Mr. Reinecke. The conversation at dinner seems to have been largely on the commerce and manufactures of Gottenburg, for a full description of both follows in the journal, with the query "Cannot the Americans undersell them in all foreign markets?" On Friday, the 27th, he notes: "I dined with Messrs. Collow, Fréres, Carmichael & Co., having been addressed by my friend Commodore Nicholson, of New York." And again, on Sunday, "I dined with Mr. Carmichael at his own house. This gentleman does great justice to the expectation of his friend Nicholson." June 30th he writes: "To-morrow we set out for Paris. My company are, Mr. Jacobson, Mr. Alsot—who is another merchant from Gottenburg — and Master George Washington Greene, a son of General Greene, twelve years old, who goes to Paris for his education, being addressed to the Marquis de Lafayette." The party travelled by carriage and arrived at Paris July 3d. He describes at length the roads, the country, the vehicles, the people, and the three different modes of travelling—by diligence, by carriage, and on horseback—comparing them with the American stage, much to the latter's disadvantage, and observes at the close, "Travelling in France, and, I believe, in any part of Europe, is really a science." He describes the manufactures of the various towns he passes through. The old church of Notre Dame at Rouen attracted him. "Nothing gives me more pleasure in these old places," he records, "than the contemplation of their Gothic cathedrals. The style of building is so totally unlike what can be seen or ever will be seen in America, that it is impossible to form the least idea of it but by the eye. This church struck me with such an air of solemnity and magnificence, and as being so much larger than any I had before seen, that I should have taken the dimensions of every part were it not

that I expected to see those that were larger and more
worthy of notice at Paris and London. I spent some time
in it, and even went up to see the bell, which, they tell
me, is the largest in Europe. This I had no right to
believe; and when the guide told me that it weighed
40,000 pounds, it only induced me to take its dimensions
that I might calculate its weight at my leisure." He
had half a day in the city, and spent it in visiting several
nunneries, churches, the bridge over the Seine, and other
"capital places." The nuns, he observes, "from their
white robes, black veils, the simplicity of their other
ornaments, and their modesty of deportment, have the
appearance of great serenity and innocence." At the
Hôtel de France, just as he is quitting the town, he meets
the two Mr. Appletons, from Boston. "They are connected with a Mr. Pew, an ingenious Scotch chemist,
who has discovered a method of converting the common
whale-oil into a substance not distinguishable from the
head matter of the spermaceti whale. The profits of
the business are immense. The Appletons expect to
make their fortunes in it." He also notes, as the invention of a mechanic of Rouen, a machine for carding cotton which divides the wool much more perfectly than
any that have yet been used, and adds: "I do not find
that extreme wretchedness and poverty among the lower
class of people in France that I had been taught to
expect." He makes no record of his first visit of nine
days to Paris. July 12th he set out with Mr. Parker for
England via Boulogne, travelling by post-chaise. They
reached London July 14th at midnight. He views England through an enemy's glasses, yet his criticisms are
not unfair. July 31, 1788, he notes: "This day, in company with Mr. Tod, a Scotch gentleman, Mr. Jarvis, an
American, a Frenchman and an Englishman whose
names I forget, I visited that ancient and renowned
fortress the Tower of London." His criticisms on the
figures of the English kings are piquant and amusing.

"In another large apartment . . . . are figures of most of the English kings from William I. to George II., sitting on horseback as large as life, and actually clad in the armor which they wore. The figures are said to be likenesses: probably all the late ones are. Many of them will disappoint you. Edward III. is a thin old man; has nothing of the appearance of a warrior. William III. is a very small man. Many others are as I expected. Edward IV. is as handsome a fellow as you will find him in the history of Jane Shore. Henry VIII. is the largest in the race of kings, and John of Gaunt is the stoutest man by far that I ever saw. . . . I was disappointed in the appearance of the beasts kept in the Tower, as I am with almost all other objects in Europe of which I have formerly met with descriptions." The old castle, the centre of the Tower, he describes as about the size of Fort Putnam at West Point.

Other jottings from the journal follow:

"*Aug.* 1. Went with my friend Cutting to see Sir Appleton Lever's Museum. It is contained in a large house near Black Friars Bridge. Sir Appleton is dead, and the Museum is now kept and shown by his successors. It is a most magnificent collection of birds and beasts, preserved with great neatness, and so as to resemble the life, with a variety of other curiosities, natural and artificial. . . . .

"We spent about two hours in the different rooms, with a satisfaction much beyond my expectations. We dined with Mr. George Howel, from America. At dinner were Mr. Trumbull, Mr. Cutting, Colonel Blount, of North Carolina, Mr. Sears, of Boston, and Dr. Muirson, of New York."

"*Aug.* 2. I dined with Mr. Caldwell, and went with him in the evening to Vaux Hall." Then follows a description of that noted resort as it appeared in 1788: "It is a garden of about 200 yards square. The borders on two sides are a wilderness. The rest is laid out in a great number of walks, some covered with elliptical arches of wood adorned with paintings, others arched with lofty elms. Near the centre is a grand orchestra, in which a band of music performs all the evening. Near one corner is a rotunda or a circular hall, 70 feet in diameter and about 40 in height, adorned with paintings. On two sides of the garden are disposed a great number of boxes for parties to sup in. The whole of this highly ornamented area is illuminated in the evening with upwards of 2000 lamps, disposed in such a manner as to have the most happy effect upon the spectator, causing a surprising degree of brilliance in the upper part next the orchestra, the rotunda, and the boxes, and leaving many long alleys and winding walks faintly illuminated, and others almost dark, exhibiting in a most romantic manner numbers of statues, obelisks, transparent paintings, etc. These gardens are open only on summer evenings in fine weather. The company is very numerous and brilliant. I should judge at least two thousand people were in the garden this night. They pay a shilling entrance."

"*Aug.* 4. Mr. Parker and myself have been to dine with Mr. Rogers at Twickenham." The gardens and grotto of Pope he declares to be the most delightful little spot he ever saw. "This is an area of about a dozen acres, fringed with a wilderness which hides the wall on the inside, and planted with a vast variety of trees of the thickest foliage, placed in the most natural and unaffected position that can be imagined. The whole is in the truest English style of gardening, rather more solemn and gloomy than what is common, but perfectly in harmony with the turn of mind that most distinguished the planter. The trees are all said to have been planted by Mr. Pope's own hand, and what is much to the credit of Sir Weldbare Ellis, the present owner, and his father-in-law, Mr. Stanhope, the late owner, not a single tree has been violated nor a new one added

since the death of Mr. Pope. The garden is perfectly
well kept, clean and neat, and everything remains precisely as the poet left it, excepting that the statues,
obelisks, and urns have grown rusty by time, and the
trees larger." "None of the temples and palaces of
Europe," he continues, "have forced themselves upon
me with such silent veneration and respect as I felt on
entering the simple gardens of Pope. Perhaps the idea
of the poet might help to make the impression, but to
my eye there is as much real taste discovered here as in
any of his writings. His grotto exceeds all description,
except the one given by him in a letter to a friend whose
name I forget. The subterraneous passage that this
affords from the waters of the Thames to the gardens
has a most surprising effect upon the spectator. It goes
under the house, which is an elegant one, and under the
road, which is a public one and much travelled. No
traveller in the road would ever mistrust that there was
a garden or a grotto here."

He watches a famous English election with the deepest interest, and thus records his impressions: "This
day (August 4) ended the long contested Westminster
election. It has lasted 15 days, and a scene of more
curiosity to an American cannot well be exhibited. . . .
Mr. Fox and Lord Hood were the members for Westminster. Hood is lately created a Lord of the Admir-
alty. His acceptance of this office vacates his seat in
Parliament, but leaves him again eligible. Hood, being
a ministerial man, was opposed in his re-election by Fox
and his party, who set up Lord John Townsend. It
was astonishing to behold the whole nation, from the
king to the cobbler, engaged in this business. It was
really no less than a contest between Charles Fox and
George the Third, and to the satisfaction of every disinterested beholder, the former has won the day and
Townsend is elected. On this occasion the Treasury
was opened, and orders were drawn directly on it for the

expense on the royal side. It is computed that the money spent on the king's side was 30,000 pounds; that on the opposition actually 20,000. Of this latter sum the Whig Club subscribed 10,000 pounds beforehand, and on the tenth day of the election, finding there would be a lack of money, the Duke of Bedford drew on his banker for 5000, and sent word that 50,000 more would be at the service of the opposition if needed. The other 5000 is supposed to have come from the Prince of Wales, and others less open in the cause of the opposition. This extraordinary expense will not appear strange when it is known that the simple article of ribbons for the cockades of the Townsend party cost 4000 pounds; that about 100 'bludgeon-men,' as they are called, were hired at five shillings per day to out-mob the mob upon the other side, and that two thirds of the voters (the whole of which in this poll were 12,000) were actually paid for their votes. Add to this that, for 15 days, 200,000 people are constantly kept in an uproar. Not a tradesman, if he is disposed, can carry on business, for he is every day haunted by both parties, and his journeymen every day drunk for the honor of the candidates. Several persons have been killed on the spot, and many more languish under broken heads or legs, and it was as much as a man's pockets were worth to come within 200 yards of the hustings. The way of conducting the business is for the canvass to begin some time before the election begins and continue till it is closed. The first nobility of both sexes employ themselves in canvassing: they go to every house, stall, shop, and dock-yard and solicit the vote and interest of every person in favor of their candidate. Then comes a card in the newspapers requesting the voters in such a street or parish to breakfast with such a duke or lord and proceed with him to the polls. Thus he puts himself upon a level with the most ragged, vile, and worthless of creation, who move in a tumultuous procession through the streets, reeling and huzzaing, with His Grace or the candidate at their head. The candidates meantime advertise in the papers their wishes to be elected, and request the votes and interest of all the *worthy and independent electors* in their favor. . . . When we hear, in common language, that such a duke *sends* 16 *members to Parliament*, and that such a gentleman *has bought a borough*, what shall we think of the political freedom of this people. A gentleman of my acquaintance, who has been an eminent merchant, has lately bought a borough for ten thousand pounds—that is, he has obtained the right of securing the election of the two members of that borough on all future occasions. He proposes to return himself as one member and sell the other place for three hundred pounds each election. As these recur but once in seven years it must be considered as a bad mercantile speculation unless there are secret profits arising from the place."

"*Aug.* 5. I went, towards evening, with Mr. Vaughan to the Marquis of Lansdowne's, in Berkeley Square. He is the late minister, Lord Shelburne, who made peace with America. He is in the Whig interest, but is not a man of great abilities or influence. His house is one of the best in London. In the evening went to see Sir Joseph Banks, President of the Royal Society. He is a large man, more able-bodied than philosophers in general are. He asked many questions about the progress of the Hessian fly and weevil in America."

"*Aug.* 19. Mr. Trumbull* and I have just returned from Windsor. . . . We went into church on Sunday, and Monday morning to prayers in the King's private chapel. The King is an active-looking man, light sandy hair and countenance, sanguine habit, stammers in his speech much as Peter Pindar has described. He is a man of great industry, uses much exercise, is said to possess all the private virtues in an eminent degree. He appears

---

* John Trumbull, the painter.

to have a quick intuitive faculty of discerning the human character. When his eye met mine I saw he marked me for a stranger, and I endeavored to outstare him, but in vain. 'Well!' thought I, 'a cat may look upon a king: by the same ascending scale a king may look upon me—and so, stare away.' The Queen is not handsome, but has the look of a very amiable woman. The four eldest princesses are thought surprising beauties. They are certainly handsome."

"*Aug.* 28. This day, at dinner at Mr. Dilley's, among several literary men, I met Dr. Gillies, author of the 'History of Greece.' I had much conversation with him, in which he discovered great learning and good sense. He is now writing the 'Roman Republic.' If he treats this history as well as he has that of Greece, no former history of that period need be read, and no future one written."

"*Aug.* 30. Dined with Dr. Bancroft. I dine abroad at least six days in the week; this, to a man of business, would be a bad economy of time, but for me it is the best way of collecting information, and does not interfere with other business."

"*Sep.* 7. Left London this morning at 11 o'clock with Mr. Parker, on our way to Calais and Brussels."

"*Calais, Sept.* 9. We are now as incontestably in France as ever Sterne was, and at the same hotel too, that of Mons. Dessein. It is old, large, and magnificent, but not remarkably cleanly. French cleanliness will never become proverbial except in the language of irony. . . . In crossing the Channel we found ourselves in company with several British officers, who are going to visit the camp at St. Omers. They are men of sense on every subject but that of America and the new government. We found, likewise, in the boat a young, well-dressed woman, travelling from London to the Austrian Flanders. There were so many tender things in her appearance that we were induced to ask her whether any gentleman pres-

ent was to be honored with her company. Being answered in the negative, and at the same time modestly
informed that it was business of a most pressing nature
of her father's, who was sick at London, which had em-
boldened her to undertake the journey alone, we begged
her to accept a seat in our chariot as far as our route will
permit. This she blushingly accepted, and we shall have
her company about one hundred and twenty miles. . . .
Count de Rochambeau is governor of Calais, but he is
out of town, which I regret, as I am addressed to him by
General Washington."

"*Brussels, Sept.* 11. This day we have travelled eighty
miles and reached the capital of the Austrian Brabant.
. . . . At ten this evening we entered Brussels. The gates
of the city were shut. We sent a servant forward to announce our names to the officer and bribe him to let us in,
who, after asking the usual questions about contraband
goods, consented to betray the great city to us for two
German shillings, and we are handsomely lodged in the
Hôtel d'Holland, where we stay about a week on business."

" *Sept.* 14. I have just returned from Antwerp, where
I went yesterday for the sake, merely, of seeing the curiosities of that justly celebrated place. . . .'"

" *Sept.* 23. Having finished all that can be done at
present with the Van Staphorsts about the lands, I go
to-morrow with Mr. Parker to Paris."

" *Cambray, Sept.* 24. We have rode to-day eighty miles,
through a most excellent country. . . . This was the seat
of Archbishop Fénelon, author of 'Telemachus.' His
palace is magnificent, the cathedral rich."

" *Paris, Sept.* 26. I have done nothing to-day except
pay my respects to Mr. Jefferson and the Marquis de
Lafayette."

" *Sept.* 27. I dined to-day at Mr. Jefferson's, where were
the Marquis, Mr. Parker, and an Italian chevalier, whose

name I never expect to remember, having been before in company with him sundry times."

"*Oct.* 3. It has rained every day since I have been in Paris till to-day. I have been dining with the Marquis, where was much company, chiefly American. The Patriots in France, I find, are very sanguine in their expectations that they shall effect a speedy and complete revolution in the government and establish a free constitution. The States General will doubtless assemble, and the opinions of all parties that something must be done will go a great way towards effecting something." He then ventures some remarks that seem strongly prophetic in view of the events of the succeeding summer.

"The government of France is in theory a despotism, but much softened in its administration by the respect which is paid to public opinion. I believe they have no written documents to prove that any class of the subjects have a right to any share in legislation, at least in legislating for the kingdom at large. Provincial rights they doubtless can prove; but these are so variant and discordant that it will be difficult, if not impossible, to bring them into practice. This is the reason why these rights have gone into disuse. It has been necessary for the energy and entirety of the kingdom that it should all be thrown into a common mass, and that one system should pervade the whole. This system must of course be derived from one head, the civil, military, legislative, and executive all being united in one person. Hence it is that France, considered as a collection of provinces or a confederacy of states, is what she is called—a heterogeneous mass. Considered as a kingdom, she is entire and energetic, but necessarily despotic. If the States General are composed of wise men they will consider that the small remnant of ancient provincial rights and the present opinions of the people are the materials with which they have to work in forming a constitution. As the former are variant and the latter variable it will be necessary to

conciliate and soften, in order to impart to the people
that portion of liberty which they can bear, and to impart
to all alike. Such wisdom, and the necessary integrity to
direct it, is hardly to be expected in a country like this.
I presume there are not to be found five men in Europe
who understand the nature of liberty and the theory of
government so well as they are understood by five hundred men in America. The friends to America in London and Paris are astonished at our conduct in adopting the New Constitution. They say we have given up
all we contended for. They are as intemperate in their
idea of liberty as we were in the year seventy-five."

" *Peronne, Oct.* 4. To-day we have travelled one hundred miles, and find ourselves in an elegant hotel at six
o'clock. We started after six in the morning. This way
of travelling is very amusing, and not in the least fatiguing, provided your carriage is strong and good. We have
our own courier, who rides on horseback and goes forward
to get the horses ready at every stage. On all the great
roads they give us good horses and good postilions, and
in this way a man may travel eight miles an hour, day
and night, for a week together if he chooses. All this
business of posts in France is reduced to one system and
farmed: it produces a revenue of 10,000,000 livres."

Oct. 10th he is at Dunkirk and makes a most interesting entry: "The French seem determined to enlarge
their naval force, and to lay the foundation of its increase
in the (whale) fishery. In the year 1783 a company was
formed to establish that business at Dunkirk. After
absorbing a considerable sum they applied to Government for assistance. Under the administration of Ca-
lonne the Government supplied them with —— livres on
loan, without interest, and agreed to take their oil at
a high price. By bad management, it is said, they have
failed, have sunk their own capital, and Government has
either lost theirs or are determined to reclaim it. Mr.

Rotch, from Massachusetts,* who is here, tells me he is now closing a contract with Government for carrying on the business upon a much larger scale. He has several vessels out this season. The King has now published an *arrêt*, prohibiting the importation of oil, except what is taken by French vessels. Rotch appears to be well acquainted with the business, and expects to make a large fortune in it. The former company have taken about 700 tons in the Brazil fishery and very little in the Greenland." † The journal ends with his return to Paris, Oct. 12, 1788.

The succeeding six years were marked by active literary employment, by intense activity in letters after 1790, when the failure of his embassy gave him more leisure, and indeed rendered him largely dependent on his pen for support. It was an age when, in France, the *literati* held their full measure of power. The philosophers of the preceding age, Fénelon, Montesquieu, Voltaire, Rousseau, had lent the calling dignity. King and nobles patronized it ; politicians courted it. That little knot of thinkers and writers,—Lagrange, Laplace, Berthollet, Garat, Bernardin St. Pierre, Daubenton, Hauy, Volney, Sicard, Monge, Thouin, La Harpe, Buache, Mentelle,— who founded the Normal School and, later, the National Institute, were builders of a mighty power in the kingdom —the power of the press. Nearly all were politicians,— Republicans of the moderate, constitutional, Girondist school. These men precipitated the Revolution, and, it may be added, at once lost control of it, as one does of a frenzied steed which his spur has set in motion. Jefferson, who had been four years in Paris as ambassador, was in friendly intercourse with these savants, and by the simple act of introduction gave his young countryman an assured position in their circle. Barlow found here con-

---

* A famous Nantucket whaling merchant.
† Mr. Rotch's enterprise also failed.

genial companionship. Deep learning, original ideas, a wide range of observation, plans of the largest philanthropy, he could appreciate, and these he found among the Girondist leaders of Paris. Just here his career assumes its most interesting phase. The Puritan lad, with generations of Puritan blood in his veins, brought up at the feet of Parson Bartlett, nurtured at Yale College—then the cradle of Federalism—bursts his chrysalis and appears in religion a liberal, in politics a pronounced Republican. It would be unjust to him to say that the change was produced solely by intercourse with the French *literati*. There is evidence in his letters that from youth up he had been dissatisfied with the iron-bound creed then in vogue. It chafed him, as the harness the spirited young colt. Tutor Buckminster sowed the seeds of this restiveness by permitting and encouraging that spirit of free inquiry in his classes, of which he spoke in his letter, and although, later, Barlow preached in their pulpits and wrote the hymnal used in their worship, a reference in one of his letters from the camps indicates that the Association of Congregational ministers of Connecticut had refused to license him for the chaplaincy from doubts as to his orthodoxy, and that he had in consequence been examined by the Council at Northampton, Mass., and had received from them his authority.

Politically we know he possessed all the elements of the Republican of the day, and awaited only an opportunity to leave the Conservative for the Progressive ranks. There is no evidence that he became a pronounced atheist, like some of his French compeers. He was hardly an apostate, although the charge was freely made against him by those of his old friends on this side the Atlantic who remained true to their early convictions, and whom his double desertion changed to bitter and calumniating enemies. But this will more fully appear in the sequel. Once enlisted, however, the young soldier engaged with ardor in the conflict : pamphlets, addresses, feuilletons in prose and verse, assailing royal and ecclesiastical privilege, poured from his pen in a constant stream, and he was soon recognized throughout Europe as one of the leaders of the Republican cause. He was in Paris at the birth of the fearful Revolution—the 14th of July, the 4th of August, the 5th of October—an interested but hopeful spectator. On the 20th of July he wrote his wife, still lingering in the rural shades of Greenfield Hill : " All the true things which you see published, however horrible, however cruel, however just, however noble, memorable, and important in their consequences, have passed under my eye, and it is really no small gratification to me to have seen two complete revolutions in favor of liberty. Everything is now quiet in Paris. I look upon the affairs of this nation as on the point of being settled on the most rational and lasting foundation." He concludes: " Nothing but the contemplation of the infinite happiness that I am sure will result to millions of human beings from these commotions could enable me to tolerate the observance of them."

After the failure of his special mission his time seems to have been pretty evenly divided between Paris and London. He was one of that body " of American citizens who, for commercial or political traffic, or both," were " sometimes resident in England and sometimes in France," and who made up mainly the London Society for Constitutional Information. One not familiar with this period of English history in its minuter details can have little conception of the disquiet and state of ferment into which the nation was plunged by the French Revolution. Societies whose chief objects were such amendments to the present constitution as would give annual sessions of Parliament and universal suffrage were formed in all the large cities of the kingdom. Pamphlets and broadsides advocating these " reforms " were sown broadcast ; public meetings were held. A single petition to this effect received 140,000 signers. In fact, the liberal movement shared with Warren Hastings the attention of Parliament, and elicited some of the finest efforts of those Commons giants, Burke, Sheridan, Fox, and Pitt. There were three important societies in London which favored the cause of the French Republicans, and lent them sympathy and substantial aid. These were, first, the "Revolution Society," originally formed to celebrate the anniversary of the landing of William III. and the famous revolution of 1688, which established the British Constitution; second, the "Constitutional Society," which had a regular organization, held stated meetings, and was devoted to the dissemination of political writings favoring a change in the existing Constitution; and third, a "Society of Constitutional Information," composed largely of Americans, which we have already noticed. Dr. Price, the reputed author of Pitt's sinking-fund system; Dr. Priestly, the learned and liberal Unitarian divine; Horne Tooke, the famous philosopher, political writer, and wit: Thomas Paine, Joel Barlow, Daniel Adams, John Frost, and Hayley the poet, and biographer of Cowper, were active members of these various organizations. All three societies openly favored French Republicanism, and at various times sent "Addresses" to the National Assembly. That from the American Society was written by Joel Barlow, and conveyed personally by himself and John Frost.* The greater part of the years 1790–92, however, were spent in London. His friends, the Girondists, had been overthrown by the Jacobins; the lions had been supplanted by the wolves, and residence in Paris for him was both unsafe and uncomfortable. He had made while in Paris extensive notes for a history of the French Revolu-

---

* An English historian, referring to this mission, speaks of Barlow as "the laureate of the United States, the author of that not-to-be-forgotten epic wherein George Washington is typified by Joshua, and the free citizens of America and their expulsion of the English by the Jews and their conquest of the Holy Land."

tion, and he was also employed during this period in writing his caustic poetical squib, " The Conspiracy of Kings." His most important work, however, was a volume of political essays entitled, "Advice to the Privileged Orders." It appears by a note in the author's copy before us, that this book was finished in London in the latter part of the year 1791, and that the first part was published in that city in February, 1792. It is safe to say that no political work of the day created so wide an interest, or was so extensively read. Charles Fox, in Parliament, passed a formal eulogium upon it. The British Government suppressed it and proscribed its author, even seized on his private letters as those of a suspect. " Mr. Burke often makes honorable mention of you in Parliament," wrote Mrs. Barlow, ironically, in January, 1793, to her husband, hiding in Paris from British emissaries. " Sometimes he calls you a prophet—the prophet Joel. . . . ." And again : " Mr. Burke said that a citizen of the name of Joel Barlow, another of the name of John Adams, and Citizen Frost were engaged in this correspondence and were answerable." Jefferson, on receiving the volume, wrote its author from America: " Be assured that your endeavors to bring the transatlantic world into the world of reason are not without their effect here." Sturdy old John Adams read it with attention, as is evidenced by his reference to its heresies in his third letter on government to John Taylor in 1814. The work which created such widespread interest was not an attack on religion and law, as the more bigoted at once declared it, but a trenchant, fearless attack on kingly and ecclesiastical tyranny and abuses. Eight chapters, or essays, on the Feudal System, the Church, the Military, the Administration of Justice, Revenue and Public Expenditure, the Means of Subsistence, Literature, Science and Art, War and Peace, compose the work. The first four chapters were published in a separate volume, as we have seen, in 1792 ; the last four nearly a year later. There was that in the work to alarm and anger many classes. Besides a sharp arraignment of church * and priestly abuses, it bitterly attacked the feudal system, and especially primogeniture. It exposed and held up to public ridicule the abuses, absurdities, and intricacies of English jurisprudence, and it was, we believe, the first publication to condemn capital punishment and the "lotteries, tontines, and annuities on separate lives," then so popular in Europe. Full on its heels the poet launched a sharper and more bitter philippic, this time in verse—"The Conspiracy of Kings." England, Holland, Naples, Sweden, and the German States had conspired to crush out Republicanism in France, and this coalition suggested the poem.

"The Conspiracy of Kings" was more popular with the Whigs of England than the prose work. Its brevity—it contains less than 300 lines—made it easy of insertion in newspapers and broadsides, and it was quickly spread among all classes of readers, eliciting the hearty applause of the Liberal and the bitter condemnation of the Conservative or Government party.

From these political broils in which the poet's warm sympathies and pugnacious instincts involved him, it will be pleasant to turn aside, and even retrace our steps a

---

* That no injustice may be done our author, we give his definition of the term "church" as he uses it : "From that association of ideas which usually connects the church with religion, I may run the risk of being misunderstood by some readers unless I advertise them that I consider no connection as existing between these two subjects, and that when I speak of 'church' indefinitely, I mean the government of a state assuming in the name of God to govern by divine authority, or, in other words, darkening the consciences of men in order to oppress them. In the United States of America there is, strictly speaking, no such thing as a church, and yet in no country are the people more religious. All sorts of religious opinions are entertained there, and yet no heresy among them all. All modes of worship are practised, and yet there is no schism. Men frequently change their creed and their worship, and yet there is no apostasy. They have ministers of religion, but no priests. In short, religion is there a personal and not a corporate concern."

little, to consider his family relations. Barlow was so domestic in tastes and habits, and so tenderly attached to his wife, that the parting from her must have been the bitterest feature of his self-imposed exile. As soon as it became apparent that his mission had failed, and that he would remain some time in Europe, he wrote in the ardent and impassioned strains of a lover, desiring her to join him in Paris at once. Mrs. Barlow, however, as was natural, demurred. She shrank with womanly dread from the long sea voyage alone, and the arrival among strangers. Aside from the absence of her husband, her life at Greenfield Hill, the most charming of rural retreats, with her brother as protector, the learned and poetic Dr. Dwight as pastor and friend, and a refined society at command, was all that could be desired. But Paris, to the average New England gentlewoman of that day, represented all that was vile, lawless, licentious, papistical, and atheistical. Several letters from him, magnificent examples of special pleading, were necessary before she could be persuaded to undertake the journey. His directions how to come and what to provide for the voyage will read strangely to modern lady travellers.

" When you come to New York," he wrote, " you will see Mrs. Adams, the Vice-President's wife ; talk with her and Mrs. Smith, her daughter." " There are four captains," he adds, " who follow the London trade and go twice a year, all of whom are the cleverest fellows in the world. They are much used to carrying passengers and ladies. They are acquainted with Prom (Abraham Baldwin) and me, and will treat you with all the attention, politeness, and kindness in the world. 2. You will find in New York, well recommended, a good maid who is used to the sea; take one with you, unless you find a female companion that you like, in which case you may do without a maid. 3. The captain will find all the customary provisions. Take on board besides, the following things (I mention them not because they are

the most necessary, but because you would be most likely
to omit them): woollen stockings, a loose woollen gown,
oat-meal, Indian-meal to make gruel, rice, chocolate, oil of
peppermint, and some stomachic medicines—rhubarb or
salts. 4. Give the captain a good price, even a double
price, and bargain with him to see you lodged at the place
I shall mention. If by contrary winds you should come
into a port a little distant from London the captain will
give you a coach and a companion. You will then go to
the house of Mrs. Rogers, No. 18 King Street, Cheap-
side, London." Then, if he was not there, she was to
write to certain gentlemen, whose addresses he enclosed,
who could advise her where he might be found. This
plan was carried out. The lady sailed with a Captain
Wolsey early in June, and arrived safely at Mrs. Rogers';
but the errant husband was not there to meet her. Instead, he wrote, saying that it was impossible for him to
leave Paris under several days.

One gains from the letters a very affecting picture of
the scene that followed—the tears, bewailings, and home-
sickness : not even the sympathy of a friend, a "charming Connecticut lady," whom he had prevailed on to go
to London " to meet her, and keep her laughing till he
came," could allay the feeling of disappointment and
wrong.

In about three weeks, however, Mrs. Barlow, with her
friend, Mrs. Blackden, passed over to Calais, where the
husband met them, and the happy pair were reunited after
two years' separation. They at once took up their abode
in Paris. How did the young, piously reared, Puritan
lady relish the gay capital, is a question that at once occurs to the reader. Fortunately, we have a letter from
her to Mrs. Dr. Dwight, which answers it satisfactorily.
When she had been in Paris about a month she wrote that
lady : " O, it is altogether disagreeable to me. It is only
existing. I have not an hour I can call my own except
when I sleep. Must at all times be dressed and see com-

pany, which you know, my dear madam, is not to my taste. We are pent up in a narrow, dirty street surrounded with high brick walls, and can scarcely see the light of the sun. We have no Sabbath : it is looked upon as a day of amusement entirely. O, how ardently do I wish to return to America, and to Greenfield, that dear, delightful village." The city became more tolerable, however, as time passed.

The bright, pretty Connecticut girl soon found that she did not appear to disadvantage, as she had feared, in the polished circles of Paris. The provincialisms quickly vanished ; she learned to speak French and Italian with ease, and soon became as great a favorite and as pronounced a Republican as her husband.

The two remained in Paris until the spring of 1791, when, as we have seen, the enormities of the Jacobins rendered residence there unsafe, and they repaired to London, taking lodgings in Litchfield Street, then the literary centre. His papers contain no reference to the striking scenes and incidents that must have attended his residence in both Paris and London during this period. He kept no journal. Notes and jottings addressed to his wife contain frequent references to some mysterious affair which was dependent on the action of the House of Lords. He was in constant communication with the French patriots. The American painters—Trumbull, Copley, and Benjamin West—were among his associates, as were also the London *literati*—Horne Tooke, Price, Priestly, Thirlwall, and William Hayley, the poet, of whom Southey said that "he was by popular election king of the English poets of his time." At Copley's, who was then living in the house No. 25 George Street, Hanover Square, so charmingly described by his granddaughter in her recent life of the artist, and which was a favorite resort for all resident or visiting Americans in London, the young poet and his wife were frequent and welcome guests.

But his chief employment, as we have seen, was the writing and publishing of his political essays, presumably under the patronage of the Constitutional Society.

Early in April, 1792, he has an important project to communicate to Lafayette, who is at Metz, in command of 35,000 men, opposing the Austrian army of invasion, and sets out to pierce the cordon of the opposing force. He details his adventures during the trip in a series of interesting letters to Mrs. Barlow. From Aix-la-Chapelle he writes: "In travelling on the Continent I find I have seen much to affect as well as much to afflict. I find myself more than ever affected with the fortunes of that dear, deluded race that we call our fellow-creatures. I say nothing of their situation in the countries where I have passed, as that would be like politics, and my letter may be opened; I reserve that till I see you. But I wished that my Ruthy could have been a witness of some scenes that have so affected me." He adds in French that news of the declaration of war—(between France and Austria)—has been received there. From Dunkirk, May 20: "Ever since I wrote from Aix last month it has been out of my power to write you, that is, to say anything that I wished to say, as I expected my letters would be opened; then I expected every day to have got into France, when I should be free to tell you all. But the cursed tyrannies of men, and the more supportable ones of the elements, have fought against me ever since. I thank God I have escaped them all, though our new philosophers in London have not taught me to subdue them. I left that seat of the 'Forsaken Villains,' Coblentz, on the 3d of May, after having concocted a good plan with my friend to render the most essential service to France. I was to make the best of my way to France to communicate my scheme to Lafayette, who was then near Metz—(cast your eye upon the map). The 4th day I had got within a mile of the parties, when I was taken up by the Austrians and sent back to Luxembourg. A

long tale hangs to this which I will tell you afterwards.
I found it impossible to get into France in that direction.
From Luxembourg, after several days' hinderance, I trav-
ersed all the frontiers as far as Ostend, not without making several attempts to reach the French army, which lay
within two or three leagues of me all the way. From
Luxembourg to Ostend is 200 miles, travelling very slow.
At Ostend I went on board a heavy, dull-sailing Dutchman to come to Dunkirk, only thirty miles; as fine a
morning as need be; but my Dutchman did not reach
Dunkirk that night, when, to be sure, nothing but a violent storm would do, and here we have been beating and
buffeting three days and three nights and a half, within
plain sight of Dunkirk, and a more terrible scene my
poor nerves never experienced. . . . O my Carissima, had
I set out one fortnight sooner, or immediately on receiving S.'s letter, everything would have been done to my
wish, and better than I had ever calculated. Had I
arrived at Luxembourg three days sooner I might have
got, without difficulty, into France. Had I sailed a tide
sooner from Ostend it would have saved me four days,
and perhaps been the saving of the scheme, which perhaps
may be once more ruined by delay. . . . Tell Mr. Johnson if either of my books are sold off to go on with
another edition as with the first." His letters he directs
addressed " Care Monsieur de Lafayette, Lieut.-Gen. *des
armées de France en son camp.*"

He continues the narrative from Paris on the 31st of
May.

"I have arrived here this moment. Lafayette sent
me to negotiate the affair of S—— with the minister. I
don't much expect it will succeed, but I am not sorry
that I pursued it, because it has led me to much information. . . ."

On the 4th of June he wrote in French that he could
not finish his affair because of Lafayette's non-arrival;
and again, on the 18th, that he should leave Paris in five

days for London, not having been able to finish the business that brought him there.

In a letter dated the 25th he gives this interesting *morceau :* "You will hear frightful stories about the riots at the Tuilleries on the 20th. You must believe but little ; there was no violence committed. This visit to the king by armed citizens was undoubtedly contrary to law, but the existence of a king is contrary to another law of a higher origin." He returned to London about the first of July.

His leisure hours on his return were spent in preparing a "Letter" to the National Convention of France, which was presented on the assembling of that body in September. This letter, which appears among his published works, will compare favorably with any state paper of the age. It was a lengthy treatise, filling some seventy printed pages, and called the attention of the legislators to such important topics as the equality of rights, the people's ability for self-government, necessity of a simple constitution, danger of a national church, distinction between a constitutional code and occasional laws, acquirement or loss of citizenship, naturalization, elections, magisterial and ministerial functions, salaries and perquisites of office, inviolability of Senators and Representatives, criminal law, the abolition of capital punishment, public instruction against public lotteries, independence of colonies, abolition of the standing army, and ratification of amendments. The paper was received with marked favor by the delegates, and led to their conferring on its author the distinguished honor of French citizenship. Dr. Joseph Warner, the English surgeon and philosopher, writes to Barlow, from Paris, Oct. 18th, on this subject : "A thousand thanks for the 'feast of reason and flow of soul' with which you have this day regaled me in your kind letter and that to the National Convention. It will, I flatter myself, do great credit to the writer and great good to the glorious cause of which he

is so able a supporter. . . . Leave the scene? No: you
must come here and be made a conventionalist—a citizen.
I think you will be whether you come or not. For in
the *Patriote* of the 25th ult. appeared the following list
of seven *Anglais* to whom the National Convention proposed to confer the title of Citizen of France: Thomas
Cooper, John Horne Tooke, John Oswald, George Borls,
Joel Barlow, Thomas Christie; and whose should the last
name be but that of your humble servant, who was not
a little pleased to see himself, with his little pretensions,
in such good company." Save Washington and Hamilton, Barlow was the only American on whom the privileges of French citizenship had been conferred. In
November the poet suddenly quitted England, it is said
to escape arbitrary arrest for his political heresies, and
several years elapsed before he again revisited her familiar
scenes. Mrs. Barlow, however, remained in London.
Arriving in Paris he found that the commissioners
appointed by the National Convention to organize Savoy
into a Department of France were about proceeding
thither, Gregoire, Bishop of Blois, Senator and Member
of the Institute, with other warm friends of the poet,
being among them, and it was arranged that the newly-
made citizen should accompany them to Savoy, and be
returned as its deputy to the Convention. Barlow details the whole plan in a letter to his wife, dated Paris,
4th December, 1792: " I am called upon this moment, and
have scarcely time to tell you of it, to go with the Commissioners of the National Convention to Savoy. That
country is united to France as an 84th Department.
These Commissioners are going to organize the internal
government, and teach them how to act in forming themselves and in choosing their deputies to the National
Convention. They intend a certain friend of your's shall
be chosen. Of this you must not be sure, but he will at
least see much of the south of France, the city of Lyons,
the Alps, etc." He then expected to be absent three

weeks, and advised his wife that she might join him if she wished at Chambery, the ancient seat of the province, where the Commission would make headquarters. In point of fact he was absent all winter. He arrived about December 15, and in a note of that date gives this flattering estimate of the Savoyards: " Here is a people, rigorous and hardy, just born to liberty. They have long struggled under the worst and most complicated species of tyranny without being broken down in their spirits or debased in their morals. Their character bears a strong resemblance to the mountains which gave them birth. They appear to be perfectly united among themselves, and enthusiastically attached to their new brothers, the French. . . . Their patriotism and morals appear to me the purest of any people I ever knew.''

Although he was received in Lyons and Savoy " with signal marks of fraternity and respect," yet, he informs her, " the object which you will suppose I had somewhat in mind will probably not be accomplished." December 15th, he writes in French, that he is occupied day and night in writing " a little work on the political situation in Piedmont, in the form of a letter to the Piedmontese, exposing (*exposant*) the advantages which would attend a revolution of government in their country," a letter which was printed and sown broadcast that winter on the Piedmontese slopes. In later letters he tells her of a " little song" which he has made on the anniversary of their wedding,* but not a whisper is breathed of the charming mock pastoral which, more than anything he ever wrote, proves his claim to the possession of true genius. For in the little inn at Chambery the poem " Hasty-Pudding" had its birth. Several expressions in the poet's letters show that the rural scenery of Savoy had brought vividly to mind the Connecticut hill slopes and the pastoral scenes of youth. '' There always was something in rural scenes too bewitching for me to enjoy

---

* See Chapter VIII.

The following is a *fac simile* of the opening page of the first draft of the poem " Hasty Pudding," in the author's handwriting :

There is a choice in spoons

Not the rude Alps that hide me from the skies
Nor Gallia's chiefs that o'er their summits rise
Not the rude Alps, where Gallia's flag unfurl'd
Bears death to kings & freedom to the world

Not the proud Alps that hide me from the skies
Can warm my soul & bid my numbers rise
Nor o'er their heights the Gallias flag that o'er their
Bears death to kings & freedom to the world

Ye Alps audacious; thro' the heavens that
the day & hide me from the skies
Ye Gallic flags, that o'er their heights unfurl'd
Bear death to kings & freedom to the world
I sing not you; a softer theme I chuse
A virgin theme unconscious of the Muse
But fruitful, rich, well suited to inspire
The frenzy of poetic fire.

Despise it not, ye Bards to terror steel'd
Who hurl your epic thunders round the field   10
Nor ye who strain your midnight throats to sing
The joys the vineyard & the Still-house bring
Or on some distant Fair   your notes employ
And speak of raptures that you ne'er enjoy.
I sing the sweets I know, the charms I feel
My morning incense & my evening meal
The sweets of Hasty-Pudding. Come dear bowl
Glide o'er my palate & inspire my soul
The milk beside thee smoking from the kine
Its substance mingled, married in with thine   20

without you," he writes to his wife. " If ever I grow peevish or indifferent, take me into the country among the rocks and trees. They will immediately transform you into an angel, and me into anything you please." " There are many things about the country which charm me," he writes again. "With you and a little farm among these romantic mountains and valleys I could be happy, content. I would care no more for the pleasures of the plain; but America—the word is sweetness to my soul; it awakens all the tenderness of my nature." The green hills and trim farm-houses of Savoy brought vividly to mind his own Connecticut hills, and the association was heightened when, on gathering with his grave compeers one day for the evening meal, he found smoking hot on the table the New Englander's national dish—Hasty-Pudding. The bard could scarce believe his eyes. He had sought it in vain in Paris, in London, at the hands of many a famous *chef*, and now, behold it under the smoky rafters of a Savoyard inn. All through the meal, it is said, he descanted to his interested colleagues on the merits of his favorite dish. When alone, these reminiscences continued to haunt him, until, under their influence, he produced what is incomparably his best poem, and which still remains one of the best examples of its peculiar style of mock heroic and pastoral verse ever produced. The poet here is natural, spontaneous, unaffected. His subject has been familiar from childhood: his tropes and figures are furnished by his surroundings, or drawn from the storehouse of memory.

He sang:

> Ye Alps audacious, through the heavens that rise,
> To cramp the day and hide me from the skies;
> Ye Gallic flags that, o'er their heights unfurl'd,
> Bear death to kings and freedom to the world,
> I sing not you. A softer theme I choose,
> A virgin theme, unconscious of the Muse,
> But fruitful, rich, well suited to inspire
> The purest frenzy of poetic fire.

Despise it not, ye bards to terror steeled,
Who hurl your thunders round the epic field;
Nor ye who strain your midnight throats to sing
Joys that the vineyard and the still house bring;
Or on some distant fair your notes employ,
And speak of raptures that you ne'er enjoy.
I sing the sweets I know, the charms I feel,
My morning incense, and my evening meal,
The sweets of Hasty-Pudding. Come, dear bowl,
Glide o'er my palate and inspire my soul.
The milk beside thee, smoking from the kine,
Its substance mingled, married in with thine,
Shall cool and temper thy superior heat,
And save the pains of blowing while I eat.

Oh! could the smooth, the emblematic song
Flow like thy genial juices o'er my tongue,
Could those mild morsels in my numbers chime,
And as they roll in substance, roll in rhyme,
No more thy awkward, unpoetic name,
Should shun the Muse, or prejudice thy fame;
But, rising grateful to the accustomed ear,
All bards should catch it and all realms revere!

Assist me first with pious toil to trace,
Through wrecks of time, thy lineage and thy race;
Declare what lovely squaw, in days of yore,
Ere great Columbus sought thy native shore,
First gave thee to the world; her works of fame
Have lived indeed, but lived without a name.
Some tawny Ceres, goddess of her days,
First learned with stones to crack the well dried maize,
Through the rough sieve to shake the golden shower,
In boiling water stir the yellow flour;
The yellow flour, bestrewed and stirred with haste,
Swells in the flood and thickens to a paste,
Then puffs and wallops, rises to the brim,
Drinks the dry knobs that on the surface swim;
The knobs at last the busy ladle breaks,
And the whole mass its true consistence takes.

Could but her sacred name, unknown so long,
Rise, like her labors, to the son of song,
To her, to them, I'd consecrate my lays,
And blow her pudding with the breath of praise.
If 'twas Oella, whom I sang before,
I'd here ascribe her one great virtue more.

Nor through the rich Peruvian realms alone
The fame of Sol's sweet daughter should be known,
But o'er the world's wide climes should live secure,
Far as his rays extend, as long as they endure.

Dear Hasty-Pudding, what unpromised joy
Expands my heart, to meet thee in Savoy!
Doomed o'er the world through devious paths to roam,
Each clime my country, and each house my home,
My soul is soothed, my cares have found an end,
I greet my long-lost, unforgotten friend.

For thee through Paris, that corrupted town,
How long in vain I wandered up and down,
Where shameless Bacchus, with his drenching hoard
Cold from his cave, usurps the morning board.
London is lost in smoke and steeped in tea;
No Yankee there can lisp the name of thee;
The uncouth word, a libel on the town,
Would call a proclamation from the crown.
From climes oblique, that fear the sun's full rays,
Chilled in their fogs, exclude the generous maize;
A grain whose rich luxuriant growth requires
Short, gentle showers and bright, ethereal fires.

But here, though distant from our native shore,
With mutual glee we meet and laugh once more,
The same! I know thee by that yellow face,
That strong complexion of true Indian race,
Which time can never change, nor soil impair,
Nor Alpine snows, nor Turkey's morbid air;
For endless years, through every mild domain,
Where grows the maize, there thou art sure to reign.

But man, more fickle, the bold license claims,
In different realms to give thee different names.
Thee, the soft nations round the warm Levant
Polenta call, the French, of course, *Polente;*
E'en in thy native regions, how I blush
To hear the Pennsylvanians call thee *Mush!*
On Hudson's banks, while men of Belgic spawn
Insult and eat thee by the name Suppawn.
All spurious appellations, void of truth—
I've better known thee from my earliest youth:
Thy name is *Hasty-Pudding!* thus my sire
Was wont to greet thee fuming from the fire;
And while he argued in thy just defence
With logic clear, he thus explained the sense :—

"In *haste* the boiling cauldron o'er the blaze
Receives and cooks the ready-powdered maize;
In *haste* 'tis served, and then, in equal *haste*,
With cooling milk, we make the sweet repast.
No carving to be done, no knife to grate
The tender ear, and wound the stony plate;
But the smooth spoon, just fitted to the lip,
And taught with art the yielding mass to dip,
By frequent journeys to the bowl well stored
Performs the hasty honors of the board."
Such is thy name, significant and clear,
A name, a sound to every Yankee dear,
But most to me, whose heart and palate chaste
Preserve my pure hereditary taste.

There are who strive to stamp with disrepute
The luscious food, because it feeds the brute;
In tropes of high-strained wit, while gaudy prigs
Compare thy nursling man to pampered pigs;
With sovereign scorn I treat the vulgar jest,
Nor fear to share thy bounties with the beast.
What though the generous cow gives me to quaff
The milk nutritious; am I then a calf?
Or can the genius of the noisy swine,
Though nursed on pudding, claim a kin to mine?
Sure the sweet song I fashion to thy praise
Runs more melodious than the notes they raise.

My song, resounding in its grateful glee,
No merit claims; I praise myself in thee.
My father loved thee through his length of days!
For thee his fields were shaded o'er with maize;
From thee what health, what vigor he possessed,
Ten sturdy freemen from his loins attest;
Thy constellation ruled my natal morn,
And all my bones were made of Indian corn.
Delicious grain! whatever form it take,
To roast or boil, to smother or to bake,
In every dish 'tis welcome still to me,
But most, my Hasty-Pudding! most in thee.

Let the green succotash with thee contend,
Let beans and corn their sweetest juices blend,
Let butter drench them in its yellow tide,
And a long slice of bacon grace their side;
Not all the plate, how famed soe'er it be,
Can please my palate like a bowl of thee.

Some talk of Hoe-Cake, fair Virginia's pride;
Rich Johnny-Cake this mouth has often tried.
Both please me well, their virtues much the same;
Alike their fabric as allied their fame,
Except in dear New England, where the last
Receives a dash of pumpkin in the paste,
To give it sweetness and improve the taste.
But place them all before me, smoking hot,
The big round dumpling rolling from the pot;
The pudding of the bag, whose quivering breast,
With suet lined, leads on the Yankee feast;
The Charlotte brown, within whose crusty sides
A belly soft the pulpy apple hides;
The yellow bread, whose face like amber glows,
And all of Indian that the bake-pan knows—
Ye tempt me not, my favorite greets my eyes,
To that loved bowl my spoon by instinct flies.

To mix the food by vicious rules of art,
To kill the stomach and to sink the heart,
To make mankind to social virtue sour,
Cram o'er each dish and be what they devour;
For this the Kitchen Muse first framed her book,
Commanding sweets to stream from every cook;
Children no more their antic gambols tried,
And friends to physic wondered why they died.
Not so the Yankee—his abundant feast,
With simples furnished, and with plainness drest,
A numerous offspring gathers round the board
And cheers alike the servant and the lord,
Whose well-bought hunger prompts the joyous task,
And health attends them from the short repast.

While the full pail rewards the milkmaid's toil,
The mother sees the morning cauldron boil;
To stir the pudding next demands her care,
To spread the table and the bowls prepare;
To feed the children as their portions cool,
And comb their heads and send them off to school.
Yet may the simplest dish some rules impart,
For nature scorns not all the aids of art:
E'en Hasty-Pudding, purest of all food,
May still be bad, indifferent, or good,
As sage experience the short process guides,
Or want of skill, or want of care presides.
Whoe'er would form it on the surest plan,
To rear the child and long sustain the man;

To shield the morals while it mends the size,
And all the powers of every food supplies—
Attend the lessons that the Muse shall bring,
Suspend your spoons, and listen while I sing.

But since, O man! thy life and health demand
Not food alone, but labor from thy hand,
First in the field, beneath the sun's strong rays,
Ask of thy Mother Earth the needful maize;
She loves the race that courts her yielding soil,
And gives her bounties to the sons of toil.

When now the ox, obedient to thy call,
Repays the loan that filled the winter stall,
Pursue his traces o'er the furrowed plain,
And plant in measured hills the golden grain.
But when the tender germ begins to shoot,
And the green spire declares the sprouting root,
Then guard your nursling from each greedy foe—
The insidious worm, the all-devouring crow.
A little ashes, sprinkled round the spire,
Soon steeped in rain, will bid the worm retire;
The feathered robber with his hungry maw
Swift flies the field before your man of straw—
A frightful image, such as schoolboys bring
When met to burn the Pope, or hang the King.

Thrice in the season, through each verdant row,
Wield the strong ploughshare and the faithful hoe—
The faithful hoe; a double task that takes,—
To till the summer corn and roast the winter cakes.
Slow springs the blade while checked by chilling rains,
E'er yet the sun the seat of Cancer gains;
But when his present fires emblaze the land,
Then start the juices, then the roots expand;
Then, like a column of Corinthian mould,
The stalk struts upward and the leaves unfold;
The bushy branches all the ridges fill,
Entwine their arms, and kiss from hill to hill.
Here cease to vex them, all your cares are done;
Leave the last labors to the parent sun;
Beneath his genial smiles the well-dressed field,
When Autumn calls, a plenteous crop shall yield.

Now the strong foliage bears the standards high,
And shoots the tall top-gallants to the sky;
The suckling ears their silky fringes bend,
And pregnant grown, their swelling coats distend;

The loaded stalk, while still the burden grows,
O'erhangs the space that runs between the rows.
High as a hop-field waves the silent grove,
A safe retreat for little thefts of love,
When the fledged roasting-ears invite the maid
To meet her swain beneath the new-formed shade :
His generous hand unloads the cumbrous hill,
And the green spoils her ready basket fill;
Small compensation for the twofold bliss,
The promised wedding and the present kiss.

Slight depredations these; but now the moon
Calls from his hollow tree the sly raccoon;
And while by night he bears his prize away,
The bolder squirrel labors through the day :
Both thieves alike, but provident of time—
A virtue rare that almost hides their crime.
Then let them steal the little stores they can,
And fill their granaries from the toils of man;
We've one advantage where they take no part :
With all their wiles they ne'er have found the art
To boil the Hasty-Pudding; here we shine
Superior far to tenants of the pine;
This envied boon to man shall still belong,
Unshared by them in substance or in song.

At last the closing season browns the plain,
And ripe October gathers in the grain;
Deep-loaded carts the spacious corn-house fill,
The sack distended marches to the mill;
The laboring mill beneath the burden groans,
And showers the future pudding from the stones,
'Till the glad housewife greets the powdered gold,
And the new crop exterminates the old.
Ah ! who can sing, what every wight must feel,
The joy that enters with the bag of meal.
A general jubilee pervades the house,
Wakes every child and gladdens every mouse.

The days grow short, but though the falling sun
To the glad swain proclaims his day's work done,
Night's pleasing shades his various tasks prolong,
And yield new subjects to my various song.
For now, the corn-house filled, the harvest home,
The invited neighbors to the *Husking* come;
A frolic scene, where work, and mirth, and play
Unite their charms to chase the hours away.

Where the huge heap lies centred in the hall,
The lamp suspended from the cheerful wall,
Brown, corn-fed nymphs and strong, hard-handed beaux,
Alternate ranged, extend in circling rows,
Assume their seats, the solid mass attack;
The dry husks rustle and the corn-cobs crack;
The song, the laugh, alternate notes resound,
And the sweet cider trips in silence round.

The laws of husking every wight can tell—
And sure no laws he ever keeps so well:
For each red ear a general kiss he gains,
With each smut ear she smuts the luckless swains;
But when to some sweet maid a prize is cast,
Red as her lips and taper as her waist,
She walks the round, and culls one favored beau,
Who leaps, the luscious tribute to bestow.
Various the sport as are the wits and brains
Of well-pleased lasses and contending swains,
Till the vast mound of corn is swept away,
And he that gets the last ear wins the day.

Meanwhile the housewife urges all her care,
The well-earned feast to hasten and prepare:
The sifted meal already waits her hand,
The milk is strained, the bowls in order stand,
The fire flames high, and, as a fool that takes
The headlong stream that o'er the mill-dam breaks,
Foams, roars, and rages with incessant toils,
So the vexed cauldron rages, roars, and boils.

First with clean salt she seasons well the food,
Then strews the flour and thickens all the flood.
Long o'er the simmering fire she lets it stand—
To stir it well demands a stronger hand:
The husband takes his turn, and round and round
The ladle flies; at last the toil is crowned;
When to the board the thronging huskers pour,
And take their seats as at the corn before.

I leave them to their feast.   There still belong
More useful matters to my faithful song;
For rules there are, though ne'er unfolded yet,
Nice rules and wise, how pudding should be eat.

Some with molasses line the luscious treat,
And mix, like Bards, the useful with the sweet.

A wholesome dish, and well deserving praise,
A great resource in those bleak, wintry days,
When the chilled earth lies buried deep in snow,
And raging Boreas dries the shivering cow.

Blest cow! thy praise shall still my notes employ:
Great source of health, the only source of joy,
Mother of Egypt's god ;—but sure for me,
Were I to leave my God I'd worship thee.
How oft thy teats these pious hands have prest!
How oft thy bounties proved my only feast!
How oft I've fed thee with my favorite grain,
And roared, like thee, to see thy children slain!

Ye swains who know her various worth to prize,
Ah! house her well from Winter's angry skies.
Potatoes, pumpkins, should her sadness cheer,
Corn from her crib, and mashes from your beer;
When Spring returns she'll well acquit the loan,
And nurse at once your infants and her own.

Milk, then, with pudding, I should always choose;
To this in future I confine my Muse,
Till she, in haste, some further hints unfold,
Good for the young, nor useless to the old.
First in your bowl the milk abundant take,
Then drop with care along the silver lake
Your flakes of pudding; these, at first, will hide
Their little bulk beneath the swelling tide;
But when their growing mass no more can sink,
When the soft island looms above the brink,
Then check your hand; you've got the portion due.
So taught my Sire, and what he taught is true.

There is a choice in spoons. Though small appear
The nice distinction, yet to me 'tis clear
The deep-bowled Gallic spoon, contrived to scoop
In ample draughts the thin diluted soup,
Performs not well in those substantial things,
Whose mass adhesive to the metal clings;
Where the strong labial muscles must embrace
The gentle curve, and sweep the hollow space.
With ease to enter and discharge the freight,
A bowl less concave, but still more dilate,
Becomes the pudding best. The shape, the size,
A secret rests, unknown to vulgar eyes;

Experienced feeders can alone impart
A rule so much above the lore of art:
These tuneful lips, that thousand spoons have tried,
With just precision could the point decide.

Though not in song; the Muse but poorly shines
In cones and cubes, and geometric lines,
Yet the true form, as near as she can tell,
Is that small section of a goose-egg shell
Which in two equal portions shall divide
The distance from the centre to the side.

Fear not to slaver; 'tis no deadly sin.
Like the fine Frenchman, from your joyous chin
Suspend the ready napkin; or, like me,
Poise with one hand your bowl upon your knee;
Just in the zenith your wise head project,
Your full spoon, rising in a line direct,
Bold as a bucket, heeds no drops that fall,
The wide-mouthed bowl will surely catch them all.

It proved a dreary winter to the little wife, however, shut up alone in great, dreary London, and made to bear the odium of being a proscribed Republican's wife. Her situation certainly was distressing. Her husband could not safely return to England, and she feared to join him abroad, for a general European war was imminent. With this war, no doubt, mingled wifely fears for her husband's welfare, both moral and physical. "Whither will these wild projects lead him," we can imagine her saying, "into the dungeons of England, of Austria, or the bloody hands of Robespierre? and into what company?" for Republicanism in that day made strange bed-fellows. This winter, too, her feelings are outraged by bitter attacks upon him in the public press, and by the silent condemnation of old friends who stand aloof.

Under date of Jan. 1, 1793, she writes from London on this subject: "Would to Heaven you had not left me— that is, unless it has given you satisfaction; if so, I have nothing to say. Here you cannot return at present; everything evil is said of you, and I am obliged to avoid company not to hear you abused. I hope you may be provided for in some eligible way in Paris, or what is to become of us? For myself it matters little; I can and shall go home in the spring. Our friends in Paris wrote that they expected me there; why should I go unless you are like to continue? . . . . Our friends the P.'s have quite withdrawn their attentions. I have not seen nor heard from them in more than a month—on account of your politics, I suppose, but am not sorry. . . ." Again, Jan. 9th: " You cannot think how much you are abused here. The *Oracle* of yesterday has promised his correspondents that on Thursday he shall publish in his paper an interesting account of the life of Joel Barlow, author of the 'Advice to the Privileged Orders.' Mr. Burke often makes honorable mention of you in Parliament; sometimes he calls you a prophet—the prophet Joel. I shall enclose you one of his sentences. You are very obnoxious here, and it is thought you cannot return with safety; the Alien Bill would prevent you, if nothing more. Mr. Burke said: 'The members of the Constitutional Society held open correspondence with certain societies in France, for the express purpose of altering the Constitution of this country. A citizen by the name of Joel Barlow, another by the name of John Adams, and Citizen Frost were engaged in this correspondence, and they had been deemed answerable.' Should England go to war, as there is now every appearance, what would you do with me? I should not like to be in Paris, and all the ports blocked up with fleets, and the frontiers surrounded with armies. I could not be safe in Boulogne, and could not go to America with safety if war is soon declared. . . . I fear, my love, you did wrong in going to Paris with Mr. F—t: his character here is so bad it has injured yours, hitherto spotless. I shall send you Mr. Fox's speech upon the Kings,* at the opening of Parliament: it is excellent." Still again, Jan. 28th:

---

*The Conspiracy of Kings (?).

"Your affairs here are all a wreck, as Mr. J—n (Johnson, his printer) will tell you. It is my present intention to go to my country early in the spring : this you will undoubtedly advise, hard as it is for us both. My heart revolts at the idea, but it must be. . . . I told you our friends the P.'s had quite withdrawn themselves from me. I have not seen nor heard from either of them in more than two months. . . . My feelings have been much wounded, as you may suppose, to see and hear my beloved, my best friend, thus scandalized as he has been here, when I know so well the goodness, the rectitude of his heart and intentions. I was going to enclose a long account of you which has been in the public papers, but on the whole thought it not worth the notice. . . . Make yourself happy and respectable ; follow entirely your own inclinations in so doing, knowing that you will always gratify me ; I know your conduct will always be directed by humanity, integrity, and a desire to promote the good of your fellow-creatures."

Feb. 1st.—"I fear every mail will be the last, as we are in daily expectation of war being declared by this country or France, as the French Minister is ordered out of this kingdom. . . ." The poet's answers to these epistles are models of conjugal tenderness, respect, and wisdom. He makes no attempt to defend his course, does not combat her design of returning home, but instead, gives a conditional promise to return with her.

The election in Savoy, for which he had been waiting, was held late in February, and Citizen Barlow was *not* returned as Deputy. He arrived in Paris on the 5th of March, 1793, fully determined, as appears by his letters, to sail for home as soon as a ship could be procured, and his wife got over from England. He had several plans for America on his return, as appears by the letters : 1st. To return to the law at Hartford; 2d. To go to Musking-mum, where he had land, received for his services in the army; 3d. To Georgia; 4th. Some possible public appointment. But he did not visit his native land that year, nor in many years. Just as he was on the point of sailing, a friend, Colonel Hitchborne, approached him with an advantageous offer, the character of which does not appear, but which, after being referred to Mrs. Barlow for approval, was accepted. It was nearly four months before the exiled husband could induce the wife to rejoin him in Paris, then the terror of Europe. " I meddle with no politics," he declares in one letter, and he seems at this time to have withdrawn from active participation in European affairs. " Paris is quiet," he says in another, " and I believe will be," and he assures her that there is no apprehension of personal danger to any peaceable person there. At length, late in June, the lady ventured to cross over, and the pair settled in lodgings for the summer at Mendon, one of the suburbs of the city. For the next three years Barlow seems to have devoted himself to commerce and speculation, with a view of retrieving his fortunes, sadly impaired by his support of the Republican cause. He is in Hamburg, Amsterdam, Antwerp, quite frequently, on "business." His ledgers of the period show accounts with many ships, captains, and cities. He invested largely in French Government consols, which rose rapidly after the victories of Napoleon and yielded him a handsome fortune. But he engaged in no more political intrigues, and published no more political writings except, in September, 1793, the last part of the "Advice to the Privileged Orders," the first chapter of which had been left with his printer on leaving London the year before. In the spring of 1793 he had received the MSS. from the printer, with a note saying that its publication and sale had been forbidden by the authorities, whereupon he completed the work and issued it from the English press in Paris. His American correspondents during this period were, chiefly, Dr. Hopkins, of the tuneful four, Oliver Wolcott, Abraham Baldwin, and Thomas Jefferson. Among his

European correspondents were Stanislaus, King of Poland, Prof. C. D. Ebeling, of the University of Göttin-
gen, Abbé Gregoire, William Hayley, the poet, Dr.
Warner, and other English Constitutionalists.

Dr. Hopkins' letters informed him of the welfare and
fortunes of certain old friends, who have been lost sight
of in the progress of our story. " I still live," he wrote
in one, "where I did when you went away, though I
ought to live in the middle of the town. I have
followed my calling with great industry the whole time ;
still keep up my medical school, and have now five
pupils—all promising young men—with me. I have not
sold my estate at Litchfield, but have exchanged it for
one in the middle of that county, that where Samuel
Sheldon kept a tavern in the war. I hope to sell my
Litchfield property timely for moving to some place
where you shall live when you return, for you know I
would make large sacrifices for the sake of enjoying my
old friends. Hartford has become a very different place
to me since you and friend Wolcott left it, and, Trumbull apart, has no more charms for me than Musking-
mum. Indeed, I believe those boundless wilds would
yield me more pleasure than any old settlement ; but
friends are the chief comforts of life. Wolcott has
taken a permanent residence at New York. Where you
will provide for your old age I know not, but I wish to
know, and hope in due time to hear from you respecting
your future plan of life. I have lately found that the
prime of our days is speeding apace ; that the transition
from middle to old age will prove short, and what can
we do better on a stage that we must quit, than strive
to leave some fair monument of melioration behind us ?
You have already erected a literary monument to your
memory, and are now preparing to make the Western
wilderness vocal in your praise. I have now no doubt of
your success, but am afraid that your extensive plans
will deprive me forever of your acquaintance. As for

myself, I grope about among the sick, and now and then ease the pain or cure the disease of a fellow-mortal; but have not yet done anything to convince posterity that I have been fairly awake. 'Tis true that, some time after you left us, I returned (as Mickle says), 'Through seas where vessel never sailed before,' even down to the Nucleus of the Earth. I found it inhabited by a race of creatures that looked queerly, and acted and reasoned queerly, but I have not yet found time to describe them or their habitation in any tolerable degree. However, I have spent six or seven sheets on that odd race of beings, and shall probably fill twenty or thirty more with the relation of this singular adventure. I calculate that we shall renew our acquaintance, in part, by looking over the manuscript.* Our friend Isaac Bronson has married his dulcinea, and where Mr. Wolcott did. Mr. Goodrich has married Mary Ann Wolcott; but she is in declining health, and I have some fears that she will not recover.

" I thought I would not write you a word about politics, but I must just say that our friend Trumbull, a few days ago, came very near being chosen a Representative to the General Assembly; that Congress have lately rejected the proposition for the assumption of the state debts; and that it seems to me that France has wrought a wonder in the earth, which, with many concurrent predispositions in Providence, must eventually break every yoke. I rejoice that you are on the theatre of their noble achievements, and I anticipate, with great pleasure, the time when I shall hear you relate them."

That the poet's Republicanism had not wholly alienated the affections of his alma mater appears from a letter written by President Stiles, in March, 1793, "introducing and recommending to his friendship and civilities" a young gentleman of Windham, Conn., a

---

* This reference is undoubtedly to the Anarchiad.

recent graduate of the college. The venerable President adds: "Your humanity and guardianship of juvenile virtue will introduce him to such acquaintance, both French and English, at Paris, as will be safe, advantageous, and agreeable to a young character who sets out in life with resolutions of endeavoring to pass through its most dangerous scenes with the preservation of virtue and honor. I commend him to your faithful counsel, advice, and friendship."

"I congratulate you," he continues, "upon the celebrity and fame which your *poetical* and *political* writings have justly merited and acquired to you, partly in procuring your conspicuous elevation and seat in the National Convention in France,* one of the most important and illustrious assemblies that ever sat on this terraqueous globe; an assembly charged with the highest bestowments, and coming up from the people with the express power and authority for the accomplishment of three great works: the form of a Constitution, the taking into their hands the public administration and national government in the interim, and sitting as a judiciary tribunal on the life of a king—works great and arduous, momentous, and of vast consequence to the cause of public liberty, the rights of sovereignty, and the indefeasible rights of man. May you, may the whole National Assembly, the authoritative and empowered representatives of 25 millions of people, be inspired with light and wisdom by the Supreme Arbiter of Public Right."

In the spring of 1795, an epoch in the poet's career the most arduous and honorable was approaching, and to this the reader's attention is now invited.

---

* The President accepts as true the English report that he was thus elected. Some of the articles in the Cyclopædias make the same statement. But we have Barlow's admission, in a letter to his wife, that the election was decided against him.

CHAPTER VI.

1795–1797.

RETURNING to Paris from a business trip to the Low Countries in the summer of 1795, Barlow found awaiting him there his old friend and companion-in-arms, Col. David Humphreys. This gentleman, whom we last saw in Hartford, had in the eight years which had elapsed also much advanced his fortunes. Joining Washington at Mt. Vernon in 1787, he had remained in his family until 1790, when he was appointed by Washington Minister to Portugal, with general supervision over Barbary affairs. Algerine piracy was then at its height of insolence and ferocity. The little bundle of wretched despotisms on the southern shore of the Mediterranean dominated all Christendom. Great Britain, France, Spain, Holland, Denmark, Sweden, and Venice paid them tribute ; Algiers alone was now waging successful war with Russia, Austria, Portugal, Naples, Sardinia, Genoa, and Malta. Her first depredation against American commerce was committed on the 25th of July, 1785, when the schooner Maria, Captain Stevens, owned by Mr. Foster, of Boston, was seized off Cape St. Vincent by a corsair and carried into Algiers. Five days later the ship Dolphin, Captain O'Brien, Messrs. Irvine, of Philadelphia, owners, was taken one hundred and fifty miles to the westward of Lisbon. Other captures followed, so that by 1795 there were fully one hundred and fifty American prisoners in the slave-pens of Algiers. These slaves, as appears from their own depositions, were treated with the utmost rigor and cruelty. The most promising were selected by the Dey for menial service in his palace ; the others were dismissed to a life of grinding, degrading slavery. They were lodged in the slave-bagnios, in the midst of filth, vermin, and loathsome diseases. Their food was black-bread and olive oil, and they toiled, chained like galley-slaves, some in the quarries, some building public works, some unloading the stores from their own captured vessels.

The steps taken by Congress for the liberation of these captives were timorous, halting, and ineffectual, and cannot be viewed even now without calling the flush of indignation to the cheek. Our frigates then in commission could easily have blown every Algerine cruiser out of the water, and have battered the Dey's crazy capital about his ears; the testimony of the prisoners proves this. But instead of an aggressive policy, the American Government preferred to follow the example of European nations, and negotiate. Its first overtures were made through Mr. John Lamb, its agent at Algiers; its second, through the General of the Mathurins, a religious order of France, instituted at an early period for the redemption of Christian captives from the Infidels. After consuming six years in negotiation both proved abortive, the Dey's valuation of a Christian being nearly double that placed upon him by Congress. In June, 1792, the celebrated John Paul Jones was appointed Consul to Algiers, with the hope of negotiating a treaty and ransoming the prisoners, but died at Paris before reaching the scene of his labors. Mr. Thomas Barclay, his successor, died at Lisbon, Jan. 19, 1793, while on his way to Algiers. After his death, Colonel Humphreys assumed the general charge of Barbary affairs, and appointed Pierre E. Skjoldebrand, a brother of the Swedish Consul, his agent at Algiers, but with no better results. Humphreys came to America in 1794, and it was then arranged that Joseph Donaldson, of Philadelphia, should be appointed agent at Tunis and Tripoli, while Joel Barlow was to be induced, if possible, to accept the mission to Algiers, and the general oversight of the Barbary States.

Humphreys and Donaldson left America in April, 1795. At Gibraltar they separated, Donaldson proceeding to his post, and Humphreys going on to Paris, to enlist his old friend in the cause, and induce the French Government, then possessing great influence with the Dey, to use its kind offices in advancing the treaty.

Barlow undoubtedly shrank at first from accepting the mission. He had great business interests, a sufficient fortune—his estate, in 1796, he valued at $126,000—a wife affectionate and beloved, a circle of choice friends, literary undertakings,—all centred in Paris. To leave these for a barbarous capital, even then smitten by the deadly plague, on a mission that from its nature must entail untold miseries, vexations, and dangers, was a sacrifice indeed. Yet the occasion seemed to demand it. There were few men so well fitted for the task as he. France was then the power highest in favor with the Dey. French was the court language. Barlow, a citizen of France as well as of America, thoroughly familiar with the French language and customs, seemed particularly well fitted for conducting these delicate negotiations. These considerations, duly urged, produced the desired effect. He accepted the mission, and entrusting to him the purchase of the presents with which it was proposed to buy a treaty and a ransom, Humphreys shortly returned to his post in Lisbon. Barlow's official correspondence while on this mission filled four large manuscript volumes, and his letters to his wife, all written in French, would fill as many more. It appears by the former that he was occupied three months in Paris selecting and purchasing the presents—which comprised "jewels and other articles," to the value of 162,530 livres—and in making his preparations for the journey. About the middle of December all was ready, and bidding his friends and his faithful wife farewell, he sat out in his own private carriage for Lyons, intending there to take the public conveyance to Marseilles and thence pro-

ceed by shipping to Algiers via Alicante.   His sole trav-
elling-companion was a *vache*, in which the 162,530 livres
worth of jewels were packed.   The carriage proceeded
southward through a level, cultivated country to the
wealthy city of Lyons on the Rhone.   He reached it
Dec. 31, 1795.   From this point, we learn by his letters,
a *diligence d'eau* (water diligence) plied down the river;
but to save time he hired a *barque de porte* (mail boat)—
quicker and surer, but more expensive.   Ponies, carriage,
postilions, and traveller embarked on this craft and
floated three days down the beautiful river to Avignon,
where they disembarked and took the post-road through
Aix to Marseilles, which they reached on the 5th of January.   Here the ambassador remained twenty days, awaiting a ship for Alicante, employing his time in writing letters to Madame Barlow, who remained at Paris, and in
questioning such Algerines as he chanced to meet on the
state of their country, and the disposition and feelings of
the Dey.

He sailed from Marseilles on the 25th of January, but
was driven by a gale into the Bay of Roses, in Spain.
From this point, anxious to get on, and head-winds continuing, he proceeded on mule-back to Alicante, a journey of ten days.   There he learned that Donaldson, who,
it will be remembered, had left Humphreys at Gibraltar
and had gone on to Algiers, on reaching his post had
found the Dey in a genial humor, and had somewhat
precipitately concluded a treaty * without awaiting the
arrival of his colleague.   The treaty had been signed
nearly six months before.   What had passed in the interim is very concisely told by Barlow in a letter written

---

* Its principal provisions were: The opening of Algerine ports to American commerce, immunity of American vessels from search or capture by
the Dey's corsairs, and the right of our war-vessels to provision at, and
send their prizes into, Algerine ports.   The cost of the treaty, according to
Treasurer Wolcott's report, was $992,463.25, of which $522,500 was paid for
the ransom of the captives.

at Alicante to James Monroe, our Minister in Paris: "On my arrival here I found no letters or orders from Mr. Humphreys, but instead of them I have collected from the best information I could obtain here the following statement of facts relative to the business in question: It appears that in the treaty made by Mr. Donaldson no precise time was fixed upon for the payment of the money stipulated to be paid by the United States, but it was understood that it would be within about three months. The treaty, I believe, was signed in the early part of September. After the expiration of the above term the Dey began to be impatient and to manifest his uneasiness that the money did not appear, and that there was no sign of its appearance, saying that he was sorry that he had made the treaty, as under present circumstances it was against the interest of the regency, but as he had signed the treaty it should be faithfully executed on his part, provided the money was paid in a reasonable time. Mr. Donaldson, being somewhat alarmed at these appearances, and at hearing nothing from the money, procured a Moorish barque and sent Mr. Sloan, his interpreter, to Alicante with despatches for Mr. Humphreys. Mr. Sloan left Algiers about the 5th of January, and arrived here about the 10th. He being obliged to perform quarantine, Mr. Montgomery, our consul here, took the despatches and proceeded himself to Lisbon, supposing the affair too pressing to admit of delay and the despatches too important to be trusted to the post. Sloan was one of the American prisoners, and had been employed as a domestic servant by the Dey. He is now here awaiting an answer from Lisbon.

"We will now look to Lisbon and the causes of the delay in that quarter. You know the credits on which the money was to be raised was lodged in London. You know, too, that Mr. Humphreys, who left Havre some time in October, had a passage of more than 40 days to Lisbon. Mr. Donaldson had despatched Captain

O'Brien from Algiers to Lisbon with the treaty early in
September. He probably arrived within that month.
Mr. Humphreys did not arrive till towards the end of
November; everything must have remained inactive during that interval. I am informed that Mr. Humphreys,
after his arrival, could not negotiate bills on London for
more than one-fourth the sum, and it appears on this
account he did not negotiate any. Of this, however, I
am not sure. But in consequence of his not being able
to raise money in that place sufficient to fulfil the contract with the Dey, he sent Captain O'Brien to London
to bring the specie from thence. O'Brien went in the
brig that Mr. Humphreys had retained in the public
service. By the last letter from Mr. Montgomery at
Lisbon of the 13th February nothing had been heard
then of O'Brien since he sailed. Indeed, if no other accident had delayed him, the contrary winds must have prevented his return. They have been without packets
from England for nearly two months. One vessel has
arrived after a passage of 76 days. It is now near six
months since the signing of the contract, and it doubtless
will be another month before the money can be paid.
But there are some other circumstances that serve to
increase my apprehensions as to the result of this affair,
as they convince me that the Dey is sincere in saying
that the treaty is against the interest of the regency.
Since this was done he has had a rupture with the English, which is now settled, as it appears, to his satisfaction. . . .

"In consequence of this new treaty with England he
has refused to accept the same consul who was there
before the rupture, but has desired that the old one may
be sent, a Mr. Logie, who was there in 1793, and who persuaded him to the truce with Portugal at that time by
holding up the advantages of going out of the straits
after the Americans. Sloan says he was present at some
of these conversations, and that he saw Logie, in the pres-

ence of the Dey, instructing the captains by the charts where to cruise for the American ships, saying he would forfeit his head if they did not catch a dozen of them in a month, provided they would follow his directions. It is certain that the most inveterate enemies we have in that place, as well as in all others under heaven, are the English. But on the 26th he received letters from Mr. Cathcart, interpreter to the Dey, and from Mr. Donaldson, both saying that the Dey had fixed one month as the ultimate term for which he would wait for the money, and records his determination to go on at once, as it can do no harm and may save the treaty."

Such were some of the unfavorable conditions attending these first essays in diplomacy. That the reader may appreciate more fully these difficulties we will describe briefly the country and ruler to whose court he was hastening, using for the purpose a letter written by Mr. Barlow to the Secretary of State soon after reaching his post. "The Regency of Algiers," he remarks, "which contains from two to three millions of inhabitants, is governed, and has been for nearly three centuries, by about 12,000 Turks. These Turks are natives of the Levant, and are enlisted and brought here as soldiers. They are generally ignorant and ferocious adventurers, and many have been guilty of crimes for which they have fled their country. Their pay is very small at first, but rises in proportion to the time they have been in service, and they are all eligible to any office under Government. They rarely marry. The laws of the Regency discourage in several ways the matrimony of the Turks.

"A married Turk receives nothing but his pay. He that is not married, in addition to his pay, is lodged in the barracks and fed. Besides, if he marries a native woman his children are not Turks, and consequently can hold no office, civil or military. . . . It is a high crime for a merchant to sell any arms or ammunition to a Moor, and the excessive rigor of this military government has accustomed them to consider the Turks as a superior race, not only as endowed with greater force, arising from the use of arms, but as favorites of the prophet and lords of the country. . . . I mention these things to show that the Algerine Turks are not patriots. . . . The proper object of each individual is to enrich himself by plunder—the poor soldiers by marauding among the country people, and the men in office by committing piracies upon all nations who do not purchase their peace by paying large sums of money to every officer in the state, and annual tributes, which go into the public treasury. The Government was formerly an aristocracy, at least in theory. The Dey was supposed to be elected by the whole body of Turks, and every soldier had an equal vote. He was Chief Magistrate and President of the Divan, which was a council composed of 42 of the most ancient officers in the army. . . . But the Government has now become a simple monarchy. The Divan has not been assembled for some years, and the Dey is subject to no other check than that which arises from the necessity he is under to distribute foreign presents, and sometimes his own money, among the principal officers, to secure himself from assassination and prevent mutinies. . . . It is necessary to observe that as the peace-presents which every nation makes, and generally to a large amount, go principally into the hands of the Dey and other great officers, and as the annual tributes only are destined to the public treasury, it is the interest of these men to break friendship with every nation as often as possible. They are sure to be enriched by every treaty, let the object of it be what it may. They use no other precaution in this kind of policy than that of allowing a nation to enjoy a peace long enough to feel the advantages of a free navigation in these seas, so far as to be willing to come forward again with this peace-offering when the rupture happens. These breaches of peace are often made on the most frivolous and unjust pretences, and, generally speaking, every nation has its turn; the only exceptions are France and England, whose great naval strength over-awes them in such a manner that their peace has been less interrupted. But even these powers, though they pretend not to pay tribute, expend a great deal of money in occasional presents. If peace with America should now take place, it will not probably last without inter-ruption 7 years. They are now going to war with Den-mark. After that it is probable they will take Venice or Sweden, or both. They will then try Holland again, and perhaps Spain, and our turn will be next. But the diffi-culties in treating with this regency at present arises not only from the constitutional character of the Govern-ment, but likewise from the personal character of the Dey, who is a man of a most ungovernable temper, pas-sionate, changeable, and unjust to such a degree that there is no calculating his policy from one moment to another. During the reign of the late Dey, who died in 1791, this man held some of the first offices in the state, and had made himself vastly rich, particularly by the Spanish peace, which was the richest treaty they ever made. The Government of Spain did not choose to make known the expense of this treaty, but I am told that it cost to make it and maintain it till this time about five millions of dollars, of which this man received about one million. By a proper distribution of money among the chiefs of the Turks, this man procured his nomina-tion, or rather proclamation, to the Deylik the moment his predecessor expired. He then caused to be arrested and banished or put to death the principal officers of state who had served under the old Dey, and created a new set of favorites, men who are mere ciphers in his council, not one of whom dares to offer an opinion con-trary to his own." To this we will add the following per-sonal description of the Dey by General William Eaton, who was sent to Algiers three years later as American Consul. Under date of Feb. 22, 12 o'clock M., General

Eaton writes in his diary: " Admitted to an audience with the Dey. Consuls O'Brien, Cathcart, and myself, Captains Geddes, Smith, Penrose, and Maley, proceeded from the American House to the courtyard of the palace, uncovered our heads, entered the area of the hall, ascended a winding maze of five flights of stairs to a narrow dark entry, leading to a contracted apartment of about 12 by 8 feet, the private audience-room. Here we took off our shoes, and, entering the cave (for so it seemed, with small apertures for light, with iron grates), we were shown to a huge, shaggy beast, sitting on his rump upon a low bench covered with a cushion of embroidered velvet, with his hind legs gathered up like a tailor or a bear. On our approach to him he reached out his fore paw as if to receive something to eat. Our guide exclaimed, ' Kiss the Dey's hand.' The Consul-General bowed very elegantly and kissed it, and we followed his example in succession. The animal seemed at that moment to be in a harmless mood; he grinned several times but made very little noise. Having performed this ceremony, and standing a few moments in silent agony, we had leave to take our shoes and other property and leave the den, without other injury than the humility of being obliged in this involuntary manner to violate the second commandment of God and offend common decency."

Such was Hassan Bashaw, Dey of Algiers, as full of whims and fancies as a sick child, as difficult to amuse and keep in a treaty-making mood as a cross bear. This was indeed the ambassador's chief business for the first six months after his arrival. The money failed to come, and the Dey grew both impatient and suspicious. He sulked and raged and threatened. When he sulked, he was inaccessible. When he threatened, he swore that the agents must go. When he raged, he declared that the treaty was off, and that he never would make peace with the Americans.

Some very piquant and interesting details of these negotiations, and of the domestic life of the Algerines, are given in the letters written by the ambassador at this time to his wife in Paris. They, with Mrs. Barlow's in reply, were written in French (one or two in Italian), and, beside the account of his labors, contained grave disquisitions, references to personal friends, and some raillery. The extracts we present are literal translations.

ALGIERS, *March* 8, 1796.

" Here we are, at the end of our voyage. The good wind, of which I spoke to you in leaving Alicante, lasted only a little while : it changed into a terrible tempest, which carried away one of our masts, with some sails. Then, after we had been cast about for three days from heaven to hell, it drove us to a port which certainly belongs to neither, since they are not men who inhabit it. This port is called Algiers. Here we entered the harbor, but the sea was so strong that I was not able to land until twenty-four hours after. Here I am, then, weakened by the most violent sea-sickness I ever suffered. . . .

" I find that our treaty is not yet lost, but lacks little of it. I hope still to save it, although the Dey is extremely irritated. I can say nothing at this moment of his inclinations in this direction. He said only what he has repeated several times in six weeks, that if the money is not soon paid it will be lost to us. You can say to Monroe that I have more hope now than when I wrote to him from Alicante the last time."

ALGIERS, *March* 14, 1796.

" I have been here nine days in the greatest uncertainty about our business. The Dey is excessively annoyed upon the subject, and I believe now that my first resolution, taken at Alicante, was the better—to remain there until this affair was settled. On my arrival he threatened very strongly to send us back, Donaldson and I, to break immediately the negotiation and to declare war anew. Then his wrath passed away a little, and the affair sleeps. I do not dare to waken it; if I can make it sleep for some weeks yet, I hope that all will go well; but that is perfectly uncertain, and I should not be at all surprised at any moment to receive orders to leave the country. . . .

"It is impossible to describe this city, and the objects which strike one on arriving. With the exception of the climate, the fruit, and the natural beauty of the vicinity, it is doubtless, in all respects, the most detestable place one can imagine. It is a city of about 100,000 inhabitants, built on the ridge of a mountain which commands the harbor. It is impossible to conceive of so much physical and moral discomfort accumulated in a single place. Properly speaking, there are no streets, but little dark alleys, which run crosswise and zig-zag among an enormous heap of houses, thrown together without order and without number. It needs a long residence before being able to walk a hundred steps in this labyrinth without losing one's self. It needs not only a guide to lead you from one house to another, but also a Turkish guide, to guarantee you from insults and from being crushed by the crowd of peasants. The houses here are badly built and almost unfurnished. Neither the Turks nor the Moors ever have chairs. Their tables are six inches high, and sometimes one does not find one in a house. Their beds are straw carpets or mats; few cooking utensils, no forks, and few table-knives. A Turk who has perhaps 100,000 piastres, and diamonds, lives in this manner. He goes bare-legged all the year, but his coat is richly gilded and his fingers adorned with brilliants.

"As to society, in the first place, one sees neither women nor girls; it is forbidden a Mohammedan woman, under penalty of a severe beating, to show her face to any man excepting her husband. If a Turk or Moor enters the house of a friend he must stop at the gate, call some one, and be announced, so that the woman of the house may be concealed during his visit. If a Mohammedan woman is taken in adultery, the law con- demns her to be placed in a sack with a large stone and be cast into the sea. And what adds to the horror of this usage, the husband asks and obtains permission to take the law into his hands, when he makes himself judge and executioner. The man in all these cases es- capes with a beating, unless the woman is of high rank, and in that case he is punished with death. The kind of punishment differs for the different sects : a Christian or Moor is hung ; a Jew is burned alive ; the Turk has the honor of being decapitated, or strangled in the house of the general executioner, who is a Turkish officer of great distinction. The present Dey has improved upon these rules, and almost everybody is beheaded, with the difference that the punishment of Infidels and Moors is public. Two days ago a Spanish slave was beheaded before the palace of the Dey for having killed two of his companions in the prison. The last victim of this act was a girl, convicted of having comforted a Christian last winter. She received the bastinado.

"The number of mosques or churches is infinite in Algiers. They are very spacious, not at all decorated within ; but well lighted during the night, for it is neces- sary to pray there five times in the twenty-four hours— twice during the night. One can look in while passing before the door, but it is forbidden an Infidel to enter. The penalty for this crime is to become a Mohammedan, or to be hanged, or burned alive, according as one is a Christian or Jew. If it happens to me, through intox- ication or some other accident, to fall into this death, I shall become a Mohammedan immediately, for I have not enough religion of any kind to make me a martyr.

"An incident occurred the other day which came near being bloody. Bacry, the Jew, our banker, a man of much merit, was with us. Some one came to call him with much agitation and he went out quickly. I sent a servant to know what was the matter. He came back and told me that the affair was most serious; that there was a stupid Jew who had cried in the street, 'Mohammed is the great prophet, I wish to become a Mussulman'; that they immediately led him before the Dey to make him keep his word and finish the conversion; that, arrived in presence of his Majesty, his courage had failed, and he refused to change his religion. The penalty written against a retraction of this kind was death, and everybody was expecting the burning of the Jew that same afternoon. Luckily for the poor man, his protector, Bacry, has great influence with the Dey, and the affair was settled by means of a little money.

ALGIERS, *April* 2, 1796.

"It seems to-day that my sojourn here draws to a close, and that the business has failed. The money has not yet come; the Dey does not wish to wait much longer. He sent us word to-day that we would be sent back in eight days; that then war would be declared; that he will then give thirty days before taking prizes, as is the custom when they declare war here; but if the money comes during these thirty days he will receive it and the peace will be concluded. We send an express courier by Tangier and Gibraltar to take this news to our compatriots. It is on this occasion that I send these letters."

April 5.—"I have most agreeable news to announce regarding our country and our miserable slaves who are here. The Dey, after some threats, some injuries, some insupportable insults, has consented to give us still three months to get our money. If it does not come within that time, to the devil with the treaty and all those who have made it fail. This business for three days has overwhelmed me with trouble and pain. The port is open. This letter goes straight to Marseilles to-morrow. M.

Andrews goes day after to-morrow. I will send you a word by him."

Under the above date—April 5—Mr. Barlow wrote to Colonel Humphreys concerning the prisoners and the treaty, which we will insert here in place of the letters to his wife referring to the same matter. The letter was also signed by Mr. Donaldson.

ALGIERS, *April* 5, 1796.

"SIR:—After finishing our despatches on the 3d inst., to send by the courier to Tangier, we found that the port was to be opened immediately. We therefore gave up that mode of conveyance for a more direct and speedy one by way of Alicante. We have now what we hope will be more agreeable news to announce. For two days past we have been witnesses to a scene of as complete and poignant distress as can be imagined, arising from the state of total despair in which our captives found themselves involved, and we without the power of administering the least comfort or hope. The threat which we mentioned to you in our last, of sending us away, had been reiterated with every mark of a fixed and final decision, and the Dey went so far as to declare that after the thirty days, if the money did not come, he never would be at peace with the Americans.

"Bacry, the Jew, who has as much art in this sort of management as any man we ever knew, who has more influence with the Dey than all the Regency put together, and who alone has been able to soothe his impatience on this subject for three months past, now seemed unable to make the least impression, and the Dey finally forbade him, under pain of his highest displeasure, to speak to him any more about the Americans. His cruisers are now out, and for some days past he has been occupied with his new war against the Danes. Three days ago the Danish prizes began to come in, and it was thought that this circumstance might put him in good humor, so that the Jew might find a chance of renewing our subject in some shape or other. And we instructed the Jew that if he could engage him in conversation on his cruisers and prizes, he might offer him a new American-built ship of twenty guns, which should sail very fast, to be presented to his daughter, on condition that he would wait six months longer for our money. The Jew observed that we had better say a ship of twenty-four guns, to which we agreed. After seeing him three or four times yesterday, under pretence of other business, without being able to touch upon this, he went this morning and succeeded. The novelty of the proposition gained the Dey's attention for a moment, and he consented to see us on the subject. But he told the Jew to tell us that it must be a ship of thirty-six guns or he would not listen to the proposition. We were convinced that we ought not to hesitate a moment. We accordingly went, and consented to his demand, and he has agreed to let everything remain as it is for the term of three months from this day, but desired us to remember that not a single day beyond that will be allowed on any account. We consider the business as now settled on this footing, and it is the best ground that we could possibly place it upon. You still have it in your power to say peace or no peace ; you have an alternative. In the other case, war was inevitable, and there would have been no hope of peace during the reign of this Dey. . . . In order to save the treaty, which has been the subject of infinite anxiety and vexation, we found it necessary some time ago to make an offer to the Jew of ten thousand sequins (18,000 dollars), to be paid eventually if he succeeded, and to be distributed by him, at his discretion, among such great officers of state as he thought necessary, and as much of it to be kept for himself as he could keep consistent with success. The whole of this new arrangement will cost the United States about fifty-three thousand dollars. We expect to incur blame because it is im-

possible to give you a complete view of the circumstances, but we are perfectly confident of having acted
right."

We continue the narrative by means of the letters to
Mrs. Barlow.

Beginning with one of April 13th : . . . . " I am now all
alone, and so crazed with business that I have not time
to think one moment of my other troubles. You will
see by this packet what work I do. But I am so much
happier since we have got our affairs on some footing
that I care nothing for the fatigue. I do not intend to
go to Tunis, but will come home as soon as possible.
My love, I don't know what I write. I have sat at this
table with very little intermission for thirty-six hours."

April 26.—" I sent you, a few days ago, a very great
packet for Monroe and the Secretary of State. I do
the like now. If these ͵two arrive safe they will give
you a tolerable idea of what I have done and thought ;
and they will prove at least, and to others as well as to
you, that I have not been idle. Nothing has come from
Humphreys since Feb. 7, and then, and before then, as
good as nothing. . . . All would have been finished before now, and $60,000 saved to the United States, if we
had had a good banker's clerk at a certain place for a
minister. . . . I told you that Donaldson was gone to
Leghorn, and Andrews back to France. I am alone.
But here is a very good society if I had time to enjoy it,
and a charming country to promenade *à pied et à cheval.*
The Dey has given me a very fine horse, and I can borrow a saddle. We are going to make a little journey
one of these days."

May 8th.—" Our business here has been about the same
for a month. No news from Lisbon nor from Liborne.
I remain alone and I work like a slave. I sent to-day a
large packet for Lisbon and for Philadelphia. If Donaldson comes with the money to finish here, he will go to
Tunis and I shall fly to your arms. If he does not come

I shall be driven from here, so I shall be free soon in any case. I shall have now very little to do after the departure of the ship which carries this. Then I shall try to amuse myself in my garden,—for I have taken a country house here for the sake of appearances, as they believe me a fixed consul, and will think when I go, it is to bring my wife and other necessities for a long residence. Ah, well! I shall bring her whenever she and I consent to bury ourselves in Barbary."

In May the plague, the scourge of the African coast, broke out in Algiers with virulence. The poet's description of it in letters to James Monroe, then our Minister to Paris, to Colonel Humphreys, and to his wife are of exceeding interest. To Mr. Monroe he wrote on the 31st of May, 1796: "My letter having been detained by the detention of the ship, I have now to add the frightful news that the plague has broken out at Algiers. It is four months later than the usual season for it to appear. It usually commences in February and begins to go off in June. The hot, dry weather kills it in this country, so that we hope it will not be severe nor last long. One of our poor fellows is attacked and will probably die. I am trying to get leave for them to quit their work and come into the country near me, where I have taken a house and garden for them, to save as many as I can."

And to Colonel Humphreys, June 12th: "Two of our finest young fellows, Nicholas Hartford, of Portsmouth, and Abraham Simmonds, of Cape Ann, have already fallen." (The Dey would not consent that the prisoners should go into the country.) "They were not yet paid for; they were therefore the property of the Regency, and if he should consent to such an unusual proceeding, he said, it would bring the Turks upon him in a body. Indeed, of all governments in the world this is perhaps the least susceptible of innovation in the most trifling usage, especially on the side fortified by religion, of which a contempt of disease, and an obstinate refusal to use precautions against the plague, are among the strongest features.''

And again, June 16th: " Since my last, Joseph Keith, a native of Newfoundland, one of our mates, has died with the plague. Lunt is still in the hospital, and John Thomas, a black man from Massachusetts. The contagion rages with greater severity than was expected." In the midst of the pestilence, stimulated thereto by the suffering and danger to which his countrymen were exposed, he succeeded in effecting their delivery, accomplishing it by a stratagem worthy of Machiavelli. An interesting account of it is contained in a letter which the liberated captives bore from him to Thomas Jefferson, Secretary of State. He wrote :—

" I have the pleasure at last to announce the liberation of our citizens from slavery in this place. To keep the peace after the expiration of the time limited for the payment, and finally to redeem our people without any money, has been a subject of more difficulty and vexation than will be imagined by those who are unacquainted with the capricious and savage character of the Dey. A few weeks after the arrangement made in April, having heard nothing from the funds, and foreseeing that they probably would not be here by the time, I thought it highly expedient to engage the Dey in a step of his own by which he should be insensibly brought to consider the peace as established on a footing different from that of the punctuality of a moment in the payment of money. Mr. Cathcart, from the office he held, enjoyed a portion of his flighty confidence. I thought it probable that if he could be engaged, as from his own mere motion, to send this man to America on the subject of the peace-presents and annual tribute, it would give a new turn to his contemplations : he would be looking to America for answers and arrivals instead of counting the days in which he was looking to me for money. But it was necessary that neither he nor Cathcart should know that the idea came from me ; and even his Jew Brobar, who was the only man who could engage him in this business, must not know my real motive. The Jew hated Cathcart and wished him away ; this was sufficient for the Jew, and I engaged him to hint the matter to the Dey in such a manner as that he should conceive the project to be his own. . . . The plan was properly managed at the time, and Cathcart was sent in the manner I stated to you in my letter by him. I believe it is in a great measure owing to the circumstance of this mission that we are now at peace with Algiers. My being able to procure the liberation of the captives at this time has been owing to an accident. Money has been extremely scarce here for some months back. The Jew house who serve as our brokers, and who do the greater part of the business here, have had their funds for some time in the hands of the French Government to the amount of half a million dollars. The operations of some other houses for a year past had centred nearly in the same point, so that there was no money left except in the public treasury. Though I had so far gained the confidence of the Jews that they declared to me that they would advance the money to the amount of the redemption if it could be raised, I had very little faith in these professions, because I believed they said so under the idea that the money could not be had in the town. The plague broke out in the latter end of May, and very much increased my anxiety for the fate of our people. Some time in June a new French Consul arrived, and by some brilliant presents revived the influence of the Republic with the Dey so as to borrow from the public treasury about $200,000, which he paid into their Jew house. I immediately insisted that they should prove the sincerity of their friendship by lending me this sum, and as much more as the redemption would amount to, for which I would give them my bills on Mr. Donaldson at Leghorn." This argument proved unanswerable to the Dey, and the strange spectacle was presentea of his lending the American Consul the very money which was paid in for the ransom of his prisoners. The prisoners once at his command, Barlow hastened to ship them out of the country before the mind of the fickle ruler should change. The American brig Sophia, Captain Calder, was then in port, and on her the redeemed captives were at once embarked and despatched to Marseilles, on their way to America. They bore a letter from their deliverer addressed to the Secretary of State, which did equal credit to his head and heart. It was as follows:

"SIR:—This will be presented to you by the remnant of our captive citizens who have survived the pains and humiliation of slavery in this place. After effecting their deliverance in the manner which I state to you in my letter of this day, without funds or even any direct intelligence that they are soon to be expected, I have another task to perform, in which it is impossible to promise myself success: it is to embark them without the infection of the plague. Five of their fellow-sufferers have died of the contagion and another who is attacked must be left behind. It still rages with such violence in the town that, although they cannot embark without risk, yet it is much more dangerous for them to stay. If they escape infection we shall be much indebted to Captain Calder, who commands the ship, and to the careful assistance of the other captains who inspect the embarkation.

"When we reflect on the extravagant sums of money that this redemption will cost the United States, it affords at least some consolation to know that it is not expended on worthless and disorderly persons, as is the case with some nations who are driven, like us, to this humiliation to the Barbary States. Our people have conducted themselves in general with a degree of patience and decorum which would become a better condition than that of slaves. And though, after they are landed in their country, it would be useless to recommend them to any additional favors from Government, yet I hope they will receive from merchants that encouragement in their professional industry which will enable them in some measure to repair their losses, and from their fellow-citizens in general that respect which is due the sufferings of honest men. Several of them are probably rendered incapable of gaining a living: one is in a state of total blindness, another is reduced nearly to the same condition, two or three carry the marks of unmerciful treatment in ruptures produced by hard labor, others have had their constitutions injured by the plague. Some of these are doubtless objects of the charity of their countrymen, but whether this charity should flow to them through the channel of the Federal Government is a question on which it would be impertinent in me to offer an opinion."

The deliverer was himself, however, far from being delivered from the perils of his position. The payment of the money borrowed was yet to be made and the treaty effected. He stayed with a fair probability of dying with the plague, or, if fortunate enough to escape that, in constant peril of losing his head from the caprice of the Dey should the money fail to come or any incident occur to excite his anger. He was kept here nearly a year longer through the criminal carelessness or indifference of his superiors, as the following letters to Mrs. Barlow show :

ALGIERS, *Aug.* 30, 1796.

" You know M. Skjoldebrand, Consul-General of Sweden to Algiers ; he will give you this letter, and will answer a thousand questions about your friend. You cannot show him too much attention or friendship. He has given the greatest service both to our affairs and to me personally, and it is necessary for me to call to my aid all my friends to fulfil the duty of being useful to him which he has imposed on me."

ALGIERS, *Sept.* 1, 1796.

" Without a patience above all trial, and indomitable courage, and a management which will never be comprehended by our Government, all would have been lost a hundred times. The Consul of Denmark said the other day in his society, ' The American agent is not a man, he is an angel that God has sent to save the interests of his country.' And our poor slaves, what tender scenes at the moment of their departure, what benedictions, what tears of gratitude! They all said that without me, and without the operations which have astonished them, they would all have perished in slavery. And that is true. As to the operations, they have attributed to me more than I have done; but they are certainly indebted to me for their liberty and their life, for if this treaty had been broken it would have been impossible to conclude another for many years, and without spending three times, perhaps ten times, as much money. I remain still without means, without money, and without credit. The affairs at Tunis are not yet arranged, nor those of the two ships taken at Tripoli. I hope to finish all business soon : but how ? I have not yet the orders to make peace with Tunis, and still less the funds. I act without orders and without money. Nothing is equal to the negligence of our public agents, unless the folly and temerity of our mariners. If it were not for interests other than theirs I would leave these people at Tripoli to their fate. They merit slavery of ten years for having come within these seas before peace was made. . . . It is true that this announces the probability of a longer absence. Unhappily, I cannot speak with any certainty of my return. If Donaldson comes with the money, as I expect every instant, I can go quickly afterward. But who can tell? His path is blockaded. . . . You will find here an Italian song, quite pretty, with the music. The Swedish Consul gave it to me. He plays very well."

ALGIERS, *Sept.* 7, 1796.

" Since my letter of the first of the month I have been overwhelmed with work. I sent to-day two packets of thirty pages of close writing to Lisbon and Philadelphia. I am the only American slave in Algiers, and I work like a dozen. I am always in perfect health. . . . I begin to see, I think, the end of my sojourn here."

ALGIERS, *Sept.* 8, 1796.

" Now that the plague is over the quarantine will not be so long. It will probably be only 25 days. You are mistaken in supposing that at Marseilles they make it on board ship. There is a very convenient lazaretto, separated like a quarter of the city. . . .

" If Trumbull remains in Paris tell him to make a very pretty portrait of you for me—large ; I will pay him. He can also prepare his brushes for a Barbaresque figure when I come myself. Do not fail to withdraw my books from Relieur. I have left my note for them. They are many and precious."

ALGIERS, *Sept.* 25, 1796.

" It is nine months to-day since my unhappy departure for this cursed country. If Hitchborn had come (as he was engaged before my arrival in Hamburg) he would have let the treaty go to the devil to get out of the business, as his son advised me very strongly. But I, who have too much obstinacy to be discouraged so quickly, and who would wish to die like a good soldier in the last ditch, have taken the part of disputing, inch by inch, and of not yielding till after the last efforts. But it seems at last that my efforts, except in liberating the prisoners, are in vain.

" Humphreys writes that he sent the money from Lisbon two months ago. The ship passed through Gibraltar 44 days ago ; the wind has been good ; the ship does not come ; it is probably taken or lost. I am waiting to know the truth. If it comes I can quickly finish the

business; if it does not come I shall be driven from
Algiers, and farewell to the peace with Barbary for a half
century, or until our wise Government finds by sure
geography that Lisbon is not Algiers. I am very well;
in perfect health and full of that energy inspired by the
feeling of having done my duty. The Government can
blame me or not, that is perfectly indifferent to me: my
happiness by no means depends on it. I do not value
the commission of any Government so much as to do
good to humanity. I have just learned, by way of Spain,
that our unfortunates have come to Marseilles to make
quarantine; and that still another one died of the plague
in the passage. Poor fellows! if they had stayed here
six weeks longer half of them would have fallen; the
sickness was very great after their departure. It has now
totally disappeared for more than a month."

ALGIERS, *Oct.* 9, 1796.

"Long live the Republic! All kinds of good fortune
have happened to me at once. O'Brien came the first
of this month with nearly two-thirds of the money that I
owe here. But it is certainly enough to establish our
business and let me withdraw. . . . . .

"Now I see clearly the end of my painful work. The
times are much changed here now. I will attempt to
picture some of these scenes for you some day. It is
necessary to tell you that O'Brien has been taken by the
Tripolitans. His was one of those two ships that I have
announced to Monroe taken by a Tripolitan corsair: and
the captain of the corsair is an English renegade, as I
said. After three weeks O'Brien was released by the Bey,
as he was afraid of the Dey of Algiers, believing that the
money belonged to him, as the ship had the passport of
the Dey. The other ship was broken up and the cargo
confiscated. When I obtained an audience to announce
to the Dey the arrival of the money, he seized my right
hand, put my left on his heart, and said, 'My friend,

you have greatly suffered by the inconceivable delay of
that money. I have troubled you much; I've treated
you with severity. I have had, however, much patience.
The enemies of your nation have done all in order to
ruin you. I have always felt something in the depth of
my heart which has told me, " This man is true and good ;
he is not capable of falsehood." Now you are well recom-
pensed for your constancy and sufferings. Your nation
is brave and worthy; so long as I live I will be your
friend in spite of the English, who were always seeking
to ruin her in my estimation. Now if there is anything
in the world I can do for you, speak.' 'My lord,' I
said to him, 'for myself it matters nothing. The interests of my nation open my mouth. The Tunisians and
the Tripolitans make a cruel war against us. For some
time I have proposed peace, asking him his terms, to the
Bey of Tunis. He told me that he would grant it for
fifty thousand piastres. I have consented to these terms
as soon as I shall be able to draw up a letter. But, in the
interval, he has taken one of our ships, so it seems that
he does not wish to keep his word. The Bey of Tripoli
has taken two of our ships. He has destroyed one of
them ; the other he wishes to return to us for fear of
being destroyed himself by your wrath. But this was
only after having scorned your passport by keeping a
long time the ship loaded with your money: and his
renegade Englishman who serves him as captain has
insulted your power by saying he does not recognize the
Dey of Algiers. Now I ask one letter from your hand to
the Bey of Tunis to force him immediately to keep his
word and conclude the peace for fifty thousand piastres,
and to return to me the prisoners and the ship. It is a
just ransom ; he has promised once to accept it. It is for
you, as the father of Justice, as you are, to hold these
people to the right and to their word, and save the honor
of Barbary.

" 'As to Tripoli, I am going to offer 40,000 piastres, in

all, for the peace and the prisoners. I ask you for a
letter for the Bey, forcing him to give me these terms
precisely, to ask your pardon for the insult done to your
passport, and to send you the head of this renegade
English captain for the outrage he has done you in not
recognizing your power and your name.'

"'My friend,' replied the Dey, 'you have not asked
enough : you have not the money : prepare your ship to
go immediately with Captain O'Brien : I give you all the
money for the two places : O'Brien will carry them. I
give you letters strong enough to make your propositions,
which are only too just, immediately accepted. It is the
last time I shall write to the Bey of Tripoli. If he does
not send me immediately with your ship the treaty of
peace and this Englishman in chains, to give me the
pleasure of cutting off his head, I will send sixty thousand
men to cut off the head of the Bey. For paying the
90,000 piastres that I give you, your nation can send
them to me when she pleases. I find that she is just—
you are wise and humble—I am her friend and yours.'

" My tears flowed in response, and I took leave.

" All is arranged ; O'Brien goes to-morrow. He will
return, I hope, in a month with the two treaties ; after
that I can quickly depart. If the Englishman comes, I
will save him. You will say this is a romance or a dream :
not at all ; this is the strictest truth."

ALGIERS, *Oct.* 12.

"O'Brien was taken by the Tripolitans, with 225,000
piastres, coming from Lisbon. I was truly on the point
of being driven from here, with war declared ; and I
should not have blamed the Dey if he had done it, putting me in chains the same time, his patience had been
so long used and abused. Suddenly O'Brien came, released from Tripoli, with his cargo. I saw the Dey of
Algiers changed from a tiger to a lamb ; transformed from
a fierce tyrant to the gentlest of men. I seized the

moment for making a great stroke: I demanded instructive and compulsory letters to the Beys of Tunis and Tripoli, that they should make peace without delay, and on the precise terms that I proposed ; . . . . in fact, O'Brien has gone with the money, with the letters, with the presents of the Dey and myself, and with the necessary power from me. I have reason to believe that he will soon return with the two treaties ; I shall then think our peace with Barbary is the most solid of all nations here ; after that I shall take leave quickly.

"There are two things which trouble me in this business : the Venetians declared war the same day O'Brien went away ; the Consul here is the victim of my success ; it lacks little that the balance should turn the other way.

"Peter Lyle, the renegade English captain, in the service of Tripoli, who took our two ships, and is a good fellow, will certainly be beheaded. I am very sorry for it. Ask Monroe if I have done wrong.

"It seems that our Government has approved all that I have done at the beginning. I do not know what it will say when it knows that, without a sou, I have sent back the captives at a time when the city was all pestilence ; that, without a sou, I have sustained the peace for three months after all limits were passed ; and that the first money which came, I borrowed from the Dey for another object. I must tell you that without the knowledge at Philadelphia, that the Tunisians had made a surprise. The President gave me orders to give them a sum four times as large as I shall probably make peace for, even while treating under the disaster of a ship taken, and including the ransom of the prize and the sailors.

"Another large ship, richly ladened, the Betsy, of Boston, Captain Sampson, has been taken at Tripoli : the crew are in slavery ; they will soon be free."

ALGIERS, *Oct.* 19.

"Our business goes on wonderfully. I shall probably leave in six weeks. I am master of the battle-field. If Victory is no more flighty than usual, she will give this field to the honor of our nation for long years."

ALGIERS, *Nov.* 20.

"I have had some trouble with Tunis and Tripoli; but all is arranged: the Dey plays well the part I have given him. I await O'Brien from day to day. They think I shall be able to leave in fifteen or twenty days."

ALGIERS, *Nov.* 20.

"Always new difficulties; still trouble with the Bey of Tunis. This man, profoundly wicked, has found some pretexts for increasing his pretensions: notwithstanding the letters of the Dey of Algiers, he has had the impudence to demand of O'Brien three times more than he himself proposed formerly. On this occasion, I put to the test the friendship and attachment which the Dey has for me, and found them stronger than ever. I played so well upon his passions, above all, self-love, honor, and friendship for me, that the Bey of Tunis is certainly lost. You would not believe that I came to Barbary to behead kings; I shall have, however, the pleasure of dethroning one. If every Jacobin could do as much, the face of the world would be changed.

"My business seems now to be perfectly arranged. The Bey has already cried for mercy, saying that peace is already made with the Americans, precisely as the Dey wished it; and he hopes to be pardoned for his indiscretion. But he is too late, he has not three months to live.

"Everybody here is astonished at this stroke of policy. There is nothing surprising, however; the Dey is of a certain temperament—difficult to manage, but easy to captivate. I have had to play here, for seven months, a *rôle* the most sad, painful, and desperate. I have conducted myself only as a man of good sense, patriotism, and humanity would have done. It surprises me a little, I confess ; I was surrounded by enemies. By a natural movement of the human heart he put himself on guard against them. Without being sure of the sincerity of our Government, he saw in my tranquillity and constancy something which won him. Finally, the end of this strange comedy—namely, the discovery of the truth of what I had said—flattered his heart, pre-occupied in my favor without knowing why. To-day he would give me his beard, hair by hair, if I should ask it ; but this humor cannot last long, for caprice is the first of his virtues ; if his favor lasts while I am obliged to remain here it is all I can hope for."

ALGIERS, *Dec.* 25.

"Nothing important."

ALGIERS, *Dec.* 30.

"What I told you, that the Bey of Tunis cried for mercy, was true at the time ; he did it in a moment of fright ; but that circumstance having passed, he broke everything. There is a long story, details of which I can-not give you ; the result is, that after many examples of perfidy on the part of the Bey, the Dey has sent fifty thousand ambassadors on horseback, well armed, to negotiate my affairs in Tunis. These good negotiators ought to bring the head of the Bey to me and his treas-ures to the Dey. At that price our peace is assured with the successor whom it shall please our friend to place on the throne of Tunis.

"All is happily ended at Tripoli. O'Brien is en route for here, and I expect from day to day the end of the affair in Tunis ; after that I shall embark immediately for Spain, and my return to Paris will be as precipitant as though I had been beaten.

"I hear, to my great regret, that our excellent friend Monroe is going to leave Paris, replaced by a man whom

I think an aristocrat. I hope this change will not happen before my arrival in Paris; I know well our Government has lost his energy with his wisdom. We had last week a great hunting-party to the Numidians. The Minister of the Marine, son of the late Dey, invited us —the consuls of England and Sweden and the father of all consuls, for so they call your poor husband—to a wild-boar hunt. It was fifteen miles distant in the forest. We were three days absent, and slept two nights under tents. We were all well mounted, hunting with the lance like the ancients. We killed fourteen *sangliers* (wild-boars) and one hyena. I must tell you, for I was there and saw all, although I did not shed a drop of blood that day. Two hours after midday I was so excessively fatigued that I dismounted, leaving all the honor to my two sons. The day of our return, the Dey asked the Minister why the American was fatigued; he said because the American had a horse hard to manage. That was a lie; the horse was excellent, but the horseman was worth nothing. But the Dey said, 'To-morrow I will send him one of the best from my stable.' Next day the horse came. He can give me two hundred, it will never make me a horseman, and I shall never go again to the chase: it is a good thing to see, but nothing more.

"You are proprietor of half of a ship; the other half belongs to a friend whom you will see some day. The ship is called the Friendship, commanded by Captain Sampson, of Boston, a brave man, recently captured at Tripoli. The ship is in good condition: I have bought it here and sold half of it; the other half I give to you. I have ordered the captain to sail with it as much as he pleases and send the gains to Wm. Biddle, at Boston; I have written to him to place the money, as it comes, in United States funds in the name of Ruthy Barlow, a woman that he once knew. Behold your fortune made!"

Feb. 6, 1797.

" I have been in despair for some time on account of
the delay of news from Tunis.   To-day I received letters
which console me, but they necessitate my remaining
here almost another month.   Another courier is needed
to finish the treaty; this one I shall send away in an
hour, and he ought to return in sixteen days—say twenty,
and then ten days to leave here !

" The Swedish Consul wrote from Paris to his brother,
Dec. 3, that he had taken tea with you, and praises your
intellect and grace.

" The brigantine Friendship came safely from Tunis,
delivered her cargo, and has been chartered at $450 a
month to my friend the Ambassador of France, to carry
him to Tripoli, and then to Naples : this service ended, it
will go to America.   It is a ship of 150 tons.

" The other ship, called the Rachel, is 250 tons.   It
went out day before yesterday to take a cargo to Spain.
Both are chartered.   I let the captains sail where they
wish, with orders to place the gains with Biddle, in
Boston.

Feb. 13*th*, 1797.

" I have had no news from Humphreys for four
months, from Philadelphia for eight.   I shall expect
them till after my departure, and then I shall cease to
trouble the affairs of Barbary.   All will go to the devil, to
whom I give it, with all those who neglect their duty so
plainly.   I have never had the least idea that the Government would follow my advice.   I did not wish, however,
to fail in giving it, but once out of Africa I promise to
keep my mouth shut.   Our engagements with Barbary
will be forgotten ; there will be war, that is the end.   It
will, no doubt, be very hard for me to see undone a
work which has cost so many sacrifices.   If Monroe goes
before I return, I pray you tell him to watch the Barbary
affairs.   If he asks what he can do at Philadelphia, beg
him only to engage the new President to read my letters

in the Bureau of the Secretary. If it is Jefferson he will not fail to be instructed, but if it is a new man of a different cast probably a Barbary war will not be the greatest evil to come."

ALGIERS, *March 4th.*

"The Swedish ship for Alicante, of which I wrote you, goes to-day without me. Nothing hinders but the delay of my courier from Tunis. This cursed affair drags on, and it is impossible to say when it will end."

April 3d.

"I received from my agent at Tunis certain news that the peace with that country is finally concluded. He has delayed my courier for a few days only, to insure the treaty. I expect him every moment. I have arranged with a good ship and captain to take me to Marseilles, and I can go in five or six days. One thing may still hinder me: I have expected for six months a ship from Philadelphia bearing presents for this nation. (It is a shameful thing for the Government, very mortifying to me and vexing to the Dey that it has not come sooner.) If it comes before my departure it will be necessary to remain here twenty days longer to unload it.

"Give a thousand thanks to my good son Powlikowski for his interesting letter."

May 13th, 1797.

"I would not have believed, fifteen days ago, that I should still be here. All is prepared: I only wait for the treaty from Tunis. The sickness of a minister, they assure me, has only hindered the registering of the signature; and they do not know the extent of my haste, so they let the affair delay. I expect every moment the arrival of the treaty."

May 25th, 1797.

"I have nearly taken leave, and the large ship is here to carry me to Marseilles, but it is necessary to remain fifteen days. The cursed ship coming with presents for the Dey from Philadelphia has been taken by the Spaniards. They shall pay for it; the Dey threatens them strongly with war. This affair has given me much trouble, but the Dey says he will send me back with great honor."

June 8th, 1797.

" My ship on which I shall go is not yet ready, having some unloading to do."

July 17th, 1797.

"Our Government has praised me much for the operations of last year. If they should reckon the sacrifices I have made, I merit still more for this one. I am almost sure of going before the end of the month."

This was the last letter from Algiers. On the 18th of July, 1797, having released the prisoners and effected treaties with Algiers, Tunis, and Tripoli, he sailed for Marseilles ; but on arriving there on the 30th found himself condemned to the lazaretto for forty days' fumigation— he had come from a port infected with the dreaded plague. A score of letters, very much stained and crumpled by the fumigation they underwent, remain as the fruit of his pen during this interval. He wrote to his wife every other day—letters gay, sparkling, exuberant in his joy at being so near her, and as ardent and lover-like as those written under the elms of New Haven. One or two of these will serve to show the character of all. " Marseilles," he exclaims in the first letter written from the lazaretto, " Marseilles ! How pretty the name is ! It is necessary to write it again—Marseilles ! There ! But it merits better writing. It is the most harmonious, the sweetest, the most charming word which can strike the ear of a returner escaped from hell. All the letters that compose it are either vowels or liquids, which roll like honey and melt in the mouth : for example, M is a liquid letter, which the infant pronounces even in nursing ; it says ' mama,' and in any language that letter is never lost from the name of that beloved person who bears and nourishes us : *Mama, mere, madre, mater, mother, moder, morimma,* etc.

"A—it is the first letter in all the alphabets, and the most easy of all the vowels.

"R — another liquid, which rolls rapidly, and which forms the principal character in the sound of my name, which is Barlow.

"S—a liquid which sighs sometimes, but rolls always.

"Ei—two vowels, which form a diphthong always agreeable in French, and especially agreeable when it stands before the two l's which come rolling to terminate with the little

"e—almost mute, the dear name of Marseilles."

August 1st, 1797.

"Behold me, then, dear friend, well established in the lazaretto since yesterday evening, in the most agreeable place in the world. It would be difficult to form an idea of the satisfaction I felt on landing. . . . . I came on my ship named the Rachel, commanded by Philip Sloan. I never had such a voyage—gentle and calm navigation of twelve days, of which I was sick only the first. . . . . The Consuls of France, Spain, and England gave me passports, and forbade the cruisers of their nations to stop me in my voyage. The Dey made me a present more superb than he has ever made, they say, on a like occasion. Then he charged me with a little present for you, something which is certainly not the custom. In presenting it to me he said, 'Carry that to your wife, and tell her to go with you to Constantinople, as she does not wish to come to Algiers.' I have another present for you from my friend Micay Baccry, and that is not all.

"I wear large mustaches—long, beautiful, and black (a little gray, however). Do you wish I shall cut them here, or do you wish to see them and cut them yourself? It is necessary to say why I let them grow. There is a prov-

erb which is only too true, although very humiliating for
humanity, ' Who makes himself mutton, the wolf eats ' :
nowhere is this so useful as in Barbary. I discovered
that on arriving there, and as I am a lamb at heart it was
necessary for me to conceal this character beneath the
exterior of some other animal, and my mustaches give
me very nearly the air of the tiger, a beast which the
wolf does not eat. They have been very useful in my
business ; I attach to them no value, except as a souve-
nir of the services they have rendered me. I place
them on your altars ; pronounce their fate.

" I have never enjoyed so perfect health as in this climate. I am not so fat as I was last year, but never so
clean before."

CHAPTER VII.

1797–1805.

ON the 11th of September the tedious quarantine was finished, and the exile hastened to his wife and friends in Paris. The city was the same, but the Republic had changed. The victories of the young general, Bonaparte, in Italy, had given her prestige, and put an entirely different face on the politics of Europe. The strained nature of French relations with America alone gave the poet uneasiness. Restored to his wife, his books, his friends, he settled down to a life of scholarly and literary retirement, enough disturbed by incursions of business, society, and politics to prevent its becoming stagnant. In a letter to Donaldson, written in 1800, he estimates his losses by the mission to Algiers at $20,000; but this was probably a hypothetical loss — the amount which he would have made had he remained. His fortune, thanks to the prudent management of his wife, had been kept intact; indeed, by the rise in French securities, of which he held or controlled a large block, it had been considerably added to. A future of happiness and contentment seemed his lot. His chief occupations for the next seven years were of a literary character, though he watched with intensest interest the progress of political movements in both Europe and America. We will notice first his literary enterprises: fiction excepted, these covered the entire range of literature—poetry, history, translations, and essays on political, economic, and scientific questions. His activity in this direction was intense. A vast array of notes and the prospectus for a contemplated " History of the French Revolution " were prepared at this time. He had published, before accepting the mission to Algiers, a superb edition of the " Vision of Columbus," and now set about the execution of a long cherished design of expanding the poem into a larger and more complete work, to be called the "Columbiad." The notes and the first draft of the epic were written during this period.

Volney's most famous work, " The Ruins," had been published in Paris in 1791, and had rapidly passed through several editions. It had been translated into English soon after its appearance; but this translation was very unsatisfactory to its author, who asserted that the translator must have been overawed by the Government or clergy from rendering his ideas faithfully. Volney at that time was travelling in the United States, and an English friend, residing in Philadelphia, hearing the remark, undertook a revision of the work. In his efforts to give the author's ideas literally, however, he made a very inelegant translation, which proved still more unsatisfactory. Volney had now returned to Paris. He and Barlow were on the most intimate terms, and the latter, at the author's suggestion, and under his supervision, undertook a new translation, which succeeded admirably, and remains to-day the best rendering of the French classic ever accomplished.*

---

* Compare the invocation in the three principal translations:

PARIS TRANSLATION (BARLOW'S).

" Hail, solitary ruins, holy sepulchres, and silent walls! You I invoke; to you I address my prayer. While your aspect averts, with secret terror, the vulgar regard, it excites in my heart the charm of delicious sentiments, sublime contemplations. What useful lessons, what affecting and profound reflections you suggest to him who knows how to consult you! When the whole earth, in chains and silence, bowed the neck before its tyrants, you had already proclaimed the truths which they abhor, and confounding the dust of the king with that of the meanest slave, had announced to man the sacred dogma of *Equality!* Within your pale, in solitary adoration of *Liberty*, I saw her genius arise from the mansions of the dead ; not such as she is painted by the impassioned multitude, armed with fire and sword, but under the august aspect of Justice, poising in her hand the sacred balance, wherein are weighed the actions of men at the gates of eternity."

Another literary work that occupied his thoughts was a history of his native country. Jefferson, as Barlow informs us in one of his letters, first broached the idea, when he was Minister at Paris. He now wrote again, returning to the attack: " We are rich ourselves in ma-

LONDON TRANSLATION.

" Solitary ruins, sacred tombs, ye smouldering and silent walls, all hail ! To you I address my invocation. While the vulgar shrink from your aspect with secret terror, my heart finds in the contemplation a thousand delicious sentiments, a thousand admirable recollections. Pregnant, I may truly call you, with useful lessons, with pathetic and irresistible advice to the man who knows how to consult you. Awhile ago the whole world bowed the neck in silence before the tyrants that oppressed it; and yet in that hopeless moment you already proclaimed the truths that tyrants hold in abhorrence. Mixing the dust of the proudest kings with that of the meanest slaves, you call upon us to contemplate this example of *equality.* From your caverns, whither the musing and anxious love of *Liberty* led me, I saw escape its venerable shade, and with unexpected felicity direct its flight and marshal my steps the way to renovated France."

PHILADELPHIA TRANSLATION.

" Hail, ye solitary ruins, ye sacred tombs and silent walls ! 'Tis your auspicious aid that I invoke; 'tis to you my soul, wrapt in meditation, pours forth its prayer ! What though the profane and vulgar mind shrinks with dismay from your august and awe-inspiring aspect, to me ye unfold the sublimest chains of contemplation and sentiment, and offer to my senses the luxury of a thousand delicious and enchanting thoughts ! How sumptuous the feast to a being that has a taste to relish, and an understanding to consult you ! What rich and noble admonitions, what exquisite and pathetic lessons do you read to a heart that is susceptible of exalted feelings ! When oppressed humanity bent in timid silence throughout the globe beneath the galling yoke of slavery, it was you that proclaimed aloud the birthright of those truths which tyrants tremble at while they detect, and which, by sinking the loftiest head of the proudest potentate, with all his boasted pageantry, to the level of mortality with his meanest slave, confirmed and ratified by your unerring testimony the sacred and immortal doctrine of *Equality.* Musing within the precincts of your inviting scenes of philosophic solitude, whither the insatiate love of true-born *Liberty* had led me, I beheld her genius ascending, not in the spurious character and habit of a bloodthirsty Fury armed with daggers and instruments of murder, and followed by a frantic and intoxicated multitude, but under the placid and chaste aspect of *Justice*, holding with a pure and unsullied hand the sacred scales in which the actions of mortals are weighed on the brink of Eternity.

terials, and can open all the public archives to you : but
your residence here is essential, because a great deal of
the knowledge of things is not on paper, but only
within ourselves for verbal communication.   John Marshall is writing the life of George Washington from his
papers.   It is intended to come out just in time to influence the next presidential election.   It is written, therefore, principally with a view to electioneering purposes.
But it will consequently be out in time to aid you with
information, as well as to point out the perversions of
truth necessary to be rectified.   Think of this, and agree
to it, and be assured of my high esteem and attachment."

Jefferson saw that the history of the great struggle
in which he had taken part was being given to posterity
entirely by his political adversaries, and was exceedingly
anxious that a competent writer should treat of it from
the Republican point of view.   Barlow accepted the
trust and made extensive preparations for it, both in
Paris and on his return to America, but his untimely
death prevented the completion of the work.   Several
hundred pages of notes on every topic in the remot-
est degree connected with it remain to attest his industry and the thoroughness of his preparation.   Nearly a
dozen essays on political matters—commerce, maritime
law, religion, science—addressed to the Governments of
England, France, the United States, and to various
learned societies, also remain to show the activity of his
pen during this period.   A curious essay, in which he
traces the origin and progress of idolatry back to the
expulsion from Eden, and another in which he demon-
strates the right of the Republicans of America to the
title of " Federalists," since they supported the Federal
Constitution, and were carrying out to their legitimate
conclusion the principles of the Revolution, both found
among his unpublished papers, may be ascribed to this
period.   He also busied himself with replying to criti-

cisms, by the leading reviews, on his " Vision of Columbus," and other works.

His services to his native country at this time cannot
be overestimated : these alone entitle him to the respect
and gratitude of his countrymen.

The years 1797–1800 were peculiarly fraught with
danger to the young Republic. The general war in
Europe destroyed her commerce, while the monarchical
tendencies of the Federalists made it probable that another revolution would be necessary before the people
could secure their rights. But the most serious danger
was the threatened collision with France. The sympathy of the mass of the American people was with
France, their old ally, now that she was engaged in a
heady struggle for her liberties against the combined
sovereigns of Europe. But the Government, then in the
hands of the Federalists, resolved on a course of strict
neutrality. Jay's treaty, which was something more
than this, almost provoked a popular uprising in
America, and with the French Directory came near being considered a *casus belli.* It favored England, they
urged, as against France, and they particularly exclaimed
against the clause giving their ancient enemy the right
to seize French goods in American bottoms, and that,
permitting freedom of trade between America and the
English colonies.

The bitter opposition of the Republican party in the
United States to this treaty, the arbitrary and high-
handed proceedings of the French Directory in retalia-
tion, and the putting of the American nation on a war-
footing by President Adams in consequence, are matters of history so familiar as to need no recapitulation.
It will be remembered that the matter was settled by
the French Directory's receding from its position, but
it is not generally known that that retrocession was
largely due to the influence of Joel Barlow, exerted
privately on the members of the Directory, and in pub-

lic on the French people through the medium of the press.*

He also wrote to Washington (on hearing that he had been appointed Commander-in-chief of the army to wage war against France) a letter presenting urgent reasons why the two Governments should refrain from the arbitrament of arms.   It was as follows :—

"PARIS, *2d October,* 1798.

"SIR:—On hearing of your late nomination as Commander-in-chief of the American armies I rejoice at it, not because I believe the war which that nomination contemplates is yet inevitable, and that it will furnish an occasion for a further display of your military talents, but because it may enable you to exert your influence to greater effect in preventing that war.   By becoming more the centre of information than you could be in your retirement, you will be better able to judge of the disposition of both countries, and to offer such counsels to your own Government as may tend to remove the obstacles that still oppose themselves to reconciliation. Were you now President of the United States I should not address you this letter, because, not knowing my inclination for the tranquillity of a retired life, you might think that I was seeking a place, or had some further object in view than the simple one of promoting peace between the two Republics.

"But I hope, under present circumstances, you will believe my motive to be pure and unmixed, and that the object of my letter is only to call your attention to the true state of facts.

"Perhaps few men who cannot pretend to be in the secrets of either Government are in a better situation

---

* Some of these articles were found among his papers.   One, designed to show that France was sharing equally with England in the commerce of the United States, was endorsed in Barlow's handwriting :   "Published by Maselet in the *Publicité,* the 25th Nivose, an 8.''

than myself to judge of the motives of both, to assign the true causes, and trace out the progress of their unhappy misunderstanding, or to appreciate their present dispositions, pretensions, and wishes. I am certain that there are none who labor more sincerely for the restoration of harmony upon terms honorable to the United States and advantageous to the cause of liberty.

"I will not in this place go over the history of past transactions; it would be of little use. The object is to seize the malady in its present stage, and try to arrest its progress. The dispute at this moment may be characterized as simply and literally a *misunderstanding*. I cannot persuade myself to give it a harsher name, as it applies to either Government.

It is clear that neither of them has an interest in going to war with the other, and I am fully convinced that neither has the inclination—that is, I believe the balance of inclination as well as interest on both sides is in favor of peace. But each Government, though sensible of this truth with respect to itself, is ignorant of it with respect to the other. Each believes the other determined on war, and ascribes all its conduct to a deep-rooted hostility. The least they can do, therefore, under this impression is to prepare for an event which they both believe inevitable while they both wish to avoid it.

" But by what fatality is it that a calamity so dreadful must be rendered *inevitable* because it is *thought* so? Both Governments have tongues, and both have ears. Why will they not speak? Why will they not listen?

"The causes that have hitherto prevented them are not difficult to assign. I could easily explain them, as I believe, to the satisfaction of all parties, and without throwing so much blame on either Government as each of them at present ascribes to the other. But I will avoid speaking of any past provocations on either side. The point that I wish to establish in your mind is that the French Directory is at present sincerely desirous of restoring harmony between this country and the United States, on terms honorable and advantageous to both parties. I wish to convince you of this, and through you the American Government, because that Government, being desirous of the same thing, would not fail to take such steps as would lead immediately to the object. In offering you my proofs of the present disposition on this side you will permit me to observe that some of them are, from their nature, incapable of being detailed, and others improper to be trusted to the casualties of a letter. But I will mention a few that are ostensible, and, so far as they go, undeniable. First, the Directory has declared that it will receive and treat with any minister from America who shall appear to be sent with a real intention of treating and terminating existing difficulties. I have no doubt but this was the intention when the last envoys were sent; but from some unfortunate circumstances the Directory did not believe it. Secondly, as a preliminary, it has declared that in the negotiation there shall be no question of a loan of money, or apologies for offensive speeches pronounced by the executive on either side. Thirdly, all commissions given to privateers in the West Indies are recalled; and when new commissions are given, the owners and commanders are to be restricted, under bonds, to the legal objects of capture. Fourthly, an embargo that was laid on the American ships within the Republic, in consequence of a report that a war was begun on the part of the United States, was taken off as soon as it was ascertained that such a war had not begun; and a new declaration was, at the same time, sent to America of the wishes of France to treat. These facts will doubtless come to your knowledge through other channels before you receive this letter. But there are other facts which, in my mind, are equally clear, though to you they will be destitute of corroborating circumstances, and must rest upon my own information and opinion.

" First, that this Government contemplates a just in-

demnity for spoliations on American commerce, to be
ascertained by commissioners, in a manner similar to the
one prescribed in our treaty with England.

" Second, that the legislation will soon be changed here
with respect to neutrals ; and that all flags will be put
on the footing of the law of nations.

" Third, that a public agent would have been sent to
Philadelphia soon after Mr. Gerry's departure were it
not for apprehension that he would not be received.
There was a doubt whether the American Government
would not have already taken such measures of hostility
as to be unwilling to listen to terms of accommodation ;
and the Directory did not like to risk the chance of seeing its offers refused.

" Fourth, that the Directory considers these declarations
and transactions as a sufficient overture on its part ; that
it has retreated to an open ground which is quite unsuspicious ; that a refusal on the part of the American Government to meet on this ground will be followed by
immediate war ; and that it will be a war of the most
terrible and vindictive kind.

" This, sir, is my view of the present state of affairs.
Should it make that impression on your mind which I
desire for the sake of humanity that it may, you will
judge whether it does not comport with the independence
of the United States and the dignity of their Government
to send another minister to form new treaties with the
French Republic. In a war there is clearly nothing to
be *gained* by us, not even honor. Honor indeed may be
saved by war, and so it may be by negotiation. But the
calamities inseparable from a war, and under present circumstances, would be incalculable. I do not say that the
United States, or any portion of them, would be conquered. But they would sacrifice great numbers of their
best citizens, burden themselves with four times their
present debt, overturn the purest system of morals, and
lose the fairest opportunity that ever a nation had of

rising to greatness and happiness on the basis of liberty. Were I writing to a young general whose name was still to be created I might deem it useless to ask him to stifle in its birth a war on which he had founded his hopes of future honors. But you, sir, having already earned and acquired all that can render a man great and happy, can surely have no object of ambition but to render your country so. To engage your influence in favor of a new attempt at negotiation before you draw your sword, I thought it only necessary to convince you that such an attempt would be well received here, and probably attended with success. I can do no more than assure you that this is my sincere opinion, and that my information is drawn from unsuspected sources. I am not accustomed to interpose my advice in the administration of any country, and should not have done it now did I not believe it my duty as a citizen of my own, and a friend to all others. I see two great nations rushing on each other's bayonets without any cause of contention but a misunderstanding. I shudder at the prospect, and wish to throw myself between the vans, and suspend the onset till a word of explanation can pass. I hope my letter will have cast some light on the subject ; but if it shall not, I know you will excuse the attempt, for you know my zeal is honest.

" I have the honor to be, sir, with great respect,

" JOEL BARLOW."

It will be interesting to follow the adventures of this letter. Though written early in October, it did not come into Washington's hands until the last day of January; the next day it was forwarded by Washington to President Adams under cover of the following note :

" I have conceived it my duty to transmit it to you without delay, and without a comment, except that it must have been written with a very good, or a very bad design ; which of the two you can judge better than I.

From the known abilities of that gentleman, such a letter could not be the result of ignorance *in him ;* nor from the implications which are to be found in it, has it been written without the privity of the French Directory. It is incumbent on me to add, that I have not been in the habit of corresponding with Mr. Barlow. The letter now forwarded is the first I ever received from him, and to him I have never written one. If, then, you should be of opinion that his letter is calculated to bring on negotiation upon open, fair, and honorable ground, and merits a reply, and will instruct me as to the tenor of it, I shall with pleasure and alacrity obey your orders ; more especially, if there is reason to believe that it would become a means, however small, of restoring peace and tranquillity to the United States upon just, honorable, and dignified terms, which I am persuaded is the ardent desire of all the friends of this rising empire."

Contrast Washington's calm and temperate language with the words of John Adams on receiving it:

" PHILADELPHIA, *Feb.* 19*th.*

" Barlow's letter had, I assure you, very little weight in determining me to this measure.* I shall make few observations upon it. But in my opinion it is not often that we meet with a composition which betrays so many and so unequivocal symptoms of blackness of heart. The wretch has destroyed his own character to such a degree that I think it would be derogatory to yours to give any answer at all to his letter. Tom Paine is not a more worthless fellow. The infamous threat which he has debased himself to transmit to his country to intimidate you and your country—'that certain conduct will be followed by war, and that it will be a war of the most terrible and vindictive kind '—ought to be answered by a Mohawk. If I had an Indian chief that I could converse with freely, I would ask him what answer he would give

---

* Sending envoys to treat with the Directory.

to such a gasconade. I fancy he would answer that he would, if they began their cruelties, cut up every Frenchman, joint by joint, roast him by a fire, pinch off his flesh with hot pincers, etc. I blush to think that such ideas should be started in this age.''

On reflection, however, the sturdy old patriot seems to have become ashamed of this ebullition of feeling. Years after, in his series of interesting letters to the *Boston Patriot*, he made this retraction :

" I, however, considered General Washington's question whether Mr. Barlow's letter was written with a very good or a very bad design ; and as, with all my jealousy, I had not sagacity enough to discover the smallest room for suspicion of any ill design, I frankly concluded that it was written with a very good one."

The above letter (to Washington) was enclosed in one addressed to the writer's brother-in-law, Abraham Baldwin, Senator from Georgia, dated Paris, 3d October, 1798, which contains the following reference to it : " Enclosed is a letter in duplicate which I have thought it my duty to address to George Washington. I wish you to seal and forward it, but first to take a copy of it ; and if you find that neither this nor any other statement of facts is likely to calm the frenzy of him and his associates, but that they continue running wild after a phantom to the ruin of their country, I should think it best to publish it with my name and his, that our countrymen may see, whenever they will condescend to open their eyes, that one of their chiefs at least has had a warning in proper time, and from an unsuspicious quarter. But the whole of this is submitted entirely to your judgment, and there are few men whose discretion I would trust in a point so delicate. As I do not contemplate its being published but in a case of extremity, when matters cannot be made worse, it may in that case not be amiss that you should appear to be the channel through which it comes. That circumstance might add to its weight ; and it might be

proper to introduce it by publishing the first paragraph
of this letter to you."

The year 1800 was the year of the fourth presidential
election. Shrewd observers saw that a crisis was approaching; that with proper exertion the Government
could be given into Republican hands. The course of
the Federal leaders toward France, as we have seen, had
been vastly unpopular, while their arrogance and contempt of all opposition had become insufferable. Barlow
watched the contest with the keenest interest, and by an
accident was made a potent factor in deciding it. Early
in March, 1799, a copy of the *Columbian Centinel*, published in Boston, the leading organ of the Federalists of
New England, fell into his hands. It contained an article which excited his interest at once, and which we feel
impelled to give entire, not as a literary curiosity (as
might be suspected), nor as an exhibition of the partisan
rage of the period, but as necessary to our narrative.
The article is presented *verbatim et literatim*, the cap-
tions and italics being the editor's own.

" JOEL BARLOW'S LETTER.

" Quos Deus vult perdere prius dementat.

" APOLOGY.

" The Editor has repelled for some time an inclination
to give insertion to the following letter. He was unwilling to promulgate the degradation of a Man whom every
American once revered for talents, patriotism, and erudition—without the strongest proofs: And it was, at first,
difficult to believe the author of the ' Vision of Columbus ' could be the vile ejector of falsehood, froth and
filth, which would cast a midnight shade over the black-
est character of his contemporary *Thomas Paine*. But
assured of the transforming qualities of the *Upas-air of
Paris*, and satisfied of the fact of the authorship, the Editor will no longer withhold from the eyes of his numer-

ous readers, evidence of a '*falling off*' compared with which that of *Judas Iscariot* is but a foible.—The latter betrayed his Master, but he repented himself of it and returned the money. The former has not only betrayed his country, but glories in his shame.

" QUINTESSENCE OF VILLANY.

"Copy of a Letter from an American Diplomatic Character in France, to a Member of Congress in Philadelphia.

"1 *March*, 1798.

"'MY DEAR FRIEND:—It is now a long time, even many years, since I have indulged myself,' etc.

"3d Paragraph.—'America by the man whose monstrous influence formed an inexplicable contrast with the weakness of his political talents.'

"Close of 4th Paragraph.—'He was a wide-mouthed brawler, and had been for two years the exaggerated echo of all the abuse in all Burke's pamphlets, and of the worst papers in *London*.'

"3d.—'Through a silence marked with resentment and contempt.'

"'This accounts for the interest which the French seemed to take in the event of that election. Their wishing you to elect Q—— E—— proves that they did not want to quarrel with you, and that they still hoped that the people of America were friends to liberty.

"'*Answer Propre* (?)

"'That in everything but wisdom I am the worst or best of the present race.'"

Then follows:

"CENTINEL COMMENTS.

"We have now discharged our duty in giving a place in the *Centinel* to the preceding epistle. It is a useful document, and will serve as an appendix to the volume of the despatches from our Envoys. It incontestably proves what the Jacobins have often desired, a fixed determination in the French Directory to dictate measures and men in the United States as they have done in Holland and Italy, and develops the causes of the French robberies of our property. It unquestionably was written in Talleyrand's bureau, while that arch apostate sat at the elbow of the duped American and dictated every word. A greater quantum of folly, arrogance, egotism and falsehood could not be condensed within equal limits. Were the United States the most insignificant, conquered colony of France, and 'Joel Barlow,' as great an advocate for 'passive obedience' and servile dependence as Thomas Hutchinson, he could not have uttered insinuations more humiliating, or have more strenuously advocated the right of the French to dictate not only the Constitutions, Laws and Treaties, but the Men who shall preside in the Councils of the country which gave him birth.—' We must,' says this Joel, ' choose first such men as will please France, for President and Ambassador, or the " five-headed monster," after devouring the European whales, will " shark " the American " shrimps,"—Buffon could not have been the parent of a more belittleing idea. Again, Citoyen 'Joel' swears, ' He will not Excuse the Executive for printing,' the despatches. O! Adams! President of the Union! Your fate is fixed! The indignation of J-o-e-l B-a-r-l-o-w will hurl you from your elevated sphere, and bury all your boasted Fame in obscurity! But what ill-starred Fiend tempted Citoyen Joel to tell the silly tale of the letter from Gen. Washington to Morris?—Barlow, the ci-devant American, Knew it was a lie;—But Barlow, the Poet, had been in the habit of fibbing; and Barlow the Frenchman must write what Talleyrand dictates."

It only remains to prove that this letter had been stolen, and then so garbled and altered that an entirely different construction could be placed on its contents, to convict its publishers of the height of moral turpitude. In the same letter to Abraham Baldwin which enclosed that to Washington, Barlow had written: "I have been apprehensive that a letter of March last—very long; 8 or 10 sheets—by William Lee, has fallen into wrong hands, as well as another by the same occasion to Thomas Jefferson. Relieve my anxiety if you can on this head."

He at once recognized in the *Centinel* extracts, garbled portions of that letter, and in answer to the comments they had called forth, addressed an open letter to his fellow-citizens of the United States, which proved one of the most effective documents of the campaign. After calling attention to the extracts in the *Centinel*, and declaring that there was not a paragraph "without some omissions, additions, or changes which vitiate or wholly destroy its meaning," he proceeds: "But the substantial character of the letter, so far as it respects my opinion on the system of policy pursued by our Executive toward France and England during the period to which it relates, must answer for itself. I see nothing in it to retract or correct. Though I always reserve to myself the right of changing my opinions, as every man who is not omniscient must often have occasion to do, yet on this subject I have not changed them during the last year. It is my belief that it would cost you dearer, even now, to settle your dispute with France, than it would have done (had your negotiations been properly managed) at the time I wrote the letter. How much you have unfortunately suffered from the piracies carried on under the French laws since that period, you can doubtless determine better than I; and what will be the final expense of the negotiation, those only will be able to decide who shall live to see it. Thus much for the sentiments originally contained in that letter. I will now rectify one or two mistakes which I have observed in the American papers, relative to the circumstances under which it was written. *First*. It is supposed by some,

who do not reflect on the chronology of dates, that I was
knowing to the attempts which had been made here to
extort from our commissioners a bribe to individuals, and
a promise of a loan to the Government. They imagine
that I wrote under this impression, and consequently approved the measure. I believe that not the most distant
hint of either of these base attempts was known or whispered (beyond the circle of those persons mentioned in
the despatches) until their publication in Philadelphia—
which happened to be on the same day that my letter
was dated in Paris. The printed despatches arrived here
in May, and no man in America could feel a greater indignation than I did at the piece of villany therein detailed, though I am far from thinking that a proper use
was made of the circumstance, either before or after it
was communicated to the American Government. The
despatches of General Pinckney, alluded to in my letter,
were not those of the three commissioners, as supposed
by the *Centinel*, but were dated the year before, and were
the fruits of his former embassy. *Secondly.* Had that
letter been designed for publication, I should not have
left it open to criticism in another point more remarkable than the one above noticed. In reviewing the errors
of the American Government I then made no mention of the French, and it has been concluded, from this
omission, that I approved the conduct of the latter; that
I saw nothing wrong in that monstrous system of piracy
and plunder exercised towards neutrals; indeed, I am
supposed to have relished all the horrors that have attended this tremendous revolution. God forbid that I
should lose my senses to such a degree! I have not
only disapproved the innumerable acts of injustice and
violence committed under the order of the 2d of March,
1797, and the law of the 18th of January, 1798, but I have
uniformly remonstrated, with as much force as an individual of little influence could do, against that order and
that law, and against the general current of resentment

which has marked the measures of this Government towards that of the United States, ever since the ratification of the British treaty. This resentment has appeared to me far greater than the occasion would justify; and I have not failed to enforce this opinion whenever I thought it could be usefully done. But Paris .is the place where it is proper to point out for correction the errors of the French Government, and *Philadelphia* those of the American. My friend was in Philadelphia. My letter was written with the simple hope of doing some immediate good, not with the design of transmitting history to future ages. Where then would have been the use of swelling it with a list of blunders, or *crimes* if you please, which no man of candor will deny, but on which his silence ought not to be construed into approbation? You might as well say I believe in the doctrines of Mahomet because I do not go out of my way to refute them. We are so constituted and circumscribed in our powers of action that most of the good or ill which we do in the world, is the result of circumstances, not always in our power to control. Whoever will give himself the trouble of obtaining a competent knowledge of the French Revolution, so as to be able to judge it with intelligence, and weigh the infinite complication of difficulties and incentives to ungovernable passions that have lain in the way of'its leaders, must indeed be shocked at their follies and their faults; but he will find more occasion to ask why they have committed so few, than why they have committed so many. A state of political insanity is not at all inconsistent with the situation in which they have been placed by the irresistible force of circumstances. And there are cases in which we ought to applaud men for the mischiefs they have not done, as well as to seek excuses for those they have brought about. I am sensible that, in your view, the wrongs committed by the French towards the United States are less excusable than those towards other nations. You form this opin-

ion not so much from national prejudice as from a consciousness of the purity of your own intentions in your
conduct towards this Republic ; from having felt a general friendship to her cause, and not perceiving a sufficient ground of complaint on which her resentment can
be founded. But you are not to learn that jealousy is
one of the strongest and blindest of the human passions ;
and I believe you will be convinced that the facts hinted
at in my letter, viewed through the mist of jealousy that
had constantly surrounded the leaders in the Revolution,
could not fail of producing effects similar to what we
now deplore. No ! my fellow-citizens ; I have too high
a sense of justice and of the rights of nations to sanction
maritime plunder from any quarter, or even to approve
the least restriction on trade. A perfect liberty of
commerce is among the most indubitable rights of man,
and it is the best policy of nations. The establishment
of this principle alone, with proper measures to preserve
it, would have a powerful tendency, if not an infallible
effect, to maintain a perpetual peace between countries
separated by the ocean. The opposers of this branch of
liberty, who do it from reflection, are not only the enemies of America, but they are the abettors of injustice
and the foes of humanity. They strive to perpetuate a
system of war, of public devastations, private rapine, fraud
and cruelty, which disturb the tranquillity of the states,
discourage honest industry, and blacken the character
of man. Those who oppose it through ignorance, and at
the same time aspire to the task of administering the
government of a free people, ought to be sent back to
school, and there taught the rudiments of the science
which solicits their ambition. Possessing these opinions,
and seeing America move nearer to this principle than
any other nation, how is it possible that I could approve
the blind policy of European plunder, or look with indifference on the tyranny of the seas? From the time
when your first vessel was taken by the English at the

beginning of the present war, I expected to see some of your great men in power come forward with something luminous on the rights of nations relative to trade. From the reputed wisdom of America I expected to see Europe at last enlightened on a subject of so much importance to the human race. In addition to the freedom of your constitution, I considered you as possessing two singular advantages for the attainment of this great object : 1st. Nature had placed a wide ocean between you and those nations to which your commercial intercourse extended. And you had not, or ought not to have, any other political intercourse abroad but what relates to commerce. 2d. From the nature of your trade, and the constant result of your accounts current, you are always indebted to those nations in sums amounting to from fifteen to thirty millions of dollars. This state of your accounts was not confined to England. It extended (before the present war) to those other countries whose manufactures you were in the habit of importing; and to France and Holland in as high a proportion, compared with their manufactures imported, as to England. The first of these advantages, being a sufficient bulwark against attacks by land, secured you from the political squabbles of Europe, leaving you vulnerable only in your commerce. The second furnished you, in your commerce itself, with a most powerful weapon of defence. The English began to plunder you in the year 1793, in a manner totally unprovoked, and without even a pretext. Here was an occasion which called for the talents of your leaders, and invited them to use with dexterity this weapon, which was the most legitimate, the most pacific, and the most effectual that was ever put into the hands of any Government. But instead of this, an embassy is despatched to London to resign this precious weapon, the only infallible one you had, into the hands of the British king, and this for no other reason than for fear that a future Congress, and another Executive might use it. Your situation, though new to you, was not difficult nor delicate; it required a declaration of neutrality, a solemn declaration and definition of the rights of neutrality, and a notification of your intention that all property taken unjustly from your citizens by any power at war should be compensated by so much property of the subjects of that power found within your jurisdiction, whether in the public funds or in the hands of private debtors. There is nothing unjust or immoral in this mode of proceeding. The aggression would be on the part of the foreign power. You compensate your own citizen, and leave that power to compensate hers; and if she does not do it the injustice is on her side, both as first aggressor and final delinquent. If she makes the compensation she will not be likely to repeat the offence, because it would be an expensive business; if she refuses compensation, she will soon be brought to reason by the clamors of her suffering subjects. England in such cases would not fail to do you justice, and that on the only principle you can count upon with certainty from any foreign nation—an attention to her own interests."

From this point he went on to notice and discuss nearly all the public measures then attracting attention—the funding of the debt, the establishment of a navy as another department of Government, the ulterior effects of the Jay treaty, the rupture with France, and other interesting topics, and concludes with the following spirited question: "What are the measures that America ought to take *to secure her own liberty, establish a permanent and equal independence from every foreign power, command the respect and gain the confidence of all mankind, and induce the commercial nations to adopt a general plan of pacific intercourse which will perpetuate itself and better the condition of society?* It is possible that these inquiries may be the subject of another letter which I may address to you, my fellow-citizens, whose interests I will never cease to cherish.   I am your brother by the close and complicated ties of blood, of early sympathies, common dangers, and common triumphs; and your happiness is naturally and habitually nearer to my heart than that of any other nation, though my general philanthropy leads me to pity the condition of every injured people, and to censure, if I cannot restrain, those who lead them into error.   Some of you have blamed me for the severity of my remarks on the conduct of your Executive.   It is because you have made them gods that you are offended with me for finding them but men.   I never doubted the patriotism of your principal leaders, that is, so far as patriotism consists in good intentions.   But I doubt the patriotism of those who lead your leaders.   I see immense fortunes made by your funding legislators out of the public funds which they funded for themselves.   I see the most perfidious measures proposed, adopted, and persisted in for hurling you from the exalted station which enabled you to give commercial law to the Governments of Europe, and for couching you under the pelican wing of the worst of those Governments.   I see the treaty that consummates this business ratified in a gust of passion, a moment of personal resentment at an intercepted letter written by an officious French Minister, which happens to speak of the western insurrection.   And when the indignation of France, though excited by repeated provocations, rises with symptoms of extravagant fury, and threatens an unjustifiable measure of revenge, I see no prudent or manly attempts on your part to allay the storm and prevent a rupture; but prevarication about facts is given for explanation, and gasconade at home keeps time with humiliation abroad.   Then comes the flood of piracy and plunder let loose upon your property; a scene of wickedness, which no man can abominate more than myself, and no man has endeavored more to prevent or mitigate.   But when I trace the deplorable effects to their proper and indubitable causes, I cannot confine my animadversion to this side of the Atlantic. Though you may choose to deify your first magistrates, the original authors of these calamities; though you enshrine them in the temple of infallibility, fence them round with sedition laws, and intoxicate them with addresses, birthday odes, and bacchanalian toasts, I see in them some of the frailties of men, and I will not join the chorus of adoration. With respect to men, I am of no party; with respect to principle, I am a Republican in theory and practice, notwithstanding the disgrace into which that principle seems to be falling in America. I consider it as my inalienable right, as well as my indispensable duty, to render a service to you wherever I find occasion. And when such service has lead me to notice what I thought wrong in the administration of your Government, I have always done it, and in such a manner as I thought would be most likely to lead to a correction of the abuse; and I shall not relinquish this right, nor neglect this duty, whoever may be the men, and whatever the party, to whom you may choose to delegate your powers. Among my endeavors to serve you as a volunteer in the cause of humanity, there is none which I have had more at heart than that of preventing a war between you and France, and of bringing about a reconciliation on terms honorable and advantageous to each. I have no doubt but that both Governments desire it; but whether they do or not, as long as I deem it for the interest of both nations, and there remains any hope of success, I will not slacken my exertions. I do not believe in the modern doctrine of your cabinet, that it is a crime in a private citizen to serve his country, or even to call in question the infallibility of its administration, and I know no man in America who did believe it as long as he remained a private citizen. I am confident, and you may be in time, that the labors of myself and a few other men, not commissioned for the purpose, have hitherto prevented a war. But how long this will continue to be the case I cannot pretend to say. . . . But if you really have no talent among you of a higher nature than what is necessary to copy precedents from old monarchies, I pity you, and call upon you to pity me; it is time to despair of the perfectibility of human society, and make up our minds to return to slavery, monarchy, and perpetual war."

One has only to contrast this cool, temperate, convincing argument with the gasconade of the *Centinel* to discover one reason for the change in parties that characterized the election of 1800. The letter was followed a few months later by another on the remaining topics of interest indicated.

Their effect on friend and foe cannot be better described than is done in the introduction to the first edition of the " Letters," published in Connecticut—which, by the way, was not until 1806, seven years after their first appearance. The bitterness with which Mr. Barlow was assailed by those who had been in youth his warmest friends is also indicated. The editor observes:

"The following letters were written in the time of terror, and although they went through several editions in Philadelphia and in the Southern States, as well as in England and France, they never found their way into Connecticut. No printer, at that time, would venture to publish them here. Such was then our liberty of the press, and such our candor in refusing to hear a man whom our Tories thought proper to condemn for adhering to those solid principles of liberty on which all our political institutions were founded! Mr. Barlow was volunteering in the most important services of his country abroad, while his former friends and companions were reviling him at home. He was laboring with all his influence to prevent a war with France, or he was risking his life in the midst of a desolating plague at Algiers to rescue our citizens from slavery and death, at the same

time that the Royalist faction, who were then in possession of the government of this country, were employed,
with a meanness and cowardice worthy of their cause,
some in forging and publishing the vilest calumnies
against him, and some in making laws to entrap him on
his return to his native country. He was one of the
objects of that memorable act of Congress imposing penalties on any private citizen who should dare to hold any
conversation with any foreign prince, government, or
ministers on our political relations with them. Happily
for his country, his disregard of that formidable effort of
legislative imbecility saved her from a war with France.
The fraudulent and hostile conduct of our Government
toward that nation had excited a spirit of vengeance,
which to a certain degree was certainly just, but which
was swelling beyond due bounds, and had fallen heavily
on our commerce. It is well known that his exertions
had a much greater effect in healing the rupture between
the two countries than those of the six ambassadors who
were sent in two triplicate assortments for that purpose.
The public will recollect his famous letter to Mr. Baldwin, which was intercepted, mutilated, and published.
It was full of weight and galling truths. They will also
recollect the use which the Pickering faction made of
that letter to throw the country into a flame. It was
that publication, and the clamor it excited, that occasioned these two addresses to his fellow-citizens. We
now publish them for the first time in this his native
state, and we beg our countrymen to read them; this is
all we ask. They require no commendation; they admit
of no comment. People of Connecticut, men of all parties, ancient schoolfellows, former friends and present
calumniators of Joel Barlow, read these letters, then call
him Jacobin, Infidel, Democrat, whatever you please; he
will force on you the conviction that he is a wise and
virtuous man. You will recognize in him the same dignified and amiable companion you once loved; the

unchangeable friend of his country, the most zealous and able defender of her rights. If you find between him and you a difference of principle that did not formerly exist, it is yours that has changed, and not his. If in all the heavy volumes that load your shelves, on the "*Defence of the American constitution,*" you find enough of solid matter to balance a dozen pages of this pamphlet, return the pamphlet to the bookseller, and he will return your money; and if you find a legislator or a magistrate who shall read these addresses, and not grow wiser and better for the reading, trust him no longer; he is unfit for his place, being unable, from his prejudices, to discern the truth."

It is a proof of the versatility and comprehensiveness of the man, that while thus deeply interested in politics and letters he was also keenly alive to the importance of that question which was a test of the statesmanship of his age—the question of internal improvements. In his Fourth of July Oration at Washington in 1809, he put into words what his prophetic eye had seen at Paris in 1800, that this great country could only be developed and made a homogeneous whole by safe, rapid, cheap communication between its most distant parts. He at once saw what a factor in effecting this the steamboat, if successful, would be, and entered, heart, soul, and purse, into the schemes of its inventors. Among the names of the pioneers of the steamboat, not the least is that of Joel Barlow. The proofs of our assertion are to be found in a large bundle of faded, time-stained letters, written at Paris by the poet, between the years 1800–1803, to Mrs. Barlow during her various absences in the provinces, and to which the reader's attention is now invited.

In 1797, Fulton, weary of assailing the deaf ears of the British Ministry with his schemes for canal and submarine navigation, crossed over to France, hoping to be more fortunate with the Directory. It is probable that he had letters of introduction to his distinguished countryman, as did most Americans who visited Paris at that time; it is at least certain that he found in him the patron which he so much needed. A warm friendship at once sprung up between the young inventor and Mr. Barlow: the latter invited him to take up his abode with him, and during the seven years that Fulton remained in Paris, a room in the poet's house, and a seat at his fireside were always reserved for him. The relations between the two men of genius during this period were those of father and son. Mrs. Barlow, too, regarded and treated her guest with maternal affection. The first essay of the two was the construction of a torpedo-boat —"a machine by which metallic cases filled with gunpowder could be projected under water to a given point and then exploded." The first experiment with this contrivance, tried on the Seine, is said to have come near drowning both the projectors, although subsequent experiments produced a very effective and formidable machine. The summer of 1800, was spent by Mrs. Barlow at Havre for the benefit of the sea air and baths, Fulton accompanying her, both as escort and to experiment with his torpedo-boat on the British frigates then blockading the port. Mr. Barlow remained in Paris. His letters to his wife during this summer, from their frequent reference to Fulton and his projects and their gossip of the poet's friends, pursuits, and surroundings, are exceedingly interesting, and worthy of publication. We content ourselves with extracts. "Toot," we may premise, was the pet name of Fulton.

Under date of 29th Thermidor (Aug. 17th) he writes: . . . . " Tell Toot he shall have the $1000 in a day or two, but Thayer has not paid according to his promise. The pictures go not well—50 or 60 livres a day for both, and at this season ! But the excessive heat prevents everybody from stirring out, especially on the Boulevard and in the day time.*   The Clos St. Lazare is still for us, but I have concluded nothing."

29th Thermidor—at night.

"I am glad to hear of Toot's success in experiment. Always repeat to him how much I love him; you cannot tell him too much of it.   I shall send him some money to-morrow."

2d Fructidor.

"Tell Toot to go to the house of Homburg Frères and there he will find $500 from Hottingner.   He will have more in a day or two.

"P. S.—Toot may wish to send for the book of which the advertisement enclosed is taken from a magazine."

11th Fructidor.

"Apropos of praise or flattery in the matrimonial state.   It is always my opinion (I don't know how often I have told you of it) that it ought to be indulged and cultivated   as far as possible.   It has a doubly good effect when hearts are well disposed: 1st. It makes the party praised improve the mind and actions to deserve that praise; and, 2d. It helps the praising party to fix in his mind a sort of standard of sentiment to which he resorts under every different feeling.   When he forgets the merits of his other moiety and feels peevish he recollects himself and says: 'But I often tell her she possesses such and such good qualities; surely I don't tell her lies.   Well, then, she does possess them; well, then, she merits my love,' and it's ten to one but all his love returns with this single reflection.

"I have written a long letter to Professor Ebeling to condole with him for the loss of Professor Bosch, to talk with him about the armed neutrality, and to propose a better way to secure the rights of neutrals."

13th Fructidor.

". . . . Tell Toot that every strain and extraordinary exertion in middle life, and cold, and damp, and twisting,

---

* Probably refers to a panorama Fulton had opened in Paris.

and wrenching, and unnatural and strained position that
our bodies are exposed to in middle life, tend to stiffen
the nerves, joints, and muscles, and bring on old age pre-
maturely, perhaps sickness or decrepitude ; that pains,
gouts, rheumatisms, and death are not things of chance,
but are all physical effects from physical causes ; that
the machine of his body is better and more worthy his
attention than any other machine he can make; that
preservation is more useful than creation ; and that unless he could create me one in the image of himself he
had better preserve his own automaton. Read this lect-
ure to him, or a better one, on the preservation of health
and vigor every morning at breakfast."

This and the following letter refer to a grand trial of
his plunging boat which Fulton was about to make.
The references will be better understood, perhaps, if we
give a short account of the machine and its perform-
ances: its construction had occupied the attention of
both the inventor and his patron from the day of the
initial experiment on the Seine in 1797. Fulton called
it the " diving or plunging boat," and later the *Nau-
tilus*. His design in inventing it was to provide a mo-
tor for his torpedo, and thus add another arm to naval
warfare ; but subsequently he designed it for general
purposes of communication. The only description of it
extant, probably, is that given by St. Aubin, a member of
the French tribunate, in one of the newspapers of the
day. He says: " The diving boat will be capacious
enough to contain eight men and provision for twenty
days, and will be of sufficient strength and power to enable him to plunge 100 feet under water if necessary.
He has contrived a reservoir of air, which will enable
eight men to remain under water eight hours. When
the boat is above water it has two sails, and looks just
like a common boat: when she is to dive, the mast and
sails are struck. In making his experiments, Mr Fulton
not only remained a whole hour under water with three

of his companions, but had the boat parallel to the horizon at any given distance.   He proved that the compass points as correctly under water as on the surface, and that while under water the boat made way at the rate of half a league an hour by means contrived for that purpose. . . . It has the advantage of sailing like the common boat, and also of diving when it is pursued.   With these qualities it is fit for carrying secret orders, to succor a blockaded fort, and to examine the force and position of an enemy in their harbors.   But who can see all the consequences of this discovery, or the improvements of which it is susceptible? Mr. Fulton has already added to his boat a machine by means of which he blew up a large boat in the port of Brest, and if by future experiments the same effect could be produced in frigates and ships of the line, what will become of maritime wars, and where will sailors be found to man ships of war, when it is a physical certainty that they may at every moment be blown into the air by means of diving boats, against which no human foresight can guard them."   Fulton made some interesting experiments with this boat in the harbor of Brest in July, 1801.   At his first experiment he attained a depth of twenty-five feet, and remained below the surface one hour.   This descent was made in darkness; a second was made with candles, but finding that these made too great inroads on his stock of air, he placed a round window of thick glass in the bow of the boat, and again descending, found that he received sufficient light from his window to discern the figures on his watch.   His next effort was to prove the sailing qualities of his craft.   "On the 26th of July he weighed his anchor and hoisted his sails; his boat had one mast, a mainsail, and jib.   There was only a light breeze, and therefore she did not move on the surface at more than the rate of two miles an hour; but it was found that she would tack, and steer, and sail on a wind, or before it, as well as any common sailing boat.   He then struck her mast and sails, to do which, and perfectly to prepare the boat for plunging, required about two minutes. Having plunged to a certain depth he placed two men at the engine which was intended to give her progressive motion, and one at the helm, while he, with a barometer before him, governed the machine which kept her balanced between the upper and lower waters. He found that with the exertion of one hand only he could keep her at any depth he pleased. The propelling engine was then put in motion, and he found upon coming to the surface that he had, in about seven minutes, made a progress of 400 metres, or about 500 yards. He then again plunged, turned her round while under water, and returned to near the place he began to move from." With this explanation we return to the correspondence, the next letter referring to Fulton's expedition against the British ships.

17th Fructidor.

. . . . "And poor Toot, I suppose, is now gone. I have not believed of late that there was much danger in the expedition, especially if they don't go over to the enemy's coast. I have certainly seen the day when I would have undertaken it without fear or apprehension of extraordinary risk. I can't say that I am now without uneasiness. I should probably have less if I was in the boat and without bodily pain. But there is really very little to fear. The weather is fine ; they are only going along the coast. He is master of all his movements, and it appears to me one of the safest of all hostile enterprises." . . . .

18th Fructidor.

" I am glad you made such good lectures to the poor boy before he went away. They will be useful to him always, whether there is any other danger but fatigue or not. I feel very anxious, but it is rather from the magnitude of the object than from that of the danger. . . .

" Volney says he is certain that Moreau will be in

Vienna in 40 days; he has received great force during the armistice. The latter campaign will be short, and, I think, will end in peace and a universal detestation of the English, the only authors, fomenters, renewers, and continuers of the war. Kleber is certainly murdered : it is thought Menon will keep Egypt."

19th Fructidor.

"DEAR FULTON:—Your letter of the 16th came yesterday about 4 o'clock, too late to see the Minister, and this morning he seems to have got up wrong end foremost. I went to his porter's lodge at 9 o'clock, and sent up a letter concise and clear, explaining the affair and telling him I should wait there for an answer, or for leave to speak to him. The porter returned and said he put the letter into his hands, and he read it and shrugged his shoulders, and when the porter asked him for the answer he said, '*Je ne puis pas, je ne puis pas,*' and that was all he could get out of him ; that he seemed to be very busy and vexed about other things. The porter, who was very civil, said it would be useless for me to wait ; he was sure I should get no answer to-day. However, as to-morrow is *de cadi,* I will go again to-day about 2 o'clock and send up another note, and write you to-morrow my success. I always doubted whether this Government would suffer your expedition to go into effect. It is possible they have reserved to themselves this method to prevent it, always in hopes before that your preparatory experiments would fail, or that your funds and patience would be exhausted."

20th Fructidor.

"TOOT :—I went to the Marine again yesterday at 3 o'clock and sent up a written request for an answer to my letter of the morning. The Minister referred me to Forestier, who, he said, had orders to attend to this affair. I went to Forestier's bureau : his *adjoint* told me that the business was done ; that the orders were sent that day by port to the *prefet* of the marine at Havre to deliver you the commission and dispense with the caution. Thus if you can rely on a class of men on whom I have learned long ago not to rely at all, the business is done. . . . . But if there is any more difficulty, which is altogether probable, explain it to me, and I will go to Forfairt with pleasure to get it removed. . . . Your old idea that these fellows are to be considered parts of the machine, and that you must have as much patience with them as with a piece of wood or brass, is an excellent maxim. It bears up my courage wonderfully every time I think of it, and makes me a better part to the machine than I should otherwise be. I have told it to several persons, who say it is a maxim to be quoted as the mark of a great mind. I will take care that it shall not be forgotten by the writer of your life, who, I hope, is not born yet."

A letter dated the 26th Fructidor ended the series. Husband and wife were reunited, and shortly after returned to their new home in Paris for the winter. The poet was chiefly busied this winter, we know, with his " Columbiad," and with aiding Fulton in his projects.

On the 26th of April, 1802, the white ponies and the little phaeton were again put in requisition, the precarious state of Mrs. Barlow's health having determined her husband on sending her to the famous medicinal springs at Plombières for treatment. Fulton was again her escort, the poet's business affairs keeping him in Paris. Again the gossipy letters commenced, fuller, more satisfactory as to his affairs than the preceding. In his first, dated May-day, 1802 (11th Florial), he gives a summary of his movements for a week, thus: "The 6th, came home and ate a little dinner here about 3 o'clock, and about 4 Mme. Villette came in to get consolation, and took me home to dine again with her, where we found Skipwith. The 7th, dined at Leavenworth's and stayed till ten at night; 8th, dined with Madame Villette; 9th, with Helen—(Helen Marie Williams, the English poetess)

—where, by the by, I am invited to spend this evening; 10th, dined with Swan with a good deal of company. To-day I have promised to go with Skipwith to Riteaux, where we shall get a little dinner. I called 13th; dined yesterday at Leavenworth's, night before at Williams', where was the usual great circle of letter folks. This evening, invited to Madame Merinskas to celebrate the an-niversary of the Polish Constitution, which has long since ceased to exist. I suppose next Vendémiaire we shall be called upon to celebrate the anniversary of the French Republic, which has never existed at all."

" 15*th*. Toot, the little rascal Cala has not yet sent off the boat; he says he had to get made a *barrelier*, and to get the boat painted several times. Here is another let-ter from London, which I opened the same as before. No news yet from St. Dominique nor America except failures of merchants and the burning of the Jersey Col-lege."

" 17*th*. I met Mme. Pestallori, and she sent her love to her *illustre rivale*, and charged me to ask her if she had yet been *sur le trone des Capucins*. She says Plombières was famous *autrefois* . . . . but then *alors* there was a convent of fat Capuchins who used to visit the baths every day to whom you must give alms. Since these beggar gentlemen are no more there, she supposes the place is no more remarkable than other mountainous places, where people eat and drink, and bathe and feel glad. . . . I am invited by Skipwith (American Consul-General) to dine to-morrow at his new country house on the plain back of Montmartre. . . . I expect another sweet little tell-tale to-night from about Chaumont. I almost see the little whites now trudging along this fine morning and turning back their short ears to hear wife and Toot talking about Hub, and then they stop and laugh to hear her say, ' Come, Lazybones, get out and walk up this hill; see how steep it is: if Hub was here he would walk up every one of these hills. *Cugner ! desçendez donnez moi les regnes.*'

Oh, I wish I was there. This night I suppose you will get to Langres and the 13th to Plombières, where I suppose these stupid letters will greet you. . . .

"Toot, I spoke to Livingston about King; he says it shall be done right. After four days' trial I met Thayer yesterday: he promises to meet me and settle the day after to-morrow. Here is a letter which, as it came by post from England, I knew pretty well I might open. Mr. Livingston has returned from London. Lee was to set out a few days after him. Doctor Darwin is dead. Sir John Sinclair's books have come; they are of no great importance—one giving an account of his improvements on his own estate, and one little piece on Longevity, which you had before.

"Toot, I believe little Cala has sent the model, but am not sure. I have run, and scolded, and arranged with the diligence, and given him the address, and he has promised time after time ; but he is a shuffler.

"*26th.* I have a letter from Jefferson—good and kind—by Dawson, a Member of Congress of Virginia, an old crony and classmate of Codman, educated at Cambridge ; is a clever, modest, sensible man ; seems a particular friend of Prom's and quite a pet of Jefferson. He is of the size of William Lee, only not so fat—not unlike him in the face: he wants to see Wifey that he has heard so much of. He is come to bring the treaty, and get the conditional ratification of Adams agreed to here, when he returns immediately, and then Chancellor Livingston is to come—minister. Poor Murray at the Hague, John Q. Adams at Berlin, Carolina Smith at Lisbon, recalled and their places suppressed. Humphreys recalled and to be replaced by Charles Pinckney, the Republican—of a different family from the General and Thomas. Poor Montflorence is done up ; Skipwith will be Consul here. All seems prosperous and happy in America ; people never seem more united. The new President quite the ton ; in danger of being spoiled by adulation."

"30*th*. Toot is calling for funds. Besides the 3000 which I must pay for him to-morrow, and 3000 more at the end of the month, he wants 3000 more still to build another new boat at Brest. I see no end to it; he is plunging deeper all the time, and if he don't succeed I don't know what will become of him. I will do all I can for him, but the best way I can serve him is to keep a sheet anchor for him at home that he might be sure to ride out a gale there if he can't keep the sea nor get into port. St. Aubin says it's a grand damage that he is not here now; Roderer is so enthusiased with his small canals that he would certainly be employed to make one. French froth!

"I sit altogether in the bedroom, so don't have to go into my room for shoes nor coat. . . . Min (the cat) and I go out and work in the garden about an hour every morning as soon as we are out of bed, while they make room and bed and breakfast; then we come in together, but Min outruns me in coming in. I breakfast always on milk and bread and two eggs—no tea, nor coffee, nor butter, nor anything else; boil the milk and toast the bread myself while I read the paper. Madame is getting better slowly."

1 *Prairial.*

"Toot:—In the House of Lords the 13th May, the galleries being uncommonly full to hear the great discussion on the treaty of peace, Lord Stanhope rose and stated that he had a matter of such importance to communicate to the House in secret as would admit of no delay, and he demanded that the galleries should be cleared. Lord Moira begged his noble friend to withdraw his motion for that day, as the object to be discussed was of such an interesting nature to the people of England as he could wish they might all hear it. Lord S. replied that certainly no man could wish more than he that the people should be instructed, but if his noble friend was possessed of the secret that he was going to communicate

he would surely not oppose the galleries being cleared.
Moira could say no more. The sovereign people then
withdrew, and their lordships were left in secret. In a
few minutes the doors were again opened. The *Morning
Chronicle* states that it is not permitted to publish what
passes in the House when the doors are closed ; but we
understand that his Lordship's communication was relative to submarine navigation, which to his certain knowledge was brought to that perfection by a person in France
as to render the destruction of ships absolutely sure, and
that that person could at any time blow up a first-rate
ship of war with 15 pounds of powder, and that there was
no way of preventing it. This is all that is stated in the
Chronicle. Grant is all in the high ropes about it, and
thinks it was a plan concerted between Stanhope and St.
Vincents, that the former should give the facts to the
House as preparatory to the latter's taking some measures
with the author of the invention. This is Harry's conjecture. Mine is a little different. Stanhope disdains any
communication with the ministers. He was possessed of
the fact, and not wishing to impart it to the ministers
alone, he probably made use of his right as a peer to lay
it before the only body with which he has official intercourse, and then as the ministers would be in possession
of it, if they neglected to make a proper use of the information they might be open to a future attack."

1 Prairial.

"I am going to dine to-day at Grant's. His wife
and daughters are interesting women, though not handsome ; free of English affectation and of American awk-
wardness. She is a Scotch woman, and very sensible
and well informed. She talks to me of the 'Vision of
Columbus' as a book of her most familiar reference and
reading and delight for many years. Now you know I
don't want a greater proof than that of a person's good
sense."

"TOOT :—Mme. Villette desires you would send Charlotte's portrait by the diligence if you can. I don't send you any subject for a drawing for the poem * this time, nor perhaps any more until you write me how you like the project, and whether you can do them properly. I wish this work could be done in the family as much as possible *pour l'honneur du Pavillon.*"

                                          3 *Prairial.*

"Ah! the old bed. I must leave it. The rightful owners of these walls have come out from their winter quarters this night for the first time. Their attack was impetuous, like that of the French at St. Domingo. But many a blood-bloated chief as well as vulgar warrior was left *sur le champ de battaille.* Still, like many other victorious generals, I think it prudent to retreat, and I establish myself this night in the blue room. When William comes I shall put him in Toot's bed ; broad or narrow he shall content himself with it. But there is no new sign of his coming. I found a little mouse this morning in the bag of Indian meal, and I murdered him. But this put me in mind of eating up the rest of the meal to save it, so I shall make Mrs. Pavis make me a *po-lenta*, as the barbarous, conceited coxcombs of the great nation call it, who know as little about a hasty-pudding as they do about a republic. As well might they call it *mush* in imitation of an obstinate, incorrigible race of men who might know better, since they inhabit a country which gave birth to the second person in the new and happy trinity, the much-inventing and life-endearing Toot.   But whatever it be called, whether pudding, *polenta*, or mush, she shall make me every other morning enough for two breakfasts, and I will eat it with my milk. It won't make me fat, but healthy."

                                          9*th Prairial.*

"DEAR TOOT:— How happy I am that you succeed so well with the drawings, and that you have it so much

---

* The " Columbiad," the drawing for which Fulton superintended.

at heart to make a splendid edition of the work. Here is another subject, which makes six—all, in my opinion, very interesting, and the last not the least."

25th Prairial.

"DEAR TOOT :—To-day I went to the National Depot of Machines with Parker to show it him, and there I met Montgolfier and there I saw a strange thing ; it was no less than your very steamboat, in all its parts and principles, in a very elegant model. It contains your wheel-oars precisely as you have placed them, except that it has four wheels on each side to guide round the endless chain instead of two.

" The two upper wheels seem to be only to support the chain ; perhaps it is an improvement. The model of the steam-engine is in its place, with a wooden boiler, cylinder placed horizontal, everything complete. I never saw a neater model. It belongs to a company at Lyons, who got out a patent about three months ago. Montgolfier says they have made their funds to the amount of two millions for building boats and navigating the Rhone. They have already spent six hundred thousand francs in establishing their *atelier* at Lyons. They have not yet tried the experiment *en grand.* I talked with M. a great deal about it, and told him it was Fulton's idea in every part except the cylinder being horizontal, which I believed would not do. He says none of it will do, and ' if M. Fulton had spoken to me of that, I would have complained to him of that defect ; and if I had 30,000 francs in that enterprise at Lyons, I would have sold them for a thousand ecus.'

"I found, however, after a long discussion, that his objections arose entirely from what you are well aware of, and have calculated exactly, using water instead of land for the *point d'apuye.* He said nothing that would be new to you. He says that common oars and all modes of moving a thing in water by pushing against water lose 99 hundredths of your power. You see he

is not aware that it is a subject of accurate calculation,
and that you may know exactly the difference between
pushing against water and against solid bodies. I shall
say nothing to Livingston of this model."

" *15th*. . . . I dined the day before at Mr. Livingston's
with a high flock of ambassadors, etc.; no American but
Hub. There I met Sir Charles Blagdon, Secretary of
the Royal Society, formerly Dr. Blagdon, who used to
see us sometimes in Litchfield Street (London). Toot,
there I met Count Rumford, and he and I were friends
in a moment. He told me a great many things both
new and good, and all the particulars about the Royal
Institution. I complimented him liberally and handsomely. He talked a great deal about the plunging
boat of Fulton's. He and Sir Charles agreed that its
effects could not be doubted, but that it would never
be brought into use, because no civilized nation would
consent to use it ; that men, governments, and nations
would fight, and that it was better for morals and general happiness of all people that the fighting should be
done on land. Here Livingston interposed with great
dignity and energy, and observed that the greater part
of modern wars were commercial wars, and that these
were occasioned by navies, and that the system ought
to be overturned ; that as to the humanity of the use
of the plunging boat, he was so convinced of it that he
had written to the American Government recommending
those experiments to be made which should prove its
efficacy, and then to adopt it as a general mode of
defence for our harbors and coasts. Volney joined in
enforcing with his usual strength of expression these
ideas. Schimmelpinnick sat by and said not a word."

" *21st*. Dined yesterday with Volney, day before at
Sumpter's, to-day with Sir Francis Burdett and his brother, Colonel Bonville, and a whole host of English Republicans ; last evening at Lady Montcastle's."

" *24th*. Toot, I see, without consulting Parker, that

you are mad; 16 miles an hour for a steamboat, *le pauvre homme!* I shall do all I can with Livingston when I come back. I don't intend to see a single acquaintance in London but Erving and Gore, nor let anybody in Paris know where I am going except Sk., Melville and Parker."

" *27th.* There is a letter for Wifey from Clara Baldwin, the eldest of Wifey's two little sisters, the handsomest girl in New Haven. Here are three New Havenites, fresh, left the 1st May : Benedict Brown, Captain Greene, and a Mr. French. They dined yesterday at L.'s.

" *26th.* Toot, the drawings appear to me very perfect. I shall not have time to show them to Denon till my return. Mme. Villette popped in on me yesterday as I was putting Charlotte into a *cadre* which I had brought home for the purpose. She was highly pleased and grieved at the sight of it. I send it her this morning with a few verses pasted on the back, as I like to have your work and mine go together."*

DOVER, *20th June.*

" I started at 4 o'clock in the courier, as I told you I should. I came with that courier only to Amiens, 31 leagues ; then the best I could do was to take the Calais courier, who, to my great mortification, goes in a *downright cart*, not a *patoche*, for that is a covered cart

---

* Charlotte Villette, a beautiful, accomplished girl of sixteen, had died a few months previous, and Fulton had been employed by her mother to paint the above portrait. The following are the lines referred to :

" Could youth, could innocence, could virtue save,
Our Charlotte sure had found a later grave.
But, hapless mother, cease : your tears but show
The poor scant measure of our common woe.
Ah ! cease that vulgar grief : a tribute find
More just, more worthy her exalted mind.
Resume the virtues that you planted there,
Reclaim that merit none with you can share ;
Reclaim her force of thought, her vermeil hue,
Your friends demand her promised life in you."

but this is an open, one-horse cart, without springs, without cover, and where the greatest luxury is to be seated on a sack of straw, exposed to the burning heat by day and the chilling damps by night; however, a good cloak, which I made the courier borrow for me, wrapped me so round in every part of my earthly substance as enabled me to sleep very sound the greater part of the short night, and this morning, at 8 o'clock, I arrived at Calais, 69 leagues. There we found a packet, and I got over here by 4 o'clock this afternoon."

On his return he wrote again from Dover, 12th Messidor:

"Arrived here this forenoon, and have got to wait till 9 this evening to embark. Toot, the business I went upon was good and solid, equal to the highest representation made of it. I did your commission as well as possible with Chapman: he will write you very fully by next post on all the points of your inquiry. He showed me the secret of his economy of powers by lessening his friction. It consists in the formation of the plate of his piston, which dilates or contracts by springs. He says that a 26-inch cylinder in what he calls a double engine gives the force of 50 horses; he says to move a boat of 6 feet wide, one foot deep in water, and 80 feet long, 8 miles an hour, will not require a cylinder of more than 14 inches. This is only a rough guess in conversation. (He can't know this because he don't know your application of the power.) He says to give a movement of 3 feet a second with the piston it is not necessary that the stroke should be more than 3 feet to make 30 double strokes a minute. He says a cylinder of 26 inches would require rather less than 2 bushels of coals an hour; that one of 14 inches would burn about 1 bushel an hour.—I obstinately avoided seeing anybody in London but the three or four persons with whom my business lay. I knew if I broke loose among my democratic friends I could not avoid running the gauntlet of all their dinners, getting my name in the papers, and becoming an object of jealousy with the Government. The Government found me out as it was, and without the friendly and unasked interference of Mr. King I should have found difficulty in getting off so easy as I have done. After all, I found in the coach last night a gentleman coming to Canterbury, a great Republican, who quickly found me out, and said he was led to the discovery by having been told the day before by Horne Tooke and Sir Francis Burdett that I was in London incog.

PARIS, 15*th Mess.*

" This, I believe, is the 4th of July. I find an invitation to dine with Livingston. Helen is moved onto the Quay Malaquai. Thomas Melville is married to a Mdlle. Fleury, niece to Recamier. Toot, you asked about Washington's and Cornwallis' hats.* I informed myself in London, but without seeing any painter or pictures, that Copley's picture of the surrender of Admiral Dewwinter to Admiral Duncan represents them both with their hats off in their left hands, Dewwinter with his right foot advanced presenting his sword to Duncan, and he receives it in a similar posture,—that is, the right foot forward and the hat in the left hand,— both with their bodies a little inclined in a respectful posture. The principal difference should be that the sword of the conqueror should be hanging by his side. The eyes of the vanquished should be a little inclined towards the earth, and those of the other a little more elevated, but not with a haughty air. I give you these details in this first letter lest you should be out of work. The letter from Calais will contain another subject, that of the Dragon."

" 17*th Mess.* Now for London. . . . I came to Charing Cross at 6 in the evening ; took a hack and drove to the Grand Hotel, Covent Garden, where I thought to be

---

* For " The Surrender of Cornwallis," in the " Columbiad."

incog., supposing that Americans did not frequent that place. Wrote immediately to Mr. Gore and Mr. Erving, the Consul, to call on me the next morning. Both came at different hours. Went to the city with E. When I returned the waiter asked me if I was not acquainted with one Mr. Cutting, an American gentleman, whose brother was Consul in Paris. I said no. Says he, ' He lodges in this house.' To see Mr. J. B. Cutting, you know, would be to give your name to the bell-man to cry it through the town. Soon after, Mr. Erving came in again. I called the waiter, paid my bill, and told him to call a coach, that this gentleman, my friend, was going to take me to his own house to lodge. My little portmanteau was put in the coach, and we drove to a hotel in Brook Street, Grosvenor Square, where I had a charming, clean, snug lodging, elegant, airy, still, and well attended. E. took me to this quarter for the sake of being near his father, who lives in George Street, Hanover Square, six doors below Copley's, because he said I must dine with his father and him every day : he lives and lodges there though his bureau is in the city. The father was a Boston refugee from our Revolution, a King's Counsellor in the time of Gage, now a good Republican and a sensible old man. His son is one of the best Republicans, and the best informed you ever met. In passing by Copley's (the other side of the street *bien entendre*) I saw, one day, his wife and daughter standing knocking at the door. Passing along Oxford Road another day, I sheered off into Litchfield Street, guided by an unaccountable attraction—I don't know why, but I couldn't help it—till I came to No. 18.* I ran up close to the door, being near sighted, and got onto the very last stone, and there stood a good while with one hand partly over my face to hide half of it, and there I read, ' *Snowdon, Cabinet Maker*,' cut on a brass plate. Above was a paper, ' *First*

---

* The Barlows' house while in London, 1792–93.

floor to let, genteelly furnished.' Never did I resist so
strong an inclination to go into a house. I wanted to
hire that lodging, if it was only to sleep one night in the
back room."

" 19*th.* Now again for London. That story was
broken off before in the middle. It was a gay time : the
town full for the season ; Parliament not then dissolved,
though midsummer ; the weather remarkably fine. But
the ladies dress astonishingly different from what ours
do. Why, they cover all their bosoms, and necks, and
gorges quite up to the chin. They wear nothing but
stays as long as one's arm. . . . The milliner shops and
haberdashers' warehouses are full of them. I would lay
any money that there are 10,000 pounds' worth of stays
in Broad Street alone now for sale—long, labored, stiff,
and armed with ribs of whale. It is a frightful thing to
think of. They don't walk so handsomely as our ladies
do, but they have handsomer streets, finer shops, and
cleaner houses. London is sensibly increased and filled
up ; the display of carriages and other signs of wealth
is very great. I was at Helen's last night ; I believe she
has a party almost every night—30, or 40, or 50, chiefly
English. There have been a good many lords and sirs
among them, and now Mr. Fox and Lord Holland are
expected here."

" 21*st.* . . . Toot, Parker and I have studied over the
memoir of experiments and calculations pretty well, and
yesterday I went to Livingston's to have a talk with
him ; but, behold ! the little new-born boy was dying and
I did not see him. In my idea the other day about Cornwallis' picture I forgot to mention that he must pos-
itively have his star on. Whether he had the order at
that time or not is a matter of no consequence. If he
had not, no admirer of your work will ever go to search
the Heralds' Office to detect this little anachronism.
Everybody knows he has the order now. It is a sort of
disgrace you must throw upon that royal mark of dis-

tinction. If you insist on having a subject from every book, I can give you a tolerable one from the 3d: it is Capac relieving his son Rocha from the burning pyre, having killed Zamor and routed the savages."

"25*th*. . . . I went, the day before I left (London), to Harry Bromfield's and found three trunks and the box of books. The two big trunks, chiefly filled with books, papers, Hub's coats, etc., seemed not to have been opened or suffered any injury from thieves. The coats were well riddled with moths, but the new black court-coat lined with silk and the silk coat were not touched by them. But, alas! Wifey's round hair trunk, where, I suppose, had been stowed and treasured up so many of her precious things of this world, offered a mournful lesson to those who put their trust in earthly trunks. Epictetus or Seneca, or Harvey, or Sancho Panza, could not have taken a better text: 'Seest thou that lady's trunk?' What a mine of moral reflection is to be found in that little mass of worms, who, after having devoured all that could nourish their frail and filthy bodies, have died themselves for want of food. Their prison is their tomb . . . . void is the spacious cave, save where lie the shreds and remnants of what once were garments. Lo, the lank skeleton of that once envied tippet! Not a hair; not a particle of soil; no sign by which it can say, 'I once warmed a martin on the frozen banks of Hudson, and then passed to the most consummate seat of earthly splendor—curled round the neck and panted on the bosom of the loveliest of her sex.' Alas, poor Tippet! a long, thin, brittle strip of untanned leather. Thy fur, thy warmth, thy pride, thy name is lost. And thy fond sister, Muff— Ah, me! her fate is thine. Long indeed it behooveth the curious searcher in this hollow house to turn them over and reshape their substance; to scan their length, their breadth, the form they must have had, before he can determine aught about them, or derive their nature or use of old. The lining of the muff is left entire, for it was made of silk. Worms eat not silk; worms eat not flax or cotton. But naught of hair, naught of soft wool, unless 'tis lined with vegetable web, can escape this garb-devouring tooth. Learn hence, my brethren, to line your souls with a conscience soft as satin, white as cambric, and strong as corduroy, and then, when it comes your turn to be closed up in that sable trunk which shall yield your bodies to the worms, they can never eat your souls.''

"*29th.* Toot, I had a great talk with Livingston. He says he is perfectly satisfied with your experiments and calculations, but is always suspicious that the engine beating up and down will break the boat to pieces. He seems to be for trying the horizontal cylinder, or for re-turning to his mercurial engine. I see his mind is not settled, and he promises now to write you, which he says he should have done long ago but he thought you were to be back every fortnight. He thinks the scale you talk of going on is much too large, and especially that part which respects the money. You converted him as to the preference of the wheels above all other modes, but he says they cannot be patented in America because a man (I forget his name) has proposed the same thing there. You will soon get his letter. Parker is highly gratified with your experiments; he wishes, however, something further to remove his doubts—about keeping the proportions and as to the loss of power in different velocities. He wishes to have another *barrelier* made, four times as strong as this or thereabouts, to see whether the proportional velocity would be the same when mov-ing by the paddles as when moving by the fixture on shore. I should like to see this, too. If you desire it, I can take this *barrelier* to Cala and see whether he can make another of the same volume four times as strong, and know what it will cost. These relative velocities can be tried in Perrier's pond on the hill.''

" Was forced to go to Helen's again last night. The most remarkable persons were Carnot, Livingston, and

Lord Holland. Fox is not yet come. . . . It begins to be the fashion there now (England) to look to America for examples of good government. Jefferson's character as a statesman, uniting honesty with talent, stands higher in England than that of any man now living."

" *5th Therm.* . . . . Toot, I have been to Denon and then to Gamble with the drawings. They both agree that for first-rate stroke engraving they must cost about 25 louis, but for good point engraving—as Godfrey has done the Psyche and Cupid of Gerard, by which he has got a great reputation—they can be done for 12 louis. He praised the composition a good deal, but found some defects in the drawing."

" *7th Therm.* Toot, your reasoning is perfectly right about inventions and the spirit of the patent laws, and I have no doubt it may be secured in America. . . . My project would be that you should pass directly over to England, *silent and steady*, make Chapman construct an engine of 12 inches, while you are building a boat of a proportionate size. Make the experiments on that scale, *all quiet and quick*. If it answers, put the machinery on board a vessel and go directly to New York (ordering another engine as large as you please to follow you), then secure your patent and begin your operation, first small and then large. I think I will find you the funds without any noise for the first operation in England, and if it promises well you will get as many funds and friends in America as you want. I should suggest a small operation first, for several reasons : it can be made without noise. There must be imperfections in the first trial which you can remedy without disgrace if done without noise ; you can easier find funds for a small experiment, etc. . . . . I have talked with P. on your observations about great boats with merchandise."

" *11th Therm.* Here, darling, is Jefferson's letter. I think it a good one, friendly and frank. I send it chiefly that Wifey may see what he says about the house, and garden, and ground to sell. I am strongly tempted to order him to buy it for Wifey, that is, if it is sufficiently modest, and not too vast, and to cost too much money. I can't tell what extent of meaning they attach to the words, *superb house and garden* and *most lovely seat.* I should like to have the place that has the garden already planted and in full bearing. I should like, too, the situation on a hill with a most extensive view of the Potomac, etc. For that climate an elevated situation would be preferable to a plain."

"13*th* . . . . I have had a long talk with John Appleton about America, and Washington City, and Georgetown, and about the society. He came from there in April. I asked him about Scott's house that Jefferson speaks of. He happened to know it and the circumstances of the property, but don't know the price. He says it must have cost from 3000 to 4000 guineas, built about 12 years ago, garden well planted and in full growth, situation delightful, house about 60 feet front, two wings, built of brick, body of the house two stories, wings one. He gave me a little sketch of the position. Appleton don't like America, for the same reasons that destroy Mme. Pichon, who dies with ennui. She says the ladies know the price of a bunch of turnips, but know nothing of the Paris opera. I have not seen M. Dupont de Nemour. He called here once with his wife, who has come too. I called there and saw her; he was out. She speaks in high terms of commendation of America, and I am told he is charmed with it. I am to dine with the Hotingers in the country day after to-morrow, and I am to call for Kosciusko, who lives half way. Toot, Grant apprises me that Smith has found a method of purifying sea-water without fire: it is done in his common fountains. G. says the Government (there, not here) will give him 30,000 pounds for the discovery."

"19*th.* Here are two letters from our little friend

Gibbs.* He is a young man of a great deal of merit, has been all over Europe, and is now going to set down in America ; a man of fortune and a gentleman—chemist and mineralogist. I go with him to-day to Guyton and other *davans* to help him complete his cabinet of mineralogy and his chemical laboratory. He don't know a great deal about it yet, but he intends to, and has got his taste decided. He may be a useful man. Hub intends to take some merit for forming his taste and fixing his attention to useful and laudable pursuits."

" *23d.* I have got the rich Quaker Johnson here from London. He is talking of buying Wifey's house, and is coming this morning at 9 o'clock with his wife to look at it and take breakfast. Toot knows him, he says. He is a great mechanician and chemist, Member of the Royal Society, and Royal Institution, and of all the societies of arts. He was proprietor of that famous establishment of polygraphic picture-copying business in Piccadilly, by which he says he made 30,000 pounds. Toot, I notice what you say of Bernadotte. I know he gave up the Louisiana scheme some time ago. It is not impossible that Bonaparte will give it up likewise. There is a project on foot that may end in our having the Floridas as far as the Mississippi, and let Louisiana return to Spain."

" *25th.* John Seyle goes off this day to America to try to get the consulate of Havre. Ed. Livingston and his wife are going right home by way of England. Sumpter is expecting his dismission—which he asked for long ago—when he quits. Tom Paine's baggage is gone to Havre ; he goes after it soon. Toot, I did not leave your memoir with L. above 3 or 4 days. I brought it home for the same reason which you suggest and locked it up, and here it is. I talked with him yesterday again. He seems to be desirous of bringing the thing forward. There is no danger of his trying to do the thing without you : he

---

* George Gibbs, American mineralogist and political writer.

has no thought of it; he sees too many difficulties in the way; he has heard unfavorable reports about Cartwright's engine; he doubts whether it will do. If you recur to Watts, it is probably best to lay it horizontal; his fears with regard to the strain on the boat from the up-and-down stroke are not without foundation."

27th Thermidor.

"We have got a great *fête* to-day for the birthday of Napoleon; the bells are ringing and cannon firing ever since sunrise—enough to deafen one; high mass and *Te Deum* all over France; more powder burnt than would serve to conquer half Europe. And this is to conquer the French people!"

1 Fructidor.

"Toot, whenever in your travels you find any minerals that are rare and valuable, and you can get them for nothing or for little, bring them along. I wish to collect as many as I can conveniently, not for my own use but for the advancement of science in America."

3d. "Toot, you are in general right, and particularly in your present ideas about the transportation of merchandise by a string of boats, hooked or chained together, with a few inches interval, but that interval should be covered by ox-hide to keep the water from coming between them. This is the best plan, too, for passage boats. The engine boat should only be sufficiently long to carry the engine and its accessories. This appears to be the Lyons plan; in that he may have infringed on your patent. . . . The effect of Livingston's shock from the stroke of the piston may doubtless be guarded against in part, and I make no account of his vacuum. But all the difficulties taken together, particularly that of the movement of the waves destroying the perpendicularity of the stroke, make me incline to think that if you take Watts' engine it may be best in all boat business to lay the cylinder horizontal. I shall lay your last letter before Parker, but I don't like your one great round wheel; you will lose force by it. In the little wheels and chains there are more buckets in the water at a time according to the weight and friction. Another thing: all paddles of this sort should be made in form of a triangle, with the long face sternward made solid, the hinder part of cork, triangular too, the other way: if not of cork, let it be of thin boards and water-tight, and tarred. Flat paddles would lose as much by the vacuum in the back-water as boats would with a square stern."

"*7th*. Toot, I am going to make you long to be in Paris. Benjamin West and his son Ben are here, and Opie and his wife, and my friend Tarell and his wife, and Kemble of the Drury Lane Theatre. I have not seen West; only knew of his coming last evening. Saw Opie at Helen's, and shall call on West. We can have his judgment about your drawings, etc."

"*13th*. Went last night to Helen's to see Mr. Fox; go again to-night to see Mr. West."

"*25th*. . . . Toot will find West here, though he seems to think he shall go the last of the present week. He and Ben are coming to breakfast with Hub this morning and to see all Toot's works, mechanical and glyphical— (there, now, you don't know what glyphical is. Glypho, in Greek, signifies to paint or draw ; hence, hieroglyphics, sacred painting)—and among the rest the designs for the poem. I now wish they were all here : he has promised to give me his observations on them, too, and on the other subjects which I shall explain to him, and to give me an account about himself, and the revolution which has been brought about in art within the last 30 years by his having broken the ancient shackles and modernized the art. He is to furnish me, too, a catalogue of his works. This is all to complete an interesting note in the poem, where Hub has said of West—

> " Spurns the cold critic rules to seize the heart,
> And boldly bursts the former bounds of Art.

He has a great affection for Toot, and says his wife has a still greater—*comme de raison.*"

The letters to Plombières ceased with that of the 27th Fructidor. With the frosts of September the white ponies bore their mistress back to the capital, and the circle at No. 50 *Rue de Vaugirard* was again complete. It remained unbroken for the next two years, except for a short absence of Mr. Barlow in England during the summer of 1803. Of authentic details of this period we have few. His letters from England contain nothing of interest, save the fact that at one time he acted as mediator between Sir Benjamin West and Mr. Fulton, the former having been very much offended at a certain proposition made to him by the latter, the nature of which does not appear. It is apparent, however, what occupied his attention during these two years. The completion of the "Columbiad," the preparation of the plates for it, his correspondence, and an active partnership in the enterprises of Fulton's busy brain, doubtless left him few leisure hours.

Amid all this business, however, his interest in his native land seems never to have lessened. To return and spend his days in America was his pet dream during every year of his exile. A score of times he is on the point of embarking, and as often an advantageous business opening, or war, or the illness of his wife, or inability to dispose of his real estate in France, interposes to prevent. At length, on the 2d November, 1804, he was able to write from London to Senator Baldwin that he was in England on his way to America. In London they remained during the winter, Mrs. Barlow continuing in delicate health, but about the middle of May they embarked for New York, and after a stormy voyage of 52 days arrived in safety.

CHAPTER VIII.

1805–1811.

AGAIN, after eighteen years absence, the poet was amid old familiar scenes. No one knew him : he had grown out of remembrance. But greater changes had occurred in his native land than in him. Vermont, Kentucky, Tennessee, and Ohio had been admitted into the Union. The centre of population had shifted far to the westward. Ohio, which he had left a wilderness, contained 75,000 souls. Politically, there were greater changes. The Constitution had been adopted, and had stood the test of nearly eighteen years of trial. Washington was dead, his tomb to be henceforth the Mecca of all devotees of liberty. With him had died Federalism, the last relic of early English domination. The old order had changed, giving place to the new. A new party was in power, with new men, new ideas, a new policy, and under its impetus the nation was going gayly on to its destiny. Necessarily it was an era of the fiercest partisan hatred and bitterness. The Federalists took their defeat sorely, and indulged in the most vituperative abuse of their opponents. Nor were the Republicans models of meekness under this torrent of invective. Barlow's arrival seems to have created quite a ripple in the political and religious world. The Republicans greeted him warmly, as the honored citizen of two Republics, the poet and philosopher of repute, the patriot who had risked life and health in perilous service to his countrymen.

The Federalists, on the other hand, so far as they were represented by their newspapers, joined in traducing him. It is a striking commentary on the vicious, debasing character of partisanship, that these sheets could see nothing noble, lovely, or praiseworthy in the man who, in the Algerine mission alone, had performed an act of as great heroism and self-abnegation as any hero or martyr of antiquity. Many old friends addressed him, expressing their pleasure at his return, and inviting him to their homes. Jefferson, among the rest, wrote this cordial and generous letter :—

MONTICELLO, *Aug.* 14*th*, 1805.

" I received on the 12th at this place your favor of the 4th, and I received it with great pleasure, and offer my congratulations on your safe return to our country. You will be sensible of a great change of manners generally, and of principles in some. The most important change, however, is the influence gained by the commercial towns on public opinion, and their exclusive possession of the press. But of these things we will speak hereafter. I do not expect to be in Washington till the end of September, and as you propose a visit to that place let me invite your extending it as far as this. The stage comes from Washington by Fred'bg to this place in two days and passes within 100 rods of my door, where we shall receive you with joy and be glad to retain you as long as your convenience will permit.

" The mountains among which I live will offer you as cool a retreat as can anywhere be found, and one enjoying as much health as any place in the Union. Pursuing the stage route you will see but a poor country till you reach our canton ; but if you take a horse and gig from Washington you will come a nearer and better route by Centerville, Fanquier Court House, Culpepper C. H., Orange C. H., and Mr. Madison's, if he be at home. From his house or from Orange C. H. take the road on the lower side of the mountain : along this route you will see a fine country, but not yet in a course of good culture ; and you can return by a different one, equally good. Believing you will have more satisfaction in this little peregrination than in whiling away the month of September in New York, I will believe that you will adopt the proposition, and *en attendant* offer you my friendly salutations and assurances of respect and esteem."

THOMAS JEFFERSON.

To MR. BARLOW.

A letter written to Abraham Baldwin, soon after his arrival, indicates his plans, so far as he had formed them.

"We intend," he says, "to pass the winter at Washington, and it is possible I shall take a short trip there in a few days to prepare the way. As the yellow-fever is in the North * I shall not go there at present. Indeed, I have no great inclination for that journey, at least until I learn from some of my friends there, if any there be, that the people will not throw stones at me. I have seen nobody here as yet, not a human face, that I ever saw before. I sent for Pierrepont Edwards this morning, but find he is gone to Connecticut. I hardly know who to strike for next. But we shall probably get into civilization as soon as we wish, or sooner."

On August 20th he wrote again: "My plan was to join you if I could find you, then come on here, and all go to the land of steady habits together. But the heats have been too great for me to travel, or to leave her in this place, and having learned that I shall meet nobody in Washington at this season we have concluded to lay wait for you in the North—that is, New Haven. We shall go slowly forward on the road to Albany, Ballston, Boston, Providence, Hartford, Middletown, Guilford, and then to New Haven, where we shall hope to meet you."

September and a large part of October seem to have been occupied in the carriage drive mentioned above. At New Haven, where the distinguished visitor remained for some days, the Republican members of the Legislature, then in session there, tendered him a public reception,

---

* Vermont, where he had lands and relatives.

which he modestly declined. Subsequently, a dinner was given in his honor by Abraham Bishop, Collector of the Port, which was attended by prominent Republicans in and out of the state. In an address presented on this occasion occurs these sentiments : " You will be received cordially and sincerely respected by an immense majority of your fellow-citizens, and your political writings will be held in honor as often as you shall submit them to the tribunal of an enlightened public." The address also expressed the hope that he would make the state his permanent residence.

The poet, in his reply, reiterated the expressions of patriotism and interest in his fellow-citizens made in his " Letters," and closed with the following reference to his calumniators :

" My friends, you have doubtless seen much more than I have of the malicious calumnies that the Monarchists of Europe and their agents here have published in the American papers against me. While I perceive with pleasure that their contemptible falsehoods have made no impression on your minds, I flatter myself that you believe with me that they have been hunted up and promulgated with no other view than to destroy my usefulness in the cause of liberty. They cannot be from personal dislike, for I do not know nor believe that I have a personal enemy in this, or any other country. If I have one, I will labor with all my might to do him good, and hope that he will find his happiness, as I do mine, so connected with that of his fellow-citizens at large that he will no longer wish to separate them.

" Our country must now be considered as the depository and guardian of the best interests of mankind—all good men in Europe view it in that light. I hope we shall be duly sensible of the importance of this sacred deposit, and that our patriotism, without diminishing its energy, may at all times partake of the broad and peaceful character of genuine philanthropy."

The poet, however, did not accept the invitation of the legislators of Connecticut to make that state his home. He had probably decided on Washington as his future residence, before leaving France. That city was the seat of Government; his intimate friends were there; there representative men from every part of the country were to be met, and there, if anywhere, the pet project of his maturer years must be carried out. This project was more honorable to him than any which his fertile brain had hitherto conceived: it was the founding, and building up under his own personal care, of a great National Institution, combining in itself the objects and functions of the Royal Institution of England and the National Institute of France, together with the instruction of youth as pursued by the colleges of the country; or, in its author's own concise statement, "the advancement of knowledge by associations of scientific minds, and the dissemination of its rudiments by the instruction of youth." As early as 1800, Barlow had conceived the idea of such an institution. In a letter to Senator Baldwin, dated Paris, Sept. 15th, 1800, he says: "I have been writing a long letter to Jefferson on quite another subject. . . . It is about learned societies, universities, public instruction, and the advantages you now have for doing something great and good if you will take it up on proper principles. If you will put me at the head of the Institution there proposed, and give it that support which you ought to do, you can't imagine what a garden it would make of the United States: I have great projects, and only want the time and means for carrying them into effect." Jefferson, and most of the leading Republicans, heartily seconded this plan, and almost the first public act of its author after arriving in America was to issue a prospectus, in which he forcibly and eloquently depicted the necessity and the advantages of such an institution. This prospectus provided for a School of Mines; a School of Roads and Bridges, which was also to include river navigation, canals, and hydraulic architecture ;* a Conservatory of Arts—the useful arts and trades ; a Museum of Natural History ; a Museum of Arts—the fine arts, painting, statuary, music ; a National Library ; a Mint ; a Military School ; a Prytaneum, or school of general science ; a School of Medicine ; a Veterinary School ; an Observatory ; and district colleges founded throughout the Union as the necessity for them should arise.

The prospectus was circulated through the country, and met with so favorable a response that, in 1806, Barlow drew up a bill for the incorporation of the Institution, which Mr. Logan, of Pennsylvania, introduced in the Senate. It passed to a second reading, was referred to a committee, which never reported, and so was lost.

The opposition of the schools and colleges already established, and the indifference of the great majority of Congressmen to anything but the material development of the country, were sufficient to defeat it.

Although the poet had settled on Washington as his future place of residence, nearly two years elapsed before he became a householder there, the intervening time being spent in travel, in visiting friends, and in attendance upon his printers in Philadelphia—for the " Columbiad " had been given to a reputable firm of printers of that city during the first year of the poet's return. His movements during this period are satisfactorily explained by a few letters culled from the mass of his correspondence. The most interesting is one from Fulton, who had been left behind in England, to urge on its Government the importance of his torpedo invention. In September, 1806, he was able to write from London : " My arbitration is finished, and I have been allowed the £10,000 which I had received, with 5000£ salary, total £15,000, though £1600 which I have received on settling accounts will just square all old debts and expenses in London, and

---

* This department was at Fulton's suggestion.

leave me about £200. My situation now is, my hands are free to burn, sink, and destroy whom I please, and I shall now seriously set about giving liberty to the seas by publishing my system of attack. I have, or will have, when Mr. Parker sends my two thousand pounds, 500 sterling a year, with a steam-engine and pictures worth two thousand pounds. Therefore I am not in a state to be pitied. I am now busy winding up everything, and will leave London about the 23d inst. for Falmouth, from whence I shall sail in the packet the first week in October, and be with you, I hope, in November, perhaps about the 14th, my birthday, so you must have a roast goose ready. Do not write me again after receiving this. The packet, being well manned and provided, will be more commodious and safe for an autumn passage, and I think there will be little or no risk ; at least, I prefer taking all the risk there is to idling here a winter. But although there is not much risk, yet accidents may happen, and that the produce of my studies and experience may not be lost to my country, I have made out a complete set of drawings and descriptions of my whole system of submarine attack, and another set of drawings with description of the steamboat. These, with my *will*, I shall put in a tin cylinder, sealed, and leave them in the care of General Lyman, not to be opened unless I am lost. Should such an event happen, I have left you the means to publish these works, with engravings, in a handsome manner, and to which you will add your own ideas —showing how the liberty of the seas may be gained by such means, and, with such liberty, the immense advantages to America and civilization : you will also show the necessity of perfecting and establishing the steamboat and canals on the inclined plane principle. I have sent you three hundred complete sets of prints for the 'Columbiad' by the Orb, directed to Mr. Tolman, New York, value £30. As the transport by land to Philadelphia will not be much, I have sent them by this opportunity, that they may arrive before the law for prohibiting such things is in force, and that the shipment and risk may not approach too near to winter. All my pictures, prints, and other things I mean to leave here, to be shipped in spring vessels, about April next, when the risk will be inconsiderable. How shall we manage this winter, as you must be in Philadelphia for the printing, and I want to be at New York to build my boat? I am in excellent health, never better, and good spirits. You know I cannot exist without a project or projects, and I have two or three of the first order of sublimity. As all your prints are soldered up I do not see how I can leave the number you desire with Phillips,* but as I leave the plates with Mr. West the necessary number can be struck off when the sheets arrive. We will talk of this in America. Mr. West has been retouching my pictures: they are charming."

March 6th, 1807, Mr. Barlow is in Washington, to attend the funeral of his friend and brother, Senator Abraham Baldwin, who had suddenly died at his post in the Senate. In a letter to his wife he thus describes the impressive event : " Were you here to witness the sympathy, interest, and affection manifested on the loss of our excellent brother it would in a great measure lighten your distress. Though he died the day after Congress closed the session, most of the Senators and many of the other members stayed to attend his funeral. We laid him yesterday by the side of his friend General Jackson,† just one year after he had followed that friend to the same place. It was a dreadfully stormy day, and five miles from the Capitol, yet everybody went that could go, and I never witnessed such solemnity and respect. The funeral was ordered by the Senate to be at the public expense. The coffin . . . . is placed in the ground in a large wooden coffer: it is in a dry, gravelly

---

* The London publisher.   † Henry Jackson.

soil, where it will remain free from wet, so that if we should have Washington's place I shall propose to have it brought to our ground, where we can have it always under our eye till we are ready to take our own lodging by his side. . . . He had suffered no pain during his last illness, and his serenity, benignity, even good-humor remained till the last. . . . He talked, as long as he could talk at all, of the affairs of the public, advising Macon, Milledge, and all his old friends, how to conduct them. 'Take care,' says he, 'hold the wagon back; there is more danger of its running too fast than of its going too slow.' Macon says he has not left his equal behind him in the United States. I did not see him till morning—twenty hours after his death. Every sentiment of conscious dignity and self-approbation seemed painted on his pale and placid face : he seemed to say, 'Here I am ; my work is finished, and have I not done it well?' My love, I can say no more to-day. I must finish the story another time. I have to write his life to-night for the paper."

This letter is almost the only memorial left us of the author of the famous instrument of 1787. May 18th he is back in Philadelphia, and writes to Phillips, afterwards the London publisher of the Columbiad : " I have received your favor of the 27th of January, and in return for your kind expressions of friendship I am in hopes of aiding you to procure a work of great consequence, and which may be very profitable to you : it is 'Lewis' Travels by the Missouri to the Pacific Ocean,' the drawings and engravings for which are now beginning in this place." The letter then goes on to commend the author and his work very highly, and concludes : " Now for another subject. I send you herewith a portfolio containing the twelve engravings made for my poem, with a few sheets of the letter-press, to give you an idea of what the work is to be. The engravings, you know, were executed in London. I have been thinking that it would be worth your while to make an edition in quarto of this poem in London. I will ask nothing for the copy of the text, and I will sell you the prints from the engravings at a reasonable rate, that is, at about the cost. I have a thousand copies of the 12 plates; they have cost me altogether about £1200 sterling, including the pictures. You shall have 3, 4, 5, or 600 sets of the prints at a guinea the set. You will see they are elegant beyond example ; no such fine engravings have ever been put into a book. The quarto edition here, as we are doing it, will not be sold under 20 dollars. As the prints were engraved and printed in London I suppose they can be entered back in England without duty ; but that will be a trifle. Please say whether these proposals will suit you (the work will not be published here till winter, so I can send you the printed sheets from the press) ; if not, say how many copies of the American edition I shall send you to sell for me. I would much rather you would publish it."

The poem for which such great preparations had been made appeared in the winter of 1807. It was a magnificent quarto volume of 450 pages, furnished with twelve splendid engravings from paintings by Fulton and Smirke, and cut by the first engravers of London and Paris. The paper was the heaviest and best, the margins wide, the binding elegant ; it was in all respects the finest specimen of bookmaking ever produced by any American press.* Yet the Columbiad was not a great poem : its defects were precisely those pointed out by Mr. Buckminster at its inception twenty-five years before. Its scope was too wide, its subjects too many and varied to be introduced without a clear sacrifice of the poetic unities. Besides, most of the events narrated were too recent to admit of poetic or heroic treatment. American historians have succeeded much more admirably in idealizing the men of the Revolution than did our earliest poet. They came later: he

---

* The publishers were Conrad & Co. ; the printers Fry & Kammerer, all of Philadelphia.

wrote to men who had enacted the scenes he described. The Columbiad long since passed out of the category of books that are read; its chief literary interest to us arises from the fact of its having been one of the earliest efforts of the American muse, and from the circumstances under which it was produced. In this connection the reader will perhaps welcome a brief description. We have before said that it was an expansion of his early poem, the Vision of Columbus, and it will be seen that the plan of that work, as sketched at Northampton in 1779, was substantially followed. The poet's design was to give a poetical review of the leading events in the discovery and settlement of America; the birth, growth, and splendid future of the Republic, and a glance also at the history of the country before its discovery by Europeans. In form it was a national, patriotic epic. Columbus is the hero, and is discovered lying in his prison at Valladolid, uttering a mournful monologue on the injustice of his king and country. To him, in this state, appears Hesper, the guardian genius of the Western World, and, conducting him to the Mount of Vision, displays before his astonished eyes, in a series of visions, all that had happened, and all that was to happen, in the new land he had discovered: the romantic, half legendary history of the Aztecs; their conquest by Cortez and Pizarro; the successive steps by which the settlement of North America was effected; the actions and the actors in the struggle of the Revolution; the republican system in America, and the benefits which should arise from it, were first portrayed. Hesper then changes the scene and favors the hero with a universal view of all nations, and the improvement of society in all the arts and sciences when the principles of the new plutocracy should have done their perfect work in leavening the whole mass.

In his last "vision" the hero beholds a general congress of the nations, assembled to provide for the settlement of all vexed questions by a Court of Arbitration,

thus inaugurating a perpetual peace. Him the genius
thus addresses :

> ' Here, then,' said Hesper, with a brilliant smile,
> ' Behold the fruits of thy long years of toil.
> To you bright borders of Atlantic day,
> Thy swelling pinions led the trackless way,
> And taught mankind such useful deeds to dare,
> To trace new seas and happy nations rear,
> Till, by fraternal hands their sails unfurled,
> Have waved at last in union o'er the world.

> ' Then let thy steadfast soul no more complain
> Of dangers braved and griefs endured in vain,
> Of courts insidious, envy's poisoned stings,
> The loss of empire, and the frown of kings,
> While these broad views thy better thoughts compose,
> To spurn the malice of insulting foes,
> And all the joys descending ages gain
> Repay thy labors and remove thy pain.'

There are many other eloquent and melodious passages,
but, as before remarked, the poem contains too many
grave defects to be considered a classic, or to receive that
recognition which awaits the work of true genius. We
shall again advert to its reception by the reading world:
meantime, while awaiting the attacks of critics, its author had provided himself with a home. Washington, we
have seen, had been decided on as the place, but the
choice of a site was a more difficult matter. For a time
he seems to have thought seriously of purchasing Mount
Vernon, but at last he decided on an old mansion lying
between Georgetown and the Capitol, on the banks of
lovely Rock Creek, probably the identical one described
by Jefferson in his letter of 1800. In all the suburbs of
Washington there cannot be found a prettier site even
now, though the city has approached and girt two sides
of its spacious grounds with streets and avenues. From
the terraced plateau on which the mansion now stands *

---

* Kalorama was used as a hospital during the late war, and was burned
toward the close of the conflict. The strong brick walls, however, re-
sisted the flames, and are included in the present mansion.

one looks down on the Potomac, the Capitol, and the wide, beautiful city encircling it.   On the west, its grounds slope gently down to the creek, beneath a park of fine old forest trees.   On the south and east there is a wider slope with fewer trees, and a driveway winds through its green lawns under beautiful shades, that owe their existence to the poet's own hand.   What it was in 1807 we prefer to let its owner tell, as he does in a letter to his nephew, Stephen Barlow, dated Dec. 15, 1807.   A prior one, dated "Belair, Nov. 6th," gives us the time of his taking possession.   The letter proceeds: "I have here a most delightful situation; it only wants the improvements that we contemplate to make it a little paradise. It is a beautiful hill, about one mile from the Potomac and 200 feet in elevation above tidewater, with Washington and Georgetown under my eye and Alexandria eight miles below, still in view, the Potomac reflecting back the sun in a million forms and losing himself among the hills that try on each side to shove him from his course.   If you have a plan of the city I can show you my very spot.   Look at the stream called Rock Creek, that divides Washington from Georgetown.   I am just outside of the city on the Washington side of the Creek, just above where it takes its last bend and begins its straight, short course to the Potomac.   My hill is that white, circular spot.   I find the name of Belair has been already given to many places in Maryland and Virginia, so by the advice of friends we have changed it for one that is quite new—*Calorama*, from the Greek, signifying 'fine view,' and this place presents one of the finest views in America."   From another part of the letter we learn that Calorama contained 30 acres of ground— half woodland, the other half in grass and garden, including orchard—and that there were roads to be cut and paths to wind through the pleasure-grounds, a barn to move, stables to fit up, two wings to be added to the house, and many other things done for its embellishment. But this modest statement does scant justice to the improvements which speedily transformed Kalorama into one of the most elegant country seats of the day. Barlow himself had a cultivated taste and sufficient wealth. Latrobe, the architect, gave his advice. Fulton, who had returned in 1806, lent his genius to the task of embellishing the house and grounds, there being in one of his letters of the period a drawing for a summer-house, which he intends, he writes, "for the grounds of our mansion." Yet no encouragement was given to display or ostentation. The natural parks were left in their simple beauty. Walks and drives, flower-beds, a fountain or two, a summer-house, were all that art added to the natural beauty of the grounds. Within, the house was furnished plainly, but comfortably, in accordance with the poet's republican simplicity of taste, a severity, however, relieved by rare paintings, curios, and bric-a-brac, which had been collected in his seventeen years' wanderings abroad. The library was, however, the chief feature of the mansion. Its collection of books is said to have been the largest and most valuable then existing in this country, and lists of works purchased, to be found in his note-books certainly bear out the assertion.*

This charming retreat became the Holland House of America. The President—Jefferson, and, later, Madison —was often there for consultation, so that Barlow may be said to have largely moulded the policy of our Government toward France through two administrations. Heads of departments, Congressmen, foreign visitors of note, authors, artists, inventors, men of ideas of every calling, frequented its parlors. Jefferson made frequent

---

* A curious hint of their character is given by an account found among his papers, by which it appears that President Madison bought of him, June 9th, 1809, "The French Encyclopedé Methodique, 101 vols., for $448.83; Lejournant, $9; Antonini, $8; Schrevelias, $3; McFingal, $2.50; Song of Canaan, $1.50; the Die Historique, 9 vols., $27," of all which the poet had duplicates.

visits, unconnected with affairs of state, on which occasions, as we learn from references in their letters, the two sages discussed philosophy, art, internal improvements, their scheme for a National Institution; and again, spoke of improved varieties of seeds, agricultural implements, and the experiments they were making on their farms. Fulton, and those other famous pioneers in steam navigation, Jonathan and Thomas Law, were also frequent visitors. Fulton is said to have constructed his model of the Clermont at Kalorama, and to have first tested its powers on the waters of Rock Creek. The poet had, too, correspondents in almost every European country, and his house became a sort of common centre for those interested in the news and gossip of the Old World, while artists and men of letters found here that sympathy and appreciation which few Americans of that day were capable of giving. " We are full of visitors " occurs very often in his correspondence of this period as an excuse for epistolary laxness.

The first important matter that pressed upon him after being fairly domiciled was the perusal of the mass of letters and reviews which the publication of the Columbiad had elicited; for the poem had proved the literary event of the day, and quickly brought its author an extended fame. Old friends wrote to congratulate him, ambitious young poets submitted their verse for criticism. The Whig newspapers noticed the work with fulsome praises, while the Federal magazines and journals fell upon it with appetites whetted by full knowledge of all their cause had suffered at its author's hands; and as most of the scholarship and literary prestige of the nation was included in their ranks the author fared ill. He attributed this treatment to partisan rancor and malice, which was no doubt largely the case. A letter which he wrote to his old friend, Josiah Meigs, now President of Georgia University, proves how deeply he felt on the subject.

"You have seen, perhaps," he remarks, "the vulgar sneers and low-lived abuse that is cast upon it in the *Anthology*. You know that in all America no notice has been taken of it that has any pretensions to decency or common-sense. And I am now threatened, as they write me from London, with an overwhelming load of invective in the *Edinburgh Review,* the hints for which have probably been sent from Boston."

A small volume might be made of the literature to which the poem gave rise. Thomas Jefferson wrote, complimenting the author on the mechanical execution, and adding that he would not do it the injustice of giving it such a reading as his situation in Washington would admit of—a few minutes at a time, and at intervals of many days—but would reserve it for that retirement after which he was panting, and not now very distant, when he might enjoy it in full concert with its kindred scenes, amid those rural delights which join in chorus with the poet, and give to his song all its magic effect. President Wheelock, of Dartmouth College, wrote a complimentary letter, acknowledging receipt of a copy of the work for his college library. The National Institute of France, through its secretary, addressed him a letter, of which the following is a translation :

NATIONAL INSTITUTE,
CLASS OF THE FINE ARTS,
PARIS, *Oct.* 15, 1808.
The Perpetual Secretary of the Class to Mr. Joel Barlow :
Sir :—

" The Institute of France has received with the highest interest the beautiful work you have presented it—your poem ' The Columbiad.' All the friends of the human race pray that your country may achieve the high destinies to which Providence seems to call her. The most illustrious minds of France desire that the United States may join to the public and private virtues, of which they have given such fine examples, the culture of letters, science, and arts, which procure glory for nations and happiness for men. You can, then, be well assured that the National Institute will always applaud with pleasure the success of savants, literary men, or artists, your compatriots.

"The edition of your poem proves that typography has made great progress in the United States. It is fortunate that one of the first monuments of this precious art should be a work which honors national genius. Those who have had the advantage of knowing you in Paris will rejoice that you are the author of this work. As to me, sir, I am happy in being the instrument of the Institute of France to offer you its thanks and the expression of its esteem."

JOACHIM LE BRETON,
Perpetual Secretary, etc.

Among the rest were two letters from his old friend, Noah Webster, one a somewhat remarkable one, which we present:

NEW HAVEN, *Oct.* 13, 1808.

"SIR:—I had intended to give to the public a short review of your 'Columbiad' before this time, but two causes have prevented me: first, a feeble state of health and much occupation during the summer past, and, secondly, a doubt whether I can execute this purpose in a manner to satisfy you and my own conscience at the same time. Of the poem, as a poem, I can conscientiously say all, perhaps, which you can expect or desire, but I cannot, in a review, omit to pass a severe censure on the atheistical principles it contains. The principles of irreligion which you avow, of which I saw a specimen in a letter you wrote to Royal Flint in 1794 or 1795, form the partition-wall which has separated you from many of your old friends. No man on earth not allied to me by nature or marriage had so large a share in my affections as Joel Barlow until you renounced the religion which you once preached, and which I believe. But with my views of the principles you have introduced into the 'Columbiad' I apprehend my silence will be most agreeable to you, and most expedient for your old friend and obedient servant,

"N. WEBSTER."

The great lexicographer seems to have been blinded somewhat by religious zeal, for neither in Barlow's published works nor in the hundreds of letters to his wife and intimate friends which the writer has consulted, is there a sentence which might fairly be construed as proving its author an atheist. In fact, to Gregoire, he confesses himself a Presbyterian. The critique in the *Edinburgh Review* appeared in due time, but was rather commendatory than otherwise. Fulton writes from New York, July 1, 1810, on this topic: "Have you seen the Edinburgh review of the 'Columbiad'? Their first principle is that polished literature is not to be expected from America more than from Manchester or Birmingham. The second position is, that the day for epic poetry is gone by; man cannot now take pleasure in poetic fiction; the mere didactic is too dry. They find much fault with compounding new words or altering the signification of old. However, they call you a giant compared to modern British bards, though not equal, they think, to Milton." Only one of his critics the poet deigned to answer. That one was his old friend, the Abbé Gregoire, who at once wrote a pamphlet, sharply criticising the Columbiad as tending to cast contempt on the Catholic religion. This letter was widely published, and called from the poet a reply which, as satisfactorily defining his religious status, and as a fine example of his reasoning powers, we append in full:

"MY DEAR GOOD FRIEND:—I have received your letter, at once complimentary and critical, on the poem I sent you. Our venerable friend, Archbishop Carroll, informs me that he has likewise received from you a copy of the same letter, and he has expressed to me in conversation, with the same frankness that you have done in writing, his displeasure at the engraving which has offended you. While I assure you that I sincerely mingle my regrets with yours, and with his, on this subject, permit me, my excellent Gregoire, to accompany them with a few observations that I owe to the cause of truth and to my own blameless character. Yes, my friend, I appeal to yourself, to our intimate intercourse of near twenty years, when I repeat this claim of character. It cannot be denied me in any country; and your letter itself, with all its expostulating severity, is a proof of the sentiment in you which justifies my appeal. The engraving in question has gone forth, and unfortunately cannot be recalled. If I had less delicacy than I really have towards you and the other Catholic Christians whom you consider as insulted by the prostration of their emblems which you therein discover, I might content myself with stating what is the fact: that this engraving, and the picture from which it was taken, were made in England while I was in America, and that I knew nothing of its composition till it was sent over to me not only engraved, but printed and prepared for publication. My portion therefore in the crime, if it is a crime, is only the act of what our lawyers term an accomplice after the fact. But my affectionate regard for an offended brother will not suffer me to meet his complaint with so short an answer. I must discuss the subject, and reply to the whole charge as though it were all my own, premising, as I have already done, that I am sorry there is occasion for it, and regret that the engraving was ever made. How much our religious opinions depend on the place of our birth! Had you and I been born in the same place there is no doubt but we should have been of the same religion; had that place been Constantinople we must have been Mussulmen. But now the Mussulmen call us infidels; we pity their weakness, and call them infidels in our turn. I was born in a place where Catholic Christians are not known but by report; and the discipline of our sect taught us to consider them, not indeed as infidels, but as a species of idolaters. It was believed by us, though erroneously, that they worshipped images. We now find that they employed them only as instruments of worship, not as the object. But there is no wonder that, to the vulgar apprehension of our people, it should appear as we were taught to believe ; and that those nations who bow the knee before these emblems of Deity, and address their prayers to them, should be considered as really worshipping them. The idea was perhaps corroborated by their prayers being uttered in an unknown tongue. The decalogue of Moses had inspired us with an abhorrence for images, and for those who bow down to them and worship them ; and hence arose our unhappy aversion to the Catholics. We were told that their churches were full of pictures, statues, and other visible representations, not only of the Blessed Virgin, of all the Apostles and many of the saints, but of every person in the Holy Trinity. Our fathers had protested against that great section of the Christian family which calls itself the Mother Church, not merely on account of the sale of indulgences, against which Luther had led the revolt, but likewise on account of its making these pretended images of the inimageable God. The sect of Puritans, in which I was born and educated, and to which I still adhere for the same reason that you adhere to the Catholics—a conviction that they are right—were the class of reformers who placed themselves at the greatest remove from the Mother Church, and retained the least respect for her emblems and the other ceremonials of her worship. They could suffer no bishops, no mitres, crosiers, crucifixes, or censers. They made no processions, carried no lighted candles through the streets at noonday ; neither did they leave them burning in their churches through the night, when no human eye was there to see them ; having entirely lost sight of this part of the institutions of Zoroaster, Isis, and Ceres. They would not allow their prayers to be written in any language, not even in Latin, though they did not understand it ; but they chose to utter their supplications extempore, like their other discourses ; to communicate their own ideas, to express their wants and offer their confessions directly to the invisible God : through a mediator indeed, but without holding him in their hand, or having him fixed in effigy on a cross before their eyes. They had no organs in their churches, no instrumental music in their worship, which they held to be always profane. These people made use of no cross, but the mystical one of mortifying their sins ; and if they had been called upon to join in a crusade to the Holy Land they must have marched without a standard. They would have fought indeed with as much bravery as Saint Louis or the lion Richard, but when they had reconquered the tomb of Christ they would have trampled on the cross with as fervent a zeal as they would upon the crescent. They were not conversant with what we call the fine arts ; they spoke to the ear, but not to the eye ; and having no reverence for images or emblems, they despised those that had, though they were doubtless wrong in so doing. I mention these things, my worthy friend, not with the least idea of levity or evasion, but to prove to you how totally you have mistaken my meaning and my motive ; to show by what chain of circumstances, mostly foreign to our own merits or demerits, our habits of opinion, our cast of character are formed ; to show how natural it is that a man of my origin and education, my course of study and the views I must have taken of the morals of nations, their causes and tendencies, should attribute much of the active errors that afflict the human race to the use of emblems, and to the fatal facility with which they are mistaken for realities by the great mass of mankind ; how the best of Christians of one sect may consider the Christian emblems of another sect as *prejudices* of a dangerous tendency, and honestly wish to see them destroyed :

and all this without the least hostility to their funda-
mental doctrines, or suspicion of giving offence. I
never supposed that those Hollanders who, to obtain
leave to carry on commerce in Japan, trampled on the
cross, as a proof that they did not belong to the same
nation with the Portuguese, who had done so much
mischief in that island, really meant to renounce their
religion as Christians when they trod upon its Catholic
emblem. The act might be reprehensible, as being done
for lucre; but it must appear extremely different in the
eyes of different sects of Christians. To a Catholic,
who identifies the cross with the Gospel, our only
hope of salvation, it must appear a horrid crime; but
to a Protestant we may easily conceive it might appear of little moment, and by no means as a renunciation
of the Gospel. You have now furnished in your own person an additional example, and a most striking one, of
identifying the symbol with the substance. In your letter to me you treat the cross and the Gospel as the same
thing. Had I been sufficiently aware of the force of that
habit of combination among the Catholics, especially in a
mind of those acute perceptions and strong sensibilities
which I know to belong to yours, I should surely have
suppressed the engraving. You must perceive by this
time that you have mistaken my principles and feelings
in another point of view. You suppose I should be
greatly offended ' to see the symbols of liberty, so dear
to me, trampled under foot before my eyes.' Not at all,
my friend. Leave to me and my country the great realities of liberty and I freely give you up its emblems.
There was no time in the American Revolution, though
I was then young and enthusiastic, when you might not
have cut down every liberty pole, and burnt all the red
caps in the United States, and I would have looked on
with tranquillity, perhaps have thanked you for your
trouble. My habits of feeling and reasoning, already ac-
counted for, had accustomed me to regard these trap-

pings rather as detrimental than advantageous to the cause they are meant to support. These images we never greatly multiplied in this country. I have seen more liberty caps at one sitting of the Jacobin Club in Paris than were ever seen in all America. You will say, perhaps, that it is the difference of national character which makes the distinction. This is doubtless true ; but what has been the cause of this difference in the character of our two nations? Has not the universal use of emblems in one, and the almost universal disuse of them in the other, had as great, if not a greater effect than all other causes in producing such difference? I do not say that our national character is better than yours , far from it. I speak frankly. I think you undervalue the French character. I have a high esteem for that nation. They are an amiable, intelligent, generous, hospitable, unsuspicious people. I say nothing of their government, whether regal, revolutionary, or imperial. In private friendship they are as disinterested and unshaken, at least, as any people I have seen. Of this I could cite numerous examples, both within my own experience and that of others ; though it would establish my position in my own mind if I were able to mention none but you. It would indeed be paying too high a compliment to any nation on earth to cite Gregoire as a sample of its moral and social character. If all Catholics had been like you, the world at this day would all be Catholics. And I may say, I hope without offence, that if all Pagans had been like you, the world had all been Pagans; there might have been no need of Catholics, no pretext for the sect of Puritans. This is an amiable discussion between you and me. The suavity of your manner does honor to the fortitude with which you defend your principles; though it is not easy to perceive against what opponent you are defending them. Your letter expatiates in a wide field, and embraces many subjects. But really, my friend, the greater part of it has nothing more to do with me than

one of Cicero's letters to Atticus. You begin by supposing that I have renounced Christianity myself, and that I
attempt to overturn the system by ridicule and insult,
neither of which is true ; for neither of which have you
the least color of proof. No, my honest accuser, the
proof is not in the book. Review the work with all the
acumen of your discernment, and you must, you will, recall the hasty accusation. I defy you and all the critics
of the English language to point out a passage, if taken
in its natural, unavoidable meaning, which militates
against the genuine principles, practice, faith, and hope
of the Christian system, as inculcated in the Gospels and
explained by the Apostles, whose writings accompany the
Gospel, in the volume of the New Testament. On the
contrary, I believe, and you have compelled me on this
occasion to express my belief, that the Columbiad,
taken in all its parts of text and notes and preface, is more
favorable to sound and rigid morals, more friendly to
virtue, more clear and unequivocal in pointing out the
road to national dignity and individual happiness, more
energetic in its denunciations of tyranny and oppression
in every shape, injustice and wickedness in all their forms,
and consequently more consonant to what you acknowledge to be the spirit of the Gospel, than all the writings
of all that list of Christian authors of the last three
ages whom you have cited as the glory of Christendom,
and strung them on the alphabet, from Addison
down to Winkleman. Understand me right, my just
and generous friend, I judge not my poem as a work
of genius. I cannot judge it, nor class it, nor compare it
in that respect, because it is my own. But I *know* it as a
moral work; I *can* judge and *dare* pronounce upon its
tendency, its beneficial effect upon every candid mind ;
and I am confident you will yet join me in opinion. But
let me repeat my prayer that you will not mistake the
spirit of this observation. It is not from vanity that I
speak ; my book is not a work of genius ; the maxims in

it are not my own; they are yours, they are those of good
men that have gone before us both; they are drawn from
the Gospel, from history, from the unlettered volume of
moral nature, from the experience and inexperience of
unhappy man in his various struggles after happiness;
from all his errors and all his objects in the social state.
My only merit lies in putting them together with fidelity.
My work is only a transcript of the tablet of my mind
impressed with these images as they pass before it. You
will see that I have nothing to do with the unbelievers
who have attacked the Christian system, either before the
French Revolution, or during, or since that monumental
period. I am not one of them. You say I resemble
them not in anything else; you will now add that I resemble them not in this. So far as you have discovered
a cause of the failure of that resolution in the renunciation of the Christian faith by those who held, in stormy,
quick succession, the reins of your government, I thank
you for the discovery. I was in want of more causes
than I had yet perceived to account for the unhappy
catastrophe of that gigantic struggle of all the virtues
against all the vices that political society has known.
You have discovered a cause; but there is such a thing
in logic as the cause of a cause. I have thought, but perhaps it is an error, that the reason why the minds of the
French people took the turn they did, on the breaking
out of the revolution, was to be found in the complicated
ceremonials of their worship, and what you yourself would
term the non-essentials of their religion. The reasonable
limits of a letter will not allow me to do justice to this
idea. To give it the proper development would require
five times the volume that I shall give to the present communication. The innumerable varieties of pomp and circumstance which the discipline of the church had inculcated and enjoined became so incorporated with the vital
principles of faith and practice, and these exteriors were
overloaded with abuses to such a degree, that to discrim-

inate and take them down without injuring the system required a nicer eye than the people can possess, a steadier hand than can comport with the hurried movement of a great revolution. The scaffolding of your church, permit me to say it, had so enclosed, perforated, overlooked, and underpropped the building, that we could not be surprised, though sorely grieved, to see the reformer lay his hand, like a blind Samson, to the great, substantial pillars, heave and overturn the whole encumbered edifice together, and bury himself in the ruins. Why did they make a goddess of Reason? Why erect a statue of Liberty, a mass of dead matter for a living, energetic principle? Have the courage, my good friend, to answer these questions. You know it was for the same cause that the people of Moses made their golden calf. The calf Apis had from time immemorial been a god in Egypt. The people were in the habit of seeing their divine protector in that substantial boval form, with two horns, four legs, and a tail; and this habit was as interwoven in the texture of their mind as to become a part of the intellectual man. The privations incident to a whole moving nation subjected them to many calamities. No human hand could relieve them; they felt a necessity of seeking aid from a supernatural agent, but no satisfaction in praying to an invisible God. They had never thought of such a being; and they could not bring themselves at once to the habit of forming conceptions of him with sufficient clearness and confidence to make him an object of adoration, to which they could address their supplications in the day of great affliction. Forty years of migration were judged necessary to suppress the habit of using idols in their worship, during which time their continual marches would render it at once inconvenient for the people to move their heavy gods, and to conceal them in their baggage, while the severity of military discipline must expose their tents and their effects to the frequent inspection of their officers. Shall I apply this principle to the French nation in her revolution? No, my friend, it is too delicate a task for a foreigner who has received her hospitality; I will leave it to your own compassionate and philanthropic mind. You will recollect how often I partook of your grief during that scene of moral degradation. No sooner did you and the other virtuous leaders in the revolution begin to speak of august liberty, *holy* reason, and the *divine* rights of man, than the artizans took up the hammer, the chisel, and the plaster-of-Paris. They must reduce these gods to form before they could present them to the people with any chance of their being understood; they must create before they could adore. Trace this principle through five years of your history, and you will find why the Catholic religion was overturned, morality laid asleep, and the object of the revolution irretrievably lost, at least for our day. My dear Gregoire, I am glad you have written me this letter, though at first it gave me pain. I was sorry to find myself so entirely misconceived by a friend so highly valued; but I see your attack is easily repelled, a thing which I know will give you pleasure, and it furnishes me an occasion at the same time to render a piece of justice to myself in relation to my fellow-citizens. You must know I have enemies in this country—not personal ones; I never had a personal enemy, to my knowledge, in any country. But they are political enemies, the enemies of republican liberty, and a few of their followers who never read my writings; that is, my writings that I wrote, but only those that I did not write; such as were forged and published for me in my absence, many of which I never have seen, and some of which I did not hear of till ten years after they had been printed in the *American Gazette*. It has even been said and published by these Christian editors (I never heard of it till lately) that I went to the bar of your Convention, when it was the fashion so to do, and made a solemn recantation of my Christian faith, declaring myself an atheist or deist, or some other anti-Christian apostate; I know not what, for I never yet have seen the piece. Now, as an active member of that Convention, a steady attendant at their sittings, and my most intimate friend, you know that such a thing could not be done without your knowledge; you know therefore that it was not done; you know I never went but once to the bar of that Convention, which was on the occasion to which you allude in the letter now before me, to present an address from the Constitutional Society in London, of which I was a member. You know I always sympathized in your grief and partook of all your resentment while such horrors and blasphemies were passing, of which these typographical cannibals of reputation have made me a participant. These calumnies, 'you see, could not be refuted by me while I did not know of their existence. But there is another reason which you will not conceive of till I inform you. The editors of newspapers, you know, ought to be considered as exercising a sacred function; they are the high-priests of public opinion, which is the high court of character, the guardian of public morals. Now I am ashamed to inform you that there are editors in this country who will publish the grossest calumny against a citizen, and refuse to publish its refutation. This is immorality unknown in France since the death of Marat. A private letter of mine, written from Paris, was mutilated in this country, made to say things that I never wrote nor thought, and published in all our anti-republican papers. I saw it a year after the date and immediately wrote an explanatory letter, which re-established my first intention. This last I then published in Paris, London, and Philadelphia. Not one editor who printed the original mutilated letter has, to this day, printed my answer; though it was published in all those places ten years ago. And perhaps not one person in twenty who read the first has ever seen the second, or yet knows of its existence, except those editors who refused

to publish it. You must not suppose from this statement
of facts that I am angry with these people. On the
contrary, I pity and forgive them. And there is no great
merit in this, for they are not my enemies. They only
do the work they are set about by their patrons and sup-
porters, the monarchists of America. Their object is
not to injure me, but to destroy the effect of my republican writings. They now publish your letter with great
avidity because they think it will tend to decry my poem.
It may have this effect in a small degree; but I still
thank them for multiplying your publication. There is
no work of yours that I do not wish to see universally
read in America; and I hope soon to find in our language and in the hands of all our readers your last very
curious and interesting treatise *De la Littérature des Nè-
gres*. It is a work of indefatigable research, and brings
to light many facts unknown in this country, where the
cause of humanity is most interested in propagating that
species of knowledge. I hope the manuscript copy of Mr.
Warden's translation is not lost; or if it is, that he will be
able to furnish our booksellers with another. If I had renounced Christianity, as your letter seems to suppose,
that letter and my reflections on your life and conversation would certainly bring me back, for you judge me right
when you say I am not ashamed to own myself possibly
in the wrong, or, in other words, to confess myself a man.
The Gospel has surely done great good in the world, and
if, as you imagine, I am indebted in any measure to that
for the many excellent qualities of my wife, I owe it
much indeed. I must now terminate my letter, or I
shall be obliged to turn from you to the public with an
apology for making it so long; since I must offer it to
the public in my country, and trust to your sense of justice to do the same in yours, and in your language, in order to give it a chance of meeting your letter in the hands
of all its readers. If, thus united, they serve no other
purpose, they will at least be a short-lived monument of

our friendship, and furnish one example of the calmness and candor with which a dispute may be conducted, even on the subject of religion."*

Your affectionate friend,

JOEL BARLOW.

KALORAMA, 13*th September,* 1809.

Aside from the annoyance caused by attacks on his poems, the days spent at Kalorama must have been of unalloyed pleasure and interest.

There was the farm, to which he had looked forward in Paris, his wife, his books, troops of friends, with whom he could discuss scientific and philosophical questions, and, for his leisure moments, the preparation of a noble and useful work—a history of the United States. Here, too, he witnessed the success of the steamboat, the triumph of the project which for seven years he had so tenderly nursed in Paris.

We can imagine with what pleasure he read, in the spring of 1807, this letter from Fulton:

"My steamboat voyage to Albany has turned out rather more favorably than I had calculated. The distance from New York to Albany is one hundred and fifty miles. I ran it up in thirty-two hours, and down in thirty. I had a light breeze against me the whole way, both going and coming, and the voyage has been performed wholly by the power of steam. I overtook many sloops and schooners beating to windward and parted with them as if they had been at anchor. The power of propelling boats by steam is now fully proved. The morning I left New York there were not, perhaps, thirty persons in the city who believed that the boat would ever move one mile an hour, or be of the least utility, and while we were putting off from the wharf, which was

---

* This letter was followed by a second from Abbé Gregoire, in which he indignantly denied the calumny that his friend had appeared before the bar of the Convention and made a public recantation of the Christian religion.

crowded with spectators, I heard a number of sarcastic remarks. This is the way in which ignorant men compliment what they call philosophy and its projectors.

" Having employed much time, money, and zeal in accomplishing this work, it gives me, as it will you, great pleasure to see it fully answer my expectations. It will give a cheap and quick conveyance to the merchants on the Mississippi, the Missouri, and other great rivers which are now laying open their treasures to the enterprise of our country ; and although the prospect of personal emolument has been some inducement to me, yet I feel infinitely more pleasure in reflecting on the numerous advantages that my country will derive from the invention."

This period was not devoid of literary and civic honors. He was elected a member of the United States Military Philosophical Society in 1807, and of the American Philosophical Society in 1809. The same year the University of Georgia conferred on him the degree of LL.D. He was also made a director of the Bank of Washington, and was frequently called upon to preside at public meetings. He delivered an oration on the Fourth of July, 1809, at Washington, which was an able effort and was afterwards printed in pamphlet form. He seems to have made no effort during this period to secure public office for himself, and only on two occasions for his friends: he secured the office of postmaster at Naugatuck, Ct., for his nephew, Stephen Barlow, and that at Lancaster, Pa., for the mathematician and astronomer Andrew Ellicott. His appeal in behalf of the latter to Gideon Granger, Postmaster-General, it is safe to say, no other public man of his day was capable of writing: it championed a class rarely recognized by Government, and it administered a stinging rebuke to what was then, and is now, the besetting sin of our country. The letter speaks for itself:

KALORAMA, *May* 3, 1809.

"DEAR SIR :—Henry Baldwin . . . . informs me that the postmaster at Lancaster is dead or dying, and wishes to have the place given to his father Ellicott. He says he has written to you on the subject, and has probably stated to you the pretensions of the applicant. But as I happen to be acquainted with Mr. Ellicott (though probably not better than you are) he thought my note might have some effect. I have certainly a great esteem for Mr. Ellicott as a mathematician and astronomer, and would suggest that in all our country there is evidently too little attention paid to men of science, as well as to men of literature. It is really discouraging to all liberal pursuits, and proves that the Government is accessory to the great national sin of our country, which I fear will overturn its liberties : I mean the inordinate and universal pursuit of wealth as a means of distinction. For example, if I find that writing the Columbiad, with all the moral qualities, literature, and science which that work supposes, will not place me on a footing with John Taylor, who is rich, why, then, I'll be rich too; I'll despise my literary labors, which tend to build up our system of free government, and I'll boast of my bank shares, which tend to pull it down, because these, and not those, procure me the distinction which we all desire. I will teach my nephews by precept, and all the rising generation by example, that merit consists in oppressing mankind and not in serving them. Excuse, my dear sir, this dull sermon and make Andrew Ellicott postmaster of Lancaster."

One other letter written by him during this period we introduce for its intrinsic interest. In July, 1809, James Cheetham, editor of the *American Citizen*, a scurrilous political sheet of New York, addressed to Mr. Barlow the following letter :

"SIR :—Not having the honor of a personal acquaintance with you the trouble this note will occasion will require some apology, and the only one I can offer regards the subject of it, and the readiness with which, your character persuades me, you will furnish me the information required as soon as you have leisure to do so.

"I am preparing to write the life of Thomas Paine, author of 'Common Sense,' etc. As you were acquainted with him in Paris, and he mentioned you in his 'Age of Reason,' your opinion of his manners and habits, the company he kept, etc., would be very acceptable.

"He was a great drunkard here, and Mr. M——, a merchant of this city, who lived with him when he was arrested by order of Robespierre, tells me he was intoxicated when that event happened.

"Did Paine ever take an oath of allegiance to France? In his letter to the French people in 1792 he thanks them for electing him a member of the Convention, and for the additional honor of making him a French citizen. In his speech on the trial of the king he speaks, he says, as a citizen of France. There is some difference between being a member of a Convention to make a constitution and a member of the same body to try the king and transact other business. I should imagine that in the latter capacities an oath of allegiance would be necessary.

"Any other information you would be pleased to communicate, which in your judgment would be useful in illustrating his character, will be gratefully received and used as you may direct."

I am, etc.,
JAMES CHEETHAM.

To which Mr. Barlow replied:

KALORAMA, *Aug.* 11, 1809.

"*To James Cheetham, Sir:*

"I have received your letter calling for information relative to the life of Thomas Paine. It appears to me that this is not the moment to publish the life of that man in this country. His own writings are his best life, and these are not read at present.

"The greater part of readers in the United States will not be persuaded, as long as their present feelings last, to consider him in any other light than as a drunkard and a deist. The writer of his life who should dwell on these topics, to the exclusion of the great and estimable traits of his real character, might indeed please the rabble of the age, who do not know him ; the book might sell, but it would only tend to render the truth more obscure for the future biographer than it was before.

"But if the present writer should give us Thomas Paine *complete*, in all his character, as one of the most benevolent and disinterested of mankind, endowed with the clearest perception, an uncommon share of original genius, and the greatest breadth of thought ; if this piece of biography should analyze his literary labors and rank him, as he ought to be ranked, among the brightest and most undeviating luminaries of the age in which he has lived, yet with a mind assailable by flattery, and receiving through that weak side a tincture of vanity which he was too proud to conceal ; with a mind, though strong enough to bear him up and to rise elastic under the heaviest hand of oppression, yet unable to endure the contempt of his former friends and fellow-laborers, the rulers of the country that had received his first and greatest services ; a mind incapable of looking down with serene compassion, as it ought, on the rude scoffs of their imitators, a new generation that knows him not ; a mind that shrinks from their society, and unhappily seeks refuge in low company, or looks for consolation in the sordid, solitary bottle, till it sinks at last so far below its native elevation as to lose all respect for itself and to forfeit that of his best friends, disposing these friends almost to join with his enemies, and wish, though from different motives, that he would hasten to hide himself in the grave—if you are disposed and prepared to write his life *thus entire*, to fill up the picture to which these hasty strokes of outline give but a rude sketch with great vacuities, your book may be a useful one for another age, but it will not be relished, nor scarcely tolerated, in this.

" The biographer of Thomas Paine should not forget his mathematical acquirements and his mechanical genius : his invention of *the iron bridge*, which led him to Europe in the year 1787, and which has procured him a great reputation in that branch of science in France and England, in both which countries his bridge has been adopted in many instances, and is now much in use.

" You ask whether he took the oath of allegiance to France. Doubtless the qualification to be a member of the Convention required an oath of fidelity to that country, but involved in it no abjuration of his fidelity to this. He was made a French citizen by the same decree with *Washington, Hamilton, Priestly, and Sir James Mackintosh.*

" What Mr. M—— has told you relative to the circumstances of his arrestation by order of Robespierre is erroneous, at least in one point. Paine did not lodge at the house where he was arrested, but had been dining there with some Americans, of whom Mr. M—— may have been one. I never heard before that Paine was intoxicated that night. Indeed, the officers brought him directly to my home, which was two miles from his lodgings and about as much from the place where he had been dining. He was not intoxicated when they came to me. Their object was to get me to go and assist them to examine Paine's papers. It employed us the rest of that night and the whole of the next day at Paine's lodgings, and he was not committed to prison till the next evening.

" You ask what company he kept. He always frequented the best, both in England and France, till he became the object of calumny in certain American papers (echoes of the English court papers) for his adherence to what he thought the cause of liberty in France—till he conceived himself neglected and despised by his former friends in the United States. From that moment he gave himself very much to drink, and, consequently, to companions less worthy of his better days.

"It is said he was always a peevish ingrate. This is possible. So was *Lawrence Sterne*, so was *Torquato Tasso*, so was *J. J. Rousseau*. But Thomas Paine, as a visiting acquaintance and as a literary friend, the only points of view from which I knew him, was one of the most instructive men I have ever known. He had a surprising memory and a brilliant fancy; his mind was a storehouse of facts and useful observations; he was full of lively anecdote and ingenious, original, pertinent remarks upon almost every subject.

"He was always charitable to the poor beyond his means, a sure protector and friend to all Americans in distress that he found in foreign countries. And he had frequent occasions to exert his influence in protecting them during the revolution in France. His writings will answer for his patriotism, and his entire devotion to what he conceived to be the best interest and happiness of mankind.

"This, sir, is all I have to remark on the subject you mention. Now I have only one request to make, and that would doubtless seem impertinent were you not the editor of a newspaper; it is, that you will not publish this letter, nor permit a copy of it to be taken."

JOEL BARLOW.

Cheetham, however, disregarded the injunction, and published the letter in full in his Life of Paine.

An interesting correspondence was also kept up with Jefferson during this period. Jefferson's letters to Barlow were carefully preserved, and give interesting details of the character and pursuits of two great men. Several of the most important are here presented. The first was written shortly before his retirement from the Presidency.

MONTICELLO, *July* 25, 1808.

" DEAR SIR :—Having been tempted by a cloudy day to leave Washington a day sooner than I intended, among other things which I omitted to do was the furnishing you an itinerary of the route to this place : it is as follows from Georgetown Ferry:

	Miles.	Cents.	
To Wren's................	6	38	
* " Fairfax Court House..	8	65	
* " Centerville, about....	7	50	Mitchell's is the best house.
* " Red House, about....	10		Mrs. Hereford's best ; Bronaugh's next.
* " Fanquier C. House...	20		Norris' best, indeed a superlatively good one.
– " Jefferson............	9	80	Kuhn's, but even that a wretched place.
* " Culpepper C. House..	13	77	Capt. Shackleford.
* " Orange C. House....	19	83	
" Mr. Madison's.......	4	17	
* " Gordon.............	8	75	
* " Walton's Tavern.....	13	58	
" Monticello...........	7	58	
	129	$6.01	

" The houses marked thus * are pretty good, comparatively ; — means bad. You asked me the best time of taking the journey, and I observed as well soon as late, but I found Mrs. Randolph in the straw, having increased her family on the 16th. Of course she will not be with us till a month from that, and for her sake as well as Mrs. Barlow's the visit will be doubly pleasing if so timed as that she should be here. In the hope that nothing may intervene to deprive us of the pleasure of possessing Mrs. Barlow and yourself here, after presenting her my respects, I salute you with friendship and great consideration."

TH. JEFFERSON.

To MR. BARLOW.

WASHINGTON, *Dec.* 25, 1808.

" DEAR SIR :—I return you Dr. Maese's letter, which a pressure of business has occasioned me to keep too long.

I think an account of the manufactures of Philadelphia would be really useful, and that the manufactures of other places should be added from time to time, as information of them should be received. To give a perfect view of the whole would require a report from every county or township of the United States. Perhaps the present moment would be premature, as they are in truth but just now in preparation. The Government could not aid the publication by the subscription suggested by Dr. Maese without a special law for it. All the purposes for which they can pay a single dollar are specified by law.

"The advantages of the veterinary institution proposed may perhaps be doubted. If it be problematical whether physicians prevent death, where the disease, unaided, would have terminated fatally, oftener than they produce it, where order would have been restored to the system by the process, if uninterrupted, provided by nature—and in the case of man who can describe the seat of his disease, its character, progress, and often its cause—what might we expect in the case of the horse, mute and yielding no sensible and certain indications of his disease ? They have long had these institutions in Europe. Has the world as yet received one iota of valuable information from them? If it has, it is unknown to me. At any rate, it may be doubted whether, where so many institutions of obvious utility are yet wanting, we should select this one to take the lead.—I return you Gibbon with thanks. I send you also, for your shelf of pamphlets, one which gives really a good historical view of our funding system, and of Federal transactions generally, from an early day to the present time.

"I salute you with friendship and respect."

TH. JEFFERSON.

To MR. BARLOW.

MONTICELLO, *Oct.* 8, 1809.

"DEAR SIR :—It is long since I ought to have acknowledged the receipt of your most excellent oration on the

4th of July. I was doubting what you could say equal to your own reputation on so hackneyed a subject, but you have really risen out of it with lustre, and pointed to others a field of great expansion. A day or two after I received your letter to Bishop Gregoire, a copy of his diatribe to you came to hand from France. I had not before heard of it. He must have been eagle-eyed in quest of offence to have discovered ground for it among the rubbish massed together on the point he animadverts on. You have done right in giving him a sugary answer, but he did not deserve it; for, notwithstanding a compliment to you now and then, he constantly returns to the identification of your sentiments with the extravagances of the revolutionary zealots. I believe him a very good man, with imagination enough to declaim eloquently, but without judgment to decide. He wrote to me also on the doubts I had expressed five or six and twenty years ago, in the 'Notes on Virginia,' as to the grade of understanding of the negroes, and sent me his book on the literature of the negroes. His credulity has made him gather up every story he could find of men of color (without distinguishing whether black, or of what degree of mixture), however slight the mention or light the authority on which they are quoted. The whole does not amount in evidence to what we know ourselves of Banneker. We know he had spherical trigonometry enough to make almanacs, but not without the suspicion of aid from Elliot, who was his neighbor and friend, and never missed an opportunity of praising him. I have a long letter from Banneker, which shows him to have had a mind of very common stature indeed. As to Bishop Gregoire, I wrote him, as you have done, a very soft answer. It was impossible for doubt to have been more tenderly or hesitatingly expressed than that was in the 'Notes of Virginia,' and nothing was, or is, farther from my intentions than to enlist myself as the champion of a fixed opinion where

I have only expressed a doubt. St. Domingo will in time throw light on the question.

" I intended ere this to have sent you the papers I had promised you, but I have taken up Marshall's fifth volume, and mean to read it carefully to correct what is wrong in it, and commit to writing such facts and annotations as the reading that work will bring into my recollection, and which have not yet been put on paper. In this I shall be much aided by my memorandums and letters, and will send you both the old and the new; but I go on very slowly. In truth, during the pleasant season I am always out of doors employed, not passing more time at my writing-table than will despatch my current business; but when the weather becomes cold I shall go out but little. I hope, therefore, to get through this volume during the ensuing winter, but should you want the papers sooner they shall be sent at a moment's warning. The ride from Washington to Monticello in the stage or in a gig is so easy that I had hoped you would have taken a flight here during the season of good roads. Whenever Mrs. Barlow is well enough to join you in such a visit it must be taken more at ease. It will give us real pleasure whenever it may take place. I pray you to present me to her respectfully, and I salute you affectionately."

TH. JEFFERSON.

MONTICELLO, *Dec.* 31, 1809.

" DEAR SIR :—In removing my effects from Washington I had the misfortune of having a trunk stolen, which, besides papers of irretrievable value, contained other things highly prized, and among them nothing more so than a dynamometer I had just received from France. The Agricultural Society of the Seine had sent me one of Guillaume's ploughs, which by that instrument was proved to require but half the force of their best ploughs, and they asked from me a plough with my mould-board. It was my wish, while doing this, to make a plough which might compete with theirs, and, I am confident, excel it. I therefore imported their dynamometer in order to prove mine with Guillaume's. I am now engaged in this work, but have lost my dynamometer. I think you have one. Could you do me the favor to lend it to me for this experiment, as well as to aid me in the construction of other articles for my farms, which now engross all my attention. It shall be carefully preserved and safely returned.

"Mr. Carr, a nephew of mine, will be going on in some days to Washington, where he will make a short stay. He will bring it on by the stage under his own particular care. As you have also the spirit of farming, perhaps if I succeed in my plough you would think one of them worthy of acceptance. In the mean time, be assured of my constant friendship and respect."

TH. JEFFERSON.

To JOEL BARLOW, ESQ.

Could Barlow's history of the men and events of his day, for which such great preparations were made, have been written, doubtless its author's fame would have shone with brighter lustre, and an entirely different complexion been given the early history of the American people. During this period the poet also conducted a correspondence with Noah Webster, of considerable literary interest. The letters, it will be observed, antedate the one of Oct. 13, 1808, in regard to the Columbiad, which Barlow never answered.

NEW HAVEN, *Oct.* 19, 1807.

"DEAR SIR:—Your favor of the 12th has given me much pleasure; not merely on the score of former friendship, but because it informs me of your favorable opinion of my Dictionary and of my further designs. The approbation of classical scholars is the most flattering reward that I can receive. By *classical scholars* I do not mean the conductors of some periodical publications in our country, whose inquiries have been bounded by the perusal of a few mod-

ern elegant writers, but men who have drunk deep of
the Pierian spring. A few gentlemen of this character,
like yourself, duly appreciate the merit of my labors,
but the number is small ; my hope and expectations are
that it will increase. You will recollect that Judge
Trumbull and yourself were the only friends who, in 1783,
ventured to encourage me to publish my *Spelling Book*.
The attempt to correct English books was thought a rash
undertaking, yet more than 200,000 copies now sell
annually. My Grammar had its run, but has been super-
seded by Murray's. Both are wrong. I have lately
published one on Horne Tooke's plan, which President
Smith, of Princeton, pronounces the best analysis of the
language ever published. If I can, I will send you a
copy. I have published three books of ' Elements of
Useful Knowledge,' containing a brief history and geographical view of America and the Eastern Continent.
This is getting into use extensively with us, and if I can
give it circulation in the Middle and Southern States the
profits will enable me to bear the expenses of my great
work. This is to me very interesting. I believe these
volumes are in Philadelphia, at David Hogan's, in Third
Street. I wish you would take a look at them. I have
in the press an abridgment of my Complete Dictionary
for common schools, omitting obsolete and technical
terms, and reducing it to a dollar book. With the profits
of these I hope to be able to finish my Complete Dictionary. If I could get two or three hundred subscribers
to advance the price of it this would be all I should
want; but I have no expectation of such patronage,
though I am confident there would be no hazard to the
subscribers except that of my life. It will require the
incessant labor of from three to five years. My views
comprehended a *whole system*, intended to lay the foundation of a more correct practice of writing and speaking,
as well as a general system of instruction in other
branches. It is time for us to begin to think for our-

selves. Great Britain is probably in her wane, and I look forward to the time when her descendants will *reflect* some light back on the parent nation. But immense hosts of prejudices are to be subdued. I agree with you that we ought to correspond and understand each other. Dr. Mitchell often suggests this union as important. I will cheerfully accord with any scheme of this kind that shall be deemed prudent and advantageous. I have suggested in brief my proposed reformation of orthography, confining my views chiefly to the reducing to uniformity such classes of words as error, favor, candor, and so forth; public, music, and so forth; theater, luster, and so forth; and, secondly, to review the original orthography of feather, tether, controller, and so forth, which have been corrupted. The Legislature of this state has adopted the latter, and in our laws we write *controller*. My plan is to correct rather than to innovate, for this is a subject of extreme difficulty. I, however, will be accommodating. I endeavor to unite other opinions with my own on many points, and shall be happy to take the advice of my friends. The proof-sheet copy of an appendix to the notes to the Columbiad was not enclosed in your letter, I suppose by mistake. I shall be happy to see it. I am looking with impatience for the Columbiad, as I have heard much of the elegance of the work, and I have no doubt you have improved the poem. I shall be happy to receive your opinion on any subject favorable to American literature, and to be of any service to you in the pursuit. On the particular points of neology, and so forth, I will write you more fully after adjournment of the Legislature. Assure Mrs. Barlow of my respect, and accept the same from your old friend."

N. WEBSTER.

The following letter would apply with equal force to our day and generation :

NEW HAVEN, *Nov.* 12, 1807.

"The subject of your letter to me I deemed of too much consequence to be passed with a slight answer, and therefore postponed a detail of my opinion till I could be more at leisure than at the time I received it. Indeed, I have so much to say that I shall not be able to write all I wish, but will compress my ideas into as small a compass as possible. For more than twenty years, since I have looked into philology, and considered the connection between language and knowledge, and the influence of a national language on national opinions, I have had it in view to detach this country as much as possible from its dependence on the parent country. It appears to me not only derogatory to us as a nation to look to Great Britain for opinions and practice on this subject, but I consider this species of dependence as extremely prejudicial, as it regards our political interest in a variety of ways which I need not *write*, because you doubtless think of the subject in all its bearings. But there is another evil resulting from this dependence which is little considered ; this is, that it *checks improvement.* Not one man in a thousand —not even of the violent political opposers of Great Britain—reflects upon this influence. Our people look to English books as the standard of truth on all subjects, and this confidence in English opinions puts *an end to inquiry.* Our gentlemen, even in the colleges and professions, rarely question facts and opinions that come from English authors of reputation ; hence we have no *spirit of investigation;* and numerous errors are daily propagated from English presses which become current in this country. I make not these remarks from prejudice against Great Britain. The fact would be the same if our people could all read French, or Spanish, and should read none but French or Spanish books. All nations have their interests and prejudices, which influence more or less all their popular writings. I have discovered many popular errors on other subjects thus propagated in the United

States from our reliance on English books. But to confine myself to the language which I best understand. I can affirm that the standard English books abound with errors which nothing could have kept in countenance in this country but a blind veneration for English authorities. Our literary men investigate so little that they do not judge correctly of the talents and erudition of English writers, many of whom are not half so learned as our people suppose. My new Grammar and the letter to Dr. Murray will show you what I think, and what I have proved, upon a small scale, in regard to the most popular works on philology. In truth, we shall always be in leading strings till we resort to original writers and original principles instead of taking upon trust what English writers please to give us. But I need not enlarge upon this subject. You must certainly understand it better than I do; you know the manner in which *book-making* is carried on in England, and how, with a due portion of puffing from the reviewers, almost anything may obtain currency in this country. Leaving therefore a consideration of the cause of the evil let us attend to the remedy. On this subject I want your opinion. In the mean time, accept a short review of what I have done, without making much noise respecting my ultimate. My plan has been to furnish our schools with a tolerably complete system of elementary knowledge in books of my own, gradually substituting American books for English, and weaning our people from their prejudices and from their confidence in English authority. For this purpose I have endeavored to make, in the first place, my spelling book as perfect as possible. To this end I have done what is not done in any other book of the kind. I have collected and classed all the more difficult and irregular words, so that after leading the child through tables of easy words I present him, in short tables, all the varieties of anomaly; and when he has mastered this little book he has overcome the chief difficulties in learning the lan-

guage ; and as our books should have special reference
to the local knowledge most necessary for us, I have introduced the names of *places* in this country. No English compilation can answer our purpose for want of such
tables. Murray's Quaker friends are taking great pains to
introduce his spelling book, which wants the best and
most necessary part of such a work, and in which the division of syllables in old Dilworth is preserved and vindi-
cated. This scheme, I trust, will fail. As books for reading, I have published a selection of essays which has been
in use with many others of a like mind. It is so easy to
make books of this sort, and so difficult to make one better than others, that I expect nothing from this compilation. But my ' Elements of Useful Knowledge ' I think
a work of more consequence. In the two first volumes I
have given a brief but correct account of the settlement
and history of the United States. The historical part
was collected from original documents, or the best histo-
ries. These volumes contain what all our children ought
to learn ; for, in addition to the history and geography
of the country, the work contains an abridgment of the
Constitution of the United States, and of the Constitutions of all the states, with an American chronological
table, which I made with ease.

" The third volume contains a geographical view of the
other parts of the Globe, from the latest discoveries.
These three volumes are so divided into sections that
they may be read in classes, and intended either as reading books or for committing to memory. In our schools
the children learn many whole chapters by heart. I
have a volume on natural history—or, rather, zoology—
nearly finished, and shall add one or two others on
other subjects. I deem it very important that these
works should be known, and, if practicable, introduced
into schools in all the states, as not only appropriately
useful in themselves, but as auxiliary to the main design.
Next comes my ' Philosophical and Practical Grammar,'

lately published, in which I have developed what appear to be the real structure and idioms of our language. I have left Louk and Johnson, and mounted to the original writers, as far back as the first Saxon laws and annals. The result is, that many of the principles of grammar as taught in Louk formerly, and now in Murray (whose book is nothing but Louk's altered and enlarged), prove to be totally false; and I affirm that those grammars now taught *introduce more errors than they correct.* It is believed to be extremely important that this subject should be immediately laid before the public. Murray is a diligent, neat compiler, but utterly destitute of that mind of erudition necessary to enable a man to adjust principles of language. Next follow my dictionaries. One of them is in your hands. An abridgment of that is nearly through the press. This is intended for common English schools—containing about 30,000 words—all, indeed, that a mere English farmer or mechanic can want; technical words are omitted. This will be sold at a dollar. Lastly will come my 'Complete Dictionary,' which, I trust, will contain all that is valuable in any and all the English books of this kind and supersede the use of them all. This is a work of vast labor, and in the execution of it I want all the advice and assistance that my friends can afford. My plan is, if possible, to condense the whole into half the size of Johnson in quarto, and to publish one large 4to or two large imperial 8vos. Our men of letters are not generally men of property, and I wish to accommodate this work to their circumstances. To do this I must very much abridge Johnson's exemplifications. Indeed, on a careful examination, I am satisfied that a large proportion of them are useless, throwing not the least light on his definitions. My improvement will consist in *adding* all the legitimate words which are now used, and which are not in the English dictionaries; 2d. In rendering the definitions far more precise, and in exhibiting what may be called the *specific* differences of signification, a thing not yet done in any language, as far as my knowledge extends ; 3d. In developing the origin and history of numerous *families* of words, which, springing from a common root or element, have ramified into many modern languages. In this part of the work much new and valuable light is to be diffused over a very curious and obscure subject; 4th. To settle the orthography of words ; when doubtful, recourse will be had to the primitive word, and the true etymology. The changes of orthography will not be numerous, and these all warranted by the original spelling and by principles of strict analogy. A few other improvements of minor importance I need not specify ; such as the scheme I have lain for rendering our citizens more and more independent. The outline was drawn more than twenty years ago, but my circumstances compelled me to suspend the execution of it, for the purpose of getting bread by other business, until within a few years last past. Even now my resources are inadequate to the work; my income barely supports my family, and I want five hundred dollars' worth of books from Europe which I cannot obtain here, and which I cannot afford to purchase. I have made my wishes known to men of letters by a circular accompanied by certificates, and have issued a subscription paper, but I have not any encouragement that one cent will be advanced by all the wealthy citizens of my country. I must therefore drudge on under all the embarrassments which have usually attended like undertakings. It is important that the friends of this species of improvement should be united, and aid each other. We have to oppose us the publishers of most of the popular periodical works in our large towns. The *Gazette of the United States* and *Portfolio* in Philadelphia, the *Evening Post* in New York, the *Anthology* in Boston, are all arrayed against *me* and my *designs*. Perhaps an apology may be found for the publishers in their utter ignorance of the subject, or of my views. The gentle-

men are among those who repose implicit confidence in
Johnson's opinions, never having examined the subject
enough to question their justness. This opposition may
be weakened immediately, and ultimately overthrown ;
but it requires some address, for I believe they are supported by the weight of public opinion—all founded on
that confidence in English authorities before mentioned.
In my favor is President Smith, of Princeton, and the
faculties of most of the Northern colleges—Dr. Mitchell,
Dr. Morse, and so forth. Indeed, the men of education
generally in the country towns, if not favorable, are at
least unprejudiced. The large towns are more thoroughly English in this respect than the country. I hope
my letter to Dr. Ramsay will have some effect in removing the veil of blindness ; but I want some *active friends;*
such I have not hitherto found. Let me suggest the
expediency of consulting men at the head of affairs on
the general topics here mentioned,—and would not a
general view of this subject from the leading public prints
be useful, accompanied perhaps by a candid review of my
books ? The public, especially in the Middle and Southern States, have never had their attention called to the
subject. If you think with me on these subjects I will
thank you for your thoughts and advice ; and, if you
wish, I will send you a copy of such of my books as you
have not.'

                                      N. WEBSTER.

Another phase of the poet's character is shown in a
series of letters written to his nephew and protégé,
Thomas Barlow, the orphan son of his favorite brother,
Col. Aaron Barlow. He placed the lad at school, first,
at Fairfield, Ct., then at Colchester, and, on his being
fitted, entered him at Yale. His letters to the lad, and
to the lad's brother, Stephen Barlow, contain maxims that
might well be heeded by all parents and guardians.

" I am surprised at what you tell me of the progress of
the boy," he writes Stephen Barlow. " Encourage him ;

tell him I rejoice to hear his praise, and that he shall not
want for the means of obtaining a good education if he
will do his best. But though you must not suffer him to
neglect his books, you must see that he does not bend over
them too much. Keep him in habits of bodily exercise
for the preservation of health, which is the first of all objects, and ought to be so considered in every plan of education ; after this, take care of his manners, his mode of
speaking; let his language in conversation be grammatical,
his utterance clear, elegant, and graceful. It is as easy at
his age to form good habits as bad ones, to acquire such
as will be ornamental and useful, as well as those that
must be unlearned with infinite difficulty, or else stay by
him all his days, and make him awkward and forbidding,
painful to himself and disagreeable to his friends."
Again : " Tell him that by next year at this time he must
be master of Homer, so as to explain it well to me ; Homer is my Magnus Apollo, and Thomas must be my little
priest to go between me and the god and expound to me
his oracles." In the fall of 1807 he is at doubt whether
to remove the lad from Fairfield. " You seem to think he
is doing well," he writes, " but one thing must be wanting
to him there—a chance for emulation. I suppose there
are few, if any, boys to class with him. I think I understood there were none pursuing the same studies, or, at
least, so far advanced as he : if so, it is a strong motive
for removing him to Colchester, which, I have understood,
was a good school, and numerous in students farther advanced. . . . We must enjoin it upon your wife to watch
over the boy's manners, dress, and behavior ; to make him
keep clean his hands, face, teeth, and linen. See that
he sits and acts well at table, walks, speaks, moves, and
even thinks with propriety, and approaching to elegance.
The letter for him I leave open for you to read if
you like. It is best to seal before you send them to him,
to teach him method and order." Again : " I don't know
whether his ambition wants winding up now and then

like a clock; if it does, you and your wife must do it. I must insist on his being a superior scholar; and not only that, but a gentleman in his manners, and sentiments, and language."

At last the boy was ready for college, and was furnished by his uncle "with several introductory letters to friends in New Haven." "His letters to Wolcott and Silliman," he adds, "I look upon as most essential. Those men may be of great use to him. Wolcott, I believe, is in the senior class, and a good scholar. Mr. Silliman I treated with particular politeness in London, for which he was thankful at the time, and I am sure he has not forgot it. He is an amiable man, and an able chemist." The President he does not like; "but it is not best," he adds, "to give Tom any unfavorable ideas of him. It may be best that he should respect him, for on some accounts he is doubtless respectable. . . . You must have a watchful eye upon Thomas at New Haven. Though the advantages there are greater than at minor schools, yet the temptations to idleness and extravagance are greater also. But few have the courage to resist these temptations. One of the best preservatives against the vices incident to such situations is a certain *poorness of purse*—not absolute poverty, but bordering upon it. It will not be difficult to guage him properly in this respect, then keep up his ambition. Let him never forget that he has got nothing but his own merit to depend upon—which is, and must be, the fact."

Several letters which passed between uncle and ward have also been preserved. The boy's related largely to the subjects of the studies he was pursuing. Barlow's in reply were models of elegance and force, directing, criticising, commending the lad's efforts. In a letter commending a dissertation on the life of Cicero which the latter had written occurs this characteristic passage: " Middleton is a very judicious writer and has employed his talents on a most important subject. Perhaps no great man has had his life so well written as Cicero, and very few have so well deserved it. Middleton's only fault, if it is a fault, is a little partiality to the moral qualities of his hero. But Cicero, as a friend of liberty, and a strenuous advocate of public justice, is such a favorite with me, that I scarcely think of his vanity, or any other of his weaknesses. They are the weaknesses of human nature in its very noblest specimen. Had I written his life I should have been more partial to him than Middleton has been, that is, I should have been more enthusiastic in his praise—but it would have been a fault."

CHAPTER IX.

1811–1813.

IN the year 1811 American relations with both France and England were of the gravest character. The two powers, engaged in the life-and-death struggle, were seizing and destroying everything that came in their way. There was scarcely a right of neutrals they had not outraged. England had opened the attack by issuing her " Orders in Council," declaring all French ports and rivers from the Elbe in Germany to Brest in France in a state of blockade, and Bonaparte had retaliated by his famous " Berlin Decree," declaring the British Islands blockaded, and that all intercourse with them by neutral vessels must cease—a decree, it may be said, directly contrary to the terms of the treaty then existing between the United States and France.

Seizure of American vessels in the English trade by French cruisers soon followed, and at the same time vigorous restrictions were placed on American commerce in French ports.

American products were heavily taxed. American vessels were compelled to receive for return cargoes certain specified goods, chiefly silks: they were subject to tedious investigations in unusual forms, and, when seized, their release could be obtained, if at all, only after great expense and delay. The repeated protests of the American minister against these enormities were disregarded. It seemed that to protect her commerce the young nation must take up the gage thrown down by the conqueror of Europe. Yet it was resolved by Madison and his advisers to make one last attempt at negotiation: it was also clearly seen that the success of the mission must depend largely on the ambassador entrusted with it. Napoleon was France: he, therefore, was the person to be acted upon. He was known to be crafty, imperious, dictatorial, changeable, but approachable by flattery, by his desire of being thought a patron of Poetry and the Arts, and by former service—for instance, by a man who had once addressed the National Convention, and who had been made a French citizen for his services in expelling the Bourbons. Instinctively the eyes of Madison and his Cabinet turned on Joel Barlow as the man most available for this mission. It was much easier to fix upon him, however, than to induce him to accept. He had reached the age when travel becomes a burden, and he knew too well the difficulties and vexations which would attend the mission; besides, he was deeply engrossed in literary pursuits. His History of the United States, under Jefferson's watchful care and encouragement, was fast assuming form, while another literary project of importance—the publication of his works in a series—had not even assumed shape. Yet at the demand of his country he consented to forego all and accept the mission. His selection seems to have been applauded by the respectable men of all parties, although Barlow at the outset had a disagreeable feeling that he would not have the hearty support of all his countrymen in his mission.*

---

* We adduce the following letter from that staunch Federalist, Judge Henry Baldwin, of the Supreme Court: "You have been much vilified in the Federal papers, but it is not the opinion of the party that you ought not to be the Minister to France. On the contrary, such men as Ross, and others of the most influential Federalists, do not hesitate to give their decided opinion that you are the fittest man that could be sent. Those only abuse you who would abuse everybody appointed by Mr. Madison, and everything he does. The opinion of such a man as Ross is of more weight than that of fifty printers, and is more clearly indicative of the real sentiments of the party. The country in general approves of your appointment, and there never could be a finer opportunity presented of giving yourself a solid and permanent standing. For as nothing could be effected by Armstrong (the retiring minister), and as little is to be expected from the faith of the French Government, every amelioration in our situation with France will

Kalorama was in a sad state of confusion during the months of May and June, 1811. The estate was leased, not sold, for the poet hoped, though he had forebodings, to return and finish his days there. A package was made of his published works and sent to Fulton, with the request that he would publish them in order, and do justice to his friend's memory in the event of that friend's not returning. Thomas Barlow was called from his class in Yale College to accompany his uncle to France, and there complete his studies. Miss Clara Baldwin, Mrs. Barlow's half-sister, the poet's especial favorite, who had been for some years a member of the family at Kalorama, was also invited to accompany them.

Early in July the arrangements had been perfected, and the ambassador only awaited his papers and instructions from the State Department before beginning his journey. On the 26th of July they were received—a commission and letter of credence, a letter of instructions, and other documents necessary to further the object of his mission. Mr. Monroe's letter of instructions very fully informed the ambassador what he was expected to accomplish. "The United States have claims on France," it said, "which it is expected her Government will satisfy to their full extent, and without delay. These are founded partly on the late arrangement, by which the non-importation law of the 1st May, 1810, was carried into effect against Great Britain, and partly on the injuries to their commerce committed on the high seas, and in French ports. To form a just estimate of the claims of the first class it is necessary to examine mi-

---

be attributed to your personal influence and exertion. Be assured that the rant of the papers on either side is not the voice of the country. I have touched on this subject lest you might think that because the great leading presses publish every calumny against you, and the little silly copyists repeat it, that one half of the country is in array against you. You go on your mission with as much of the public confidence as any other man could possess in these times, and with a great prospect of securing additional fame."

nutely their nature and extent. The present is a proper time to make this examination, and to press a compliance with the arrangement in every circumstance, on its just principles, on the Government of France. The President, conscious that the United States have performed every act that was stipulated on their part with the most perfect good faith, expects a like performance on the part of France. He considers it peculiarly incumbent on him to request such explanations from her Government as will dissipate all doubt of what he may expect from it in future on this and every other question depending between the two nations. By the act of May 1, 1810, it was declared that in case Great Britain or France should, before the 3d day of March, 1811, so revoke or modify her edicts as that they should cease to violate the neutral commerce of the United States, which fact the President should declare by proclamation; and if the other nation should not, within three months thereafter, revoke or modify its edicts in like manner, then the 3d, 4th, 6th, 7th, 8th, 9th, 10th, and 18th sections of the act entitled, 'An act to interdict the commercial intercourse between the United States and Great Britain and France,' should, from and after the expiration of three months from the date of the proclamation aforesaid, be revived and have full force and effect, so far as relates to the dominions, colonies, and dependencies of the nation thus refusing or neglecting to revoke or modify its edicts in the manner aforesaid. This act, having been promulgated and made known to the Governments of Great Britain and France, the minister of the latter, by note bearing date on the 5th August, 1810, addressed to the Minister Plenipotentiary of the United States at Paris, declared that the decrees of Berlin and Milan were revoked, the revocation to take effect on the 1st day of November following, but that this measure was in compliance with the law of 1st May, 1810, to take advantage of the condition contained in it, and in full confidence that that condition would be enforced against Great Britain if she did not revoke her Orders in Council, and renounce the new principles of blockade. This declaration of the Emperor of France was considered a sufficient ground for the President to act on. It was explicit as to its object, and equally so as to its import. The decrees of Berlin and Milan, which had violated our neutral rights, were said to be repealed, to take effect at a subsequent day, at no distant period ; the interval was apparently intended to allow full time for the communication of the measure to this Government. The declaration had, too, all the formality which such an act could admit of, being through the official organ on both sides—from the French Minister of Foreign Affairs to the Minister Plenipotentiary of the United States at Paris. In consequence of this note from the French Minister of Foreign Affairs of the 5th August, 1810, the President proceeded on the 2d November following, to issue the proclamation enjoined by the act of May 1st of the same year, to declare that all the restrictions imposed by it should cease, and be discontinued in relation to France and her dependencies. And in confirmation of the proclamation of the President, Congress did, on the 2d March, 1811, pass an act whereby the non-importation system provided for by the 3d, 4th, 5th, 6th, 7th, 8th, 9th, 10th, and 18th sections of the act entitled, 'An act to interdict the commercial intercourse between the United States and Great Britain and France, and their dependencies,' was declared to be in force against Great Britain, her colonies, and dependencies, with a provision in favor of such vessels or merchandises as might be seized before it was known that Great Britain had revoked or modified her edicts within the time and in the manner required by the said act, if such should be the case ; and with a provision also in favor of any ships or cargoes owned wholly by citizens of the United States, which had cleared out for the

Cape of Good Hope, or for any other port beyond the same, prior to the 2d day of November, 1810. Both of these provisions were, in strict justice and good faith, due to the parties to be affected by the law. They were also conformable to the spirit of the arrangement to execute which the law was passed. As Great Britain did not revoke or modify her edicts in the manner proposed the first provision had no effect.

"I will now inquire whether France has performed her part of this arrangement.

"It is understood that the blockade of the British Isles is revoked. The revocation having been officially declared, and no vessel trading to them having been condemned or taken on the high seas that we know of, it is fair to conclude that the measure is relinquished. It appears that no American vessel has been condemned in France for having been visited at sea by an English ship, or for having been searched or carried into England, or subjected to impositions there. On the sea, therefore, France is understood to have changed her system. Although such is the light in which the conduct of France is viewed in regard to the neutral commerce of the United States since the 1st of November last, it will, nevertheless, be proper for you to investigate fully the whole subject, and to see that nothing has been, or shall be, omitted on her part, in future, which the United States have a right to claim.

"Your early and particular attention will be drawn to the great subject of the commercial relation which is to subsist in future between the United States and France. The President expects that the commerce of the United States will be placed in the ports of France on such a footing as to afford to it a fair market, and to the industry and enterprise of their people a reasonable encouragement. An arrangement to this effect was looked for immediately after the revocation of the decrees, but it appears from the papers in this department that that was not the case; on the contrary, that our commerce has been subjected to the greatest discouragement, or rather to the most oppressive restraints; that the vessels which carried coffee, sugar, etc., though sailing directly from the United States to a French port, were held in a state of sequestration, on the principle that the trade was prohibited, and that the importation of those articles was not only unlawful, but criminal; that even the vessels which carried the unquestionable productions of the United States were exposed to great and expensive delays, to tedious investigations in unusual forms, and to exorbitant duties; in short, that the ordinary usages of commerce between friendly nations were abandoned. When it was announced that the decrees of Berlin and Milan were revoked, the revocation to take effect on the 1st November last, it was natural for our merchants to rush into the ports of France, to take advantage of a market to which they thought they were invited. All these restraints, therefore, have been unjust in regard to the parties who suffered by them; nor can they be reconciled to the respect which was due this Government. If France had wished to exclude the American commerce from her ports she ought to have declared it to this Government in explicit terms; in which case due notice would have been given of it to the American merchants, who would either have avoided her ports or gone there at their own hazard. But to suffer them to enter her ports under such circumstances, and to detain them there under any pretext whatever, cannot be justified. It is not known to what extent the injuries resulting from these delays have been carried. It is evident, however, that for every injury thus sustained the parties are entitled to reparation. If the ports of France and her allies are not opened to the commerce of the United States on a liberal scale, and on fair conditions, of what avail to them, it may be asked, will be the revocation of the British Orders in Council. In contending for the revocation of those Orders, so far as it was an object of interest, the United States had in view a trade with the continent. It was a fair and legitimate object, and worth contending for, while France encouraged it. But if she shuts her ports on our commerce, or burdens it with heavy duties, that motive is at an end.

"That France has a right to impose such restraints is admitted ; but she ought to be aware of the consequences to which they necessarily lead. The least that ought to be expected to follow would be such countervailing restrictions on the French commerce as must destroy the value of the intercourse between the two countries, and leave to the United States no motive of interest to maintain their right to that intercourse by a sacrifice of any other branch of their commerce. Adequate motives to such a sacrifice could only be found in considerations distinct from any reasonable pretensions on the part of France. To the admission of every article, the product of the United States, no objection is anticipated, nor does there appear to be just cause for any to the admission of colonial produce. A supply of that produce will be annually wanted in France, and other countries connected with her, and the United States alone can furnish her during the war. It will doubtless be to the interest of France and her allies to avail herself of the industry and capital of the American merchants, in furnishing those articles by which the wants of her people will be supplied, and their revenue increased. Several of the colonies belonged to France and may again belong to her. Great Britain, by securing to her own colonies the monopoly of the home market, lessens the value of the produce of the conquered colonies. France cannot be indifferent to the distresses of her late colonies, nor ought she to abandon, because she cannot protect them. In pressing this important object on the Government of France, it will not escape your attention

that several important articles in the list of colonial productions are raised in Louisiana, and will, of course, be
comprised among those of the United States.

" You will see the injustice, and endeavor to prevent the
necessity of bringing in return for American cargoes sold
in France an equal amount in the produce or manufactures of that country. No such obligation is imposed
on French merchants trading to the United States.
They enjoy the liberty of selling their cargoes for cash,
and taking back what they please from this country in
return, and the right ought to be reciprocal. It is indispensable that the trade *be free;* that all American
citizens engaged in it be placed on the same footing:
and with this view, that the system of carrying it on
by licenses granted by French agents, be immediately
annulled. You must make it distinctly understood by
the French Government, that the United States cannot
submit to that system, as it tends to sacrifice one part of
the community to another, and to give a corrupt influence to the agents of a foreign power in our towns,
which is, in every view, incompatible with the principles
of our Government. It was presumed that this system
had been abandoned some time since, as a letter from
the Duke of Cadore, of ——, to Mr. Russell gave assurance
of it. Should it, however, be still maintained, you will
not fail to bring the subject without delay before the
French Government, and to urge its immediate abandon-
ment. The President having long since expressed his
strongest disapprobation of it, and requested that the
consuls would discontinue it, it is probable, if they still
disregard his injunction, that he may find it necessary to
revoke their exequators. I mention this that you may
be able to explain the motive to such a measure should
it take place, which, without such explanation, might
probably be viewed in a mistaken light by the French
Government.

" It is important that the rate of duties imposed on our

commerce, in every article, should be made as low as possible. If they are not, they may produce the effect of a
prohibition. They will be sure to depress the article,
and discourage the trade.

"You will be able to ascertain the various other claims
which the United States have on France for injuries done
to their citizens under decrees of a subsequent date to
those of Berlin and Milan, and you will likewise use
your best exertions to obtain an indemnity for them.
It is presumed that the French Government will be
disposed to do justice for all these injuries.

"In looking to the future, the past ought to be fairly
and honorably adjusted. If that is not done, much dissatisfaction will remain here, which cannot fail to produce a very unfavorable effect on the relations which are
to subsist in future between the two countries. The
first of these latter decrees bears date at Bayonne, on the
17th of March, 1808, by which many American vessels
and their cargoes were seized and carried into France ;
and others, which had entered her ports in the fair course
of trade, were seized and sequestered or confiscated by
her Government.

"It was pretended, in vindication of this measure, that
as, under our embargo law, no American vessel could nav-
igate the ocean, all those who were found on it were
trading on British account, and therefore lawful prizes.
The fact, however, was otherwise. At the time the
embargo was laid a great number of our vessels were at
sea, engaged in their usual commerce, many of them on
distant voyages. Their absence, especially as no previous notice could be given them, was strictly justifiable
under the law; and as no obligation was imposed on
them by the law to return, they committed no offence by
remaining abroad. Other vessels, inconsiderable in number, left the United States in violation of law ; the latter
committed an offence against their country, but none
against foreign powers. They were not *disfranchised*

by the act. They were entitled to the protection of their Government, and it had a right to inflict on them the penalty which their conduct had exposed them to. The Government of France could withdraw them from neither of these claims. The absence of none of these vessels was a proof that they were trading on British account. The cargoes which they carried with them, the value of which was much enhanced by the embargo, were alone an ample capital to trade on. As the pretext under which these vessels were taken is no justification of the act, you will claim an indemnity to our citizens for every species of injury arising from it.

" The Rambouillet Decree was a still more unjustifiable aggression on the rights of the United States and invasion of the property of their citizens. It bears date on the 23d March, 1810, and made a sweep of all American property within the reach of French power. It was also retrospective, extending back to the 20th May, 1809. By this decree every American vessel and cargo, even those which had been delivered up to the owners, by compromise with the captors, were seized and sold.

" The law of March 1, 1809, commonly called the non-intercourse law, was the pretext for this measure, which was intended as an act of reprisal.

" It requires no reasoning to show the injustice of this pretension. Our law regulated the trade of the United States with other powers, particularly with, France and Great Britain, and was such a law as every nation has a right to adopt. It was duly promulgated, and reasonable notice given of it to other powers. It was also impartial as related to the belligerents. The condemnation of such vessels of France and England as came into the ports of the United States in breach of this law was strictly proper, and could afford no cause of complaint to either power. The seizure of so vast a property as was laid hold of, under that pretext, by the French Government places the transaction in a very fair light. If an indemnity had been sought for an imputed injury, the measure of the injury should have been ascertained, and the indemnity proportioned to it. But, in this case, no injury had been sustained on principle. A trifling loss only had been incurred, and for that loss all the American property which could be found was seized, involving in indiscriminate ruin innocent merchants who had entered the ports of France in the fair course of trade. It is proper that you should make it distinctly known to the French Government that the claim to a just reparation for these spoliations cannot be relinquished, and that a delay in making it will produce very high dissatisfaction with the Government and people of the United States.

" It has been intimated that the French Government would be willing to make this reparation, provided the United States would make one in return for the vessels and property condemned under, and in breach of, our nonintercourse law. Although the proposition was objectionable in many views, yet this Government consented to it, to save so great a mass of the property of our citizens. An instruction for this purpose was given to your predecessor, which you are authorized to carry into effect. The influence of France has been exerted to the injury of the United States in all the countries to which her power has extended. In Spain, Holland, and Naples it has been sensibly felt. In each of these countries the vessels and cargoes of American merchants were seized and confiscated under various decrees, founded on different pretexts, none of which had even the semblance of right to protect them. As the United States never injured France, that plea must fail; and that they had injured either of those powers was not pretended., You will be furnished with the documents which relate to these aggressions, and you will claim of the French Government an indemnity for them. The United States have also just cause of complaint against France for many injuries that were committed by persons acting under her authority. Of these, the most distinguished and least justifiable are the examples which have occurred of burning the vessels of our citizens at sea. Their atrocity forbids the imputation of them to the Government. To it, however, the United States must look for reparation, which you will accordingly claim. It is possible that in this enumeration I may have omitted many injuries of which no account has yet been transmitted to this department. You will have it in your power to acquire a more comprehensive knowledge of them at Paris, which it is expected you will do, and full confidence is reposed in your exertions to obtain of the French Government the just measure of redress. France, it is presumed, has changed her policy towards the United States. The revocation of her decrees is an indication of that change, and some recent acts more favorable to the commercial intercourse with her ports, the evidence of which will be found in the copy of a letter from her minister here of —— strengthens the presumption. But much is yet to be done by her to satisfy the just claims of this country. To revoke blockades of boundless extent, in the present state of her marine, was making no sacrifice. She must indemnify us for past injuries, and open her ports to our commerce on a fair and liberal scale. If she wishes the profit of neutral commerce she must become the advocate of neutral rights, as well by her practice as her theory. The United States, standing on their own ground, will be able to support those rights with effect ; and they will certainly fail in nothing which they owe to their character or interest. The papers relative to the *Impètueux*, the *Revanch de Cerf*, and the French privateer seized at New Orleans will be delivered to you. They will, it is presumed, enable you to satisfy the French Government of the strict propriety of the conduct of the United States in all those occurrences."

Such were the vexed questions which the ambassador was expected to settle agreeably to the best interests of both countries. The historic frigate Constitution, commanded by Captain Hull, had been ordered to Annapolis to transport him to France, and thither he repaired with his party on the 1st of August. Many friends had assembled to bid them God speed, and when the last good-byes were said the gallant vessel spread her sails, and gay with bunting, and responding heartily to the salutes of the forts on shore, swept down the bay. To know the poet's reflections on beginning this his second exile would be interesting, and fortunately we have them in a letter to Fulton, dated Hampton Roads, Aug. 2, 1811. " Here we are," he wrote, " 24 hours from Annapolis— a most delightful passage down the Chesapeake. We are just coming to anchor to give Captain Hull time to receive 100 men from the Essex, lying at Norfolk. I shall go on shore and stay the night. My wife is in excellent spirits, the captain and all the officers very amiable, the most perfect harmony, discipline, cleanliness, and comfort prevails. Never was a fairer prospect of a good passage ; but my heart is heavy. I have left my country, possibly—and why not probably ?—forever. But if such should be the result it will not be my fault; that is, the fault of my inclination or wishes. I go with an ardent wish, but without much hope, of doing good, and with the full intention, though with a feeble hope, of living to return."

The Constitution reached Cherbourg on the 8th of September, whence the ambassador proceeded directly to Paris. He arrived at a most inauspicious moment for a hearing. Napoleon, foiled by Russia in his designs on the German principalities, was making ready for his invasion of that powerful country. Maps, plans, military reports, the organization of an army of a million of men, and the intrigues of a score of courts, occupied his attention, to the exclusion of the affairs of the little republic three thousand miles away. The business, which might have been concluded in a few days, occupied months and years. Barlow's correspondence with the French Emperor and his ministers during this period would fill a volume; it shows him making desperate efforts to hold them to something definite, and they in turn making the smoothest promises, but never reaching the decisive point—which was the signing of a treaty practically conceding all that the United States asked. Many things he accomplished, such as the release of American vessels unjustly seized and held, and the abrogation of many of the restrictions on American commerce; but the Emperor seemed to have a strange reluctance to signing the treaty, although assenting individually to its conditions.

It was not until the 11th of October, 1812, that Bassano, the Minister of Foreign Relations, could be made to appoint a definite time and place for the signing of the treaty. On that date he wrote from Wilna—Napoleon then being engaged in his disastrous invasion of Russia —this letter:

"SIR:—I have had the honor to make known to you how much I regretted, in the negotiation commenced between the United States and France, the delays which inevitably attend a correspondence carried on at so great a distance. Your Government has desired to see the epoch of this arrangement draw near. His Majesty is animated by the same dispositions, and willing to assure to the negotiation a result the most prompt, he has thought that it would be expedient to suppress the intermediaries, and to transfer the conference to Wilna. His Majesty has, in consequence, authorized me, sir, to treat directly with you, and if you will come to this town I dare hope that, with the desire which animates us both to conciliate such important interests, we will immediately be enabled to remove all the difficulties which until now have appeared to impede the progress of the negotiation. I have apprised the Duke of Dalberg that his mission was thus terminated, and I have laid before his Majesty the actual state of the negotiation, to the end that when you arrive at Wilna, the different questions being already illustrated, either by your judicious observations, or by the instructions I shall have received, we may, sir, conclude an arrangement so desirable, and so conformable to the mutually amicable views of our two Governments."

Accept, sir, etc.

THE DUKE OF BASSANO.

To this note Mr. Barlow replied:

PARIS, *October* 25, 1812.

" SIR :—In consequence of the letter you did me the honor to write me on the 11th of this month, I accept your invitation, and leave Paris to-morrow for Wilna, where I hope to arrive in fifteen or eighteen days from this date. The negotiation on which you have done me the honor to invite me at Wilna is so completely prepared in all its parts between the Duke of Dalberg and myself, and, as I understand, sent on to you for your approbation about the 18th of the present month, that I am persuaded, if it could have arrived before the date of your letter, the necessity of this meeting would not have existed, as I am confident his Majesty would have found the project reasonable and acceptable in all its parts, and would have ordered that minister to conclude and sign both the treaty of commerce, and the convention of indemnities."

JOEL BARLOW.

A year of anxious, unwearied labor had been spent in bringing the treaty thus far : now in the little Polish town where Napoleon was directing the march of his legions into Russia the most gratifying success seemed awaiting him. He at once began preparations for the journey; but before detailing its hardships and tragic ending, it is proper to return and fill out the bare outlines of the poet's third residence in Paris with a few touches of color. On arriving in the city, after seven years' ab-

sence, they found their old house in the Rue de Vaugirard empty, and at once installed themselves in it. Old
friends were there to welcome them, and their old servants hastened to tender their fealty.

"We have been here about a week," Mr. Barlow wrote
Alexander Wolcott, Sept. 26th, "and the reception we
have had from our old friends is affectionate and affecting. Our ancient servants are pressing around us with
tears of gratitude and attachment, and even the old
coach horses, which we gave to a friend in the country on
condition that they should be kept on his farm as long
as they should live, would certainly try to come back to
us if they were not dead. But they, with some other of
our friends, have died of old age." And again, in November, a letter containing this passage: "We have
moved into our comfortable, airy, handsome, well-situated
house, which is really one of the best in Paris. The garden, planted with my own hand, is doubly interesting
from our absence of seven years, especially as the trees
and shrubs are grown up into thickets. Our old French
friends, too, are very affectionate, and we find more of
them than we expected. How much more cordial and
friendly my reception is here than it was in any part of
our own country (except at your house and one or two
others)." In a letter to Stephen Barlow he introduces
an old acquaintance: "Tom is as happy as a prince. He
is sucking the milk and honey from three colleges, all at
once. He takes chemistry from one, natural philosophy
from another, and astronomy from a third; and I had like
to have forgotten, that at the fourth—that is, where he
lives—he takes his mathematics, his fencing, dancing,
drawing, and French language. All this business is done
at once, while he grows fat under it, and comes to dine
with us every Sunday." The poets, philosophers, and
other men of ideas, also soon found their way back to the
Rue Vaugirard. Helen Marie Williams and her coterie of
literary people were still there to welcome him. Volney,

from his quiet retreat at Saville, often invited him out to dine, and as often visited him in town. Letters from various members of the family show that they mingled much in the gay society of the capital during this period. " Our girls will write you about courts, and fashions, and finery," wrote the poet to Mrs. Madison, soon after his arrival. " My tour of duty is over. I am now initiated in the mysteries." Mrs. Barlow wrote to the same lady, with whom she regularly corresponded while abroad : " Mr. Brooks has given us many little (as well as great) anecdotes respecting Washington and our friends there. We had an account of the French and English ministers' balls, with all the little etcs., the sleighing parties and the general gayety which reigned there." In the same letter she invites Mrs. Washington, Mrs. Madison's sister, to spend the next winter with them in Paris. " I want to send you some pretty things in embroidery which are the high style here," she continues ; " gold and silver with silk done on mull. Mr. Lee has sent you so much of every kind of dress, and it is so difficult to send to the port, and then to get any one to take charge of valuable things, that I shall send nothing." Poor lady ! something far different from visits, dress, and pretty things the coming winter was to bring her. Through the bright days of October the ambassador was employed, as we have seen, in preparing for the journey into the Polish wastes. It was to be performed in his own carriage, and Thomas Barlow was to accompany him as his secretary and travelling companion. " His journey will be long and cold, 650 leagues, half the way through a country of bad roads and almost destitute of everything," wrote Mrs. Barlow to Mrs. Madison a few days after his departure. " He set off, however," she adds, " with great courage and high-raised expectations (which he thought well founded) of succeeding to his wish, and to the satisfaction of our Government." It appears, from letters written by Thomas Barlow, that the course of the travellers

was through the provinces of Champaign, Lorraine, and
the old [principality of Massau to Frankfort-on-the-
Main, where they arrived Oct. 30th. They reached Berlin Nov. 5th, having passed directly over the battle-field
of Jena, where, six years before, Napoleon had put an
end to the power of the Prussian monarchy.

"A monument," the letter writer observes, "is erected
on the spot where the Duke of Brunswick was mortally
wounded." They arrived at Koenigsberg on Nov. 11th,
after "riding all day along the banks of the Baltic."
"Uncle is perfectly well," the secretary adds, "and
though we have rode for the greater part of the time
since we left Paris, day and night, I believe neither of
us are more fatigued than when we first stepped into the
carriage. There has been scarcely a day without rain
since that time, which has made the roads very bad, and
the nights dark and unpleasant. The weather has been
very moderate, and we have had no ice or frost but once
—the night after we left Frankfort. But they tell us
here they have had no frost this season, which is very
remarkable." Mr. Barlow, in a letter to Miss Baldwin
from Koenigsberg, dated Nov. 12th, gives a more pictur-
esque account of the journey. From its importance we
insert it entire : " I know of no good reason why I should
not write you a letter unless I promised to do it, and no
great man ought to keep his word. But I will break
over this rule, because no man can be very great in the
view of his intimate friends, who see his weaknesses. It is
better in his own house to be good than great. If it had
not been for my uncommon health and spirits this would
have been a dreary journey. My patriotism created a
great anxiety to get on fast, and that anxiety gave out a
constant supply of animal spirits, which, when tempered
with a due care of the organic frame of the man, is a
great contributor to his health. Thus you see the love
of country has some substantial benefits—when it con-
tributes to the health and comfort of the individual.

These roads have probably never been so cut up since the wars of Wittikind and Charlemagne,* and you could not make a set of darker nights, or call out of heaven with all your prayers a more unceasing succession of rain. Eight of these nights we have been on the road, four in succession at one time, and three at another. Three other nights we stopped after midnight, and were going again as soon as day broke. The worst of it was, that the universality and great preponderance of the mud prevented me from getting out of the carriage to walk up hill or down hill. Even the inside of the post-houses, where I got myself hoisted in once a day to eat my boiled milk, was often too muddy for my nice, clean, boots, whose habitual position on the long wool of my sheepskin on the floor of the carriage rendered it highly proper that they should be kept clean. Thus my position within my nice, strong, comfortable carriage (not a pin's head of which has started to this day, over these eleven hundred miles of racking, rending, slumping, slouching, rocks and mud) was monotonous but tolerable. Tom was all the while sucking in ideas like a calf; his soul seemed to fatten. I have given him a great many lessons on life and manners, history and politics, science and literature. Among the rest I am teaching him the German language, which he shall have well before he gets back; in return, he has read to me the whole of Robertson's 'Charles the Fifth,' from beginning to end : and from here to Wilna I believe he must read the same book backwards, from end to beginning, for we have little else to read, except the 'Columbiad' and 'Iliad,' and those are too sacred to be mangled and chopped up by unhallowed lips and untuneful tones of voice. I hope Tom has given you and sister some account of the instructive part of our travels, such as tombs, temples,

---

* Napoleon's Russian army of invasion had passed over them a short time before.

and monuments, especially those moving monuments of the wisdom of war—the hundreds of wagon loads of invalid soldiers returning from Russia, covered with glory, rags, and mud." Nov. 20th, Thomas Barlow wrote from Wilna: "We arrived on the 18th, three weeks from Paris. . . . I wrote you from Koenigsberg that we had had no cold weather, but the evening after, the weather suddenly changed, and next morning when we started the ground was frozen hard enough to bear our carriage. The cold continued very severe for several days, and froze over all the rivers; but it is now moderated, and we have had a little snow. The first day after the frost the roads were very rough, but soon became smoother on account of the great number of wagons passing to and from the army, and have now become much better than before the cold weather. . . . Our road, after leaving Koenigsberg, ran along the river Praegel, which we crossed four or five times. We passed through Gambiner, a place where the Emperor stayed a day or two and issued several orders. Soon after leaving this place we came into Poland, that part which belongs to the King of Saxony, and here we begin to perceive a difference in the appearance and manners of the people. They generally live in log huts, and have the appearance of the greatest poverty; but the scarcity of provisions on the way was not as great as we expected, as we found everything necessary to eat and drink. So far, we have always found beds where we have stayed, but they now begin to be unfashionable, so we are obliged to make our beds of straw, when we are so lucky as to find it. We crossed the Niemen on the morning of the 17th at Kowno. We arrived on the bridge in the night, and found the gates shut, so we were obliged to sleep in our carriage on the bridge. This bridge is new, built of wood, and has been finished but two weeks. Kowno is the first town we came to in Russia, or what belonged to Russia before the present war.

It is full of soldiers, and, besides those stationed there, we met a great number of sick and wounded men retreating from the army. After crossing the river, from Kowno to Wilna, the country is everywhere devastated and many of the houses destroyed. The people have the appearance of the greatest poverty and distress, for their log huts are so open as to expose them to the snow and rain. The country is not cultivated, and part is covered with fir trees and pines. The horses are as much to be pitied as the people, for their appearance is much worse, and we saw hundreds lying dead in the roads. As we approached Wilna we saw the road, sometimes a mile in length, crowded with wagons loaded with clothing and provisions for the army. As we came near the entrance to the town the crowd became still greater, and after entering the gate, the streets were so crowded with wagons loaded with baggage, together with sick and wounded soldiers, that we were an hour or two getting to the place where we lodge. . . . Wilna contains about 37,000 inhabitants, and some parts are well built, but it is scarcely possible to get the conveniences of life. The Emperor is expected here in a few days, and it is probable that this will be the headquarters during the winter."

On the 22d he writes again: " The Poles appear to be a very gay and lively people, but have no idea how to live, nor are the log huts they live in much better than those of our Western savages. They generally wear their hair and beard long, dress in sheepskins, and have a kind of fur cap which is difficult to describe. . . . . Kowno is a considerable town, but the inhabitants appear very poor and miserable, and together with the sick and wounded soldiers, with which the town is filled, present a wretched sight. This, however, was but the beginning of the scene, for after this we saw such sights of misery and distress that even the description of it would sicken you. The country is everywhere devastated, many of the houses burned, others half unroofed, and the miserable inhabitants left exposed to the snow and rain : but this was nothing when we looked at the scenes the sick, dying, and dead soldiers presented on the way. Every few rods we found dead horses in the road, and some just dropped down and dying. To see poor soldiers, half naked, crawling into houses, and asking for a shelter to die under, that they may not be left in the street, is a shocking sight, but is what happens every day on the road, and, I am told, even in this town. I never knew what misery and distress was before. . . . You know, I suppose, that the Emperor has evacuated Moscow, and is on his way to Wilna. The Russians have an army on each side of him, and are trying to cut off his retreat, though it is thought he will drive them back; but at present all communication between him and this place is cut off."

Nov. 29th he continues the narrative : "We are in a hotel which has been reserved for foreign ministers, and where several are lodged. The Danish minister, who is a very pleasant man, is on the same floor with us, and we eat at the same table. Wilna is a much larger and finer town than I expected. The houses are mostly built of stone, and some of the churches are very fine. The town is situated in a valley, and just out of the gates, in the faubourgs, runs the Wilia, a small, rapid river, which furnishes excellent fish. The hills on every side are very high, and some are crowned, the ruins of old towers or fortifications presenting a scene truly romantic. From the tops of some of these hills are the finest prospects I ever saw, presenting a view of the whole city and all the neighboring country. . . . Yesterday a courier arrived here from the Emperor, which is the first that has passed for about two weeks. We have news that he has had a skirmish with the Russians, and drove them back a little; but we have not the particulars, though it is supposed that he has opened his way so that he may arrive here in the course of the week. The town is already filled with troops, so I cannot see what they will do for lodging when the headquarters are established. The crowd is now so great that I can scarcely walk through the streets without being run over, but it must be much greater in a few days. This is said to be the most destructive war known in modern times, and I could give you some accounts which would confirm this. It is not very cold here, but everything is covered with snow, and looks like a Connecticut winter. The roads, I believe, are now very good, and I hope that before they become bad again we shall be ready to return."

Six days longer the ambassador lingered, hoping that his restless, uncertain antagonist might retreat on Wilna and make that his depot for the winter, in which case there would be a chance of saving the treaty. But on the 4th of December a weary, half-frozen courier dashed into the town with despatches for Bassano. Napoleon was at length heard from. The bloody battle of Beresina had been fought, the French defeated, the army not in retreat but in disgraceful flight, and the Emperor riding post-haste for France. He had retired from the battle-field in a square battalion, which defended him from the attacks of the Cossacks, who dashed upon it repeatedly, crying out, " King of France, surrender yourself." Getting out of the immediate vortex he had cowardly abandoned his army, and now, in a close carriage on sleigh runners, and under an assumed name, was hastening on to Paris. The courier bore an order to the Duke to meet him for consultation two leagues to the eastward of Wilna. Manifestly the treaty was lost: furthermore, it was a matter of the gravest importance to leave the town before the flying army with its savage pursuers should reach it, and involve all in their ruin. Preparations were therefore made for immediate departure ; but for details of the retreat we must again have recourse to our young chronicler.   Under date of December 13th, 1812, he writes his aunt: "The distance on the road that we were obliged to take is about 380 miles. . . . . The Emperor arrived at Wilna on the 6th, the day after we left.   He is now on his way to Paris, where, I suppose, he will arrive before this letter, as he travels night and day without guards.   He passed us on the road, and stayed at Warsaw but four hours.   It is well we stayed no longer at Wilna, for the report is that the Russians are already there, and the road between here and that place is no longer safe.   The second night after we left Wilna was the coldest I ever knew, and we rode all night without getting out of the carriage; Fahrenheit's thermometer stood at 13° or 14° below zero, or 45 or 46 below freezing point.   I never felt air that stung like this: it continued so for two days, but it is now more moderate.   The roads are now very good, as they are covered with snow and worn smooth.   We crossed the Niemen, this time at Grodno, about 150 miles this side of Wilna, and as the bridge had been broken down we were obliged to cross on the ice."

He continues, on the 17th, in a letter to Miss Clara: "I suppose you already know that we have arrived at Warsaw, and I can now tell you when we shall leave it for Paris: that will be to-morrow morning at 4 o'clock. We shall go by the way of Cracow, Vienna, and Munich. It is a little farther than the northern route by Dresden, but the roads are much better, and the country more interesting, if, indeed, there is anything interesting in a temperature of 12° or 14° below zero, the points that my thermometer has marked for many days.   I think we shall risk losing our noses if we put them out of the carriage to look at the country as we pass.   M. Petry, who is now here, will accompany us. . . . But instead of telling you what we are going to see I had better tell you what we have seen. . . . I have found by experience that it is best, when travelling in Poland, to have a light carriage, for their post-horses, particularly in Lithuania, are not much larger than rats, so it requires a consider-able number of them to draw a carriage. To verify this I will tell you what happened to us and the Danish min-ister the day we left Wilna. We were to start together at 9 o'clock in the morning, and ordered horses for that hour, eight for his carriage and six for ours, as his was the heaviest. The Danish minister started, and in a few minutes we tried to follow him, but our six horses could not draw us out of the town : they fell down in the streets, and our postilion ran off. We were till 3 o'clock in the streets of Wilna before we could procure horses strong enough to draw the carriage. At length the gov-ernor of the town ordered 6 good horses for us from the artillery, and then we went on very well. At 5 o'clock, about 10 miles from Wilna, we found the Danish min-ister at the foot of a small hill, with 13 horses to his car-riage, and could get no farther. We lent him 3 more, which made 16. He then managed to get up the hill, and as there was no more rising ground before com-ing to the next post he got along very well. . . . Prince Poniotowski is now here, wounded. He first commanded 74,000 men, the whole of the Polish army, of which it is said about 1000 are alive. We see many colonels return without a man of their regiments left. The late battles near the Beresina have been very bloody: nothing to equal them in modern wars. They have lost nearly all of their horses, and most of them have been eaten by the army. The soldiers were very glad to find dead horses, those which had perhaps starved to death, that they might eat them. The officers fared no better. I heard an officer say that he had seen soldiers cut pieces out of live horses to eat, and without killing them."

On the 18th of December the party left Warsaw in their close carriage. It consisted of Mr. Barlow, Thomas, the secretary, and M. Petry, an official of the French Government, and an old friend of the former in Paris.

The weather continued as cold, the privations of the journey quite as severe. The buoyant hope and " patriotism " which had borne the ambassador up on his outward journey had given place to the bitterness of defeat : before the first stage of the journey was past it became evident to his companions that he was seriously ill. At Zarnowiec,* a little village on the farther side of Cracow, his disorder had so far developed that it was found necessary to stop there and call in medical assistance : but it was too late ; the disease rapidly developed into acute inflammation of the lungs, and in five days resulted in his death. He died December 24, 1812. Very full and affecting particulars of the event are given in the following letter, written from Paris by Miss Clara Baldwin to Mrs. President Madison, on behalf of her sister.

PARIS, 16*th February*, 1813.

" Death has entered our happy family and torn from it its head, its support, its all, and left us a prey to sorrow and unavailing regret. My poor sister is overwhelmed with anguish, and the melancholy task of writing to those friends who best knew and loved the dear departed devolves on me; and after our family, you, our much esteemed friend, will most sensibly feel this cruel bereavement. The death of Mr. Barlow is attended with almost every circumstance of aggravation which can be combined. He undertook the journey to Wilna with a reluctance he could not conquer; before he yielded he was assailed by all the great men here with every argument likely to shake his firmness ; and convinced at last that his duty to his country required it, and that his Government would blame him if he did not go, he could say no more. Patriotism alone could have induced him to have undertaken at that season such a long, fatiguing journey, over the worst roads ever travelled, into those

---

* The name is variously spelled. The above is that given by Thomas Barlow in his letter.

frozen, inhospitable regions devastated by war, where the common necessaries of life were difficult to procure, and a little clean straw for a bed, without any covering, a luxury every traveller was not so fortunate as to procure. All hardships, inconveniences, and deprivations he disregarded and travelled with astonishing rapidity, never stopping night or day unless storms and darkness rendered it dangerous to proceed. The unexpected, unfortunate turn of affairs in the north rendered his journey as useless to his country as it was fatal to himself · and at the very moment, too, when complete success seemed ready to crown his labors.

"His sufferings after he left Wilna, from the intense cold, vast quantity of snow, and for want even of a hovel to shelter under at night, obliged to travel constantly and eat during that time frozen bread and drink frozen wine,—the limits of a letter will not allow me to describe, and few constitutions, however robust, could bear with impunity. Illness compelled him to stop at Zarnowitch, near Cracow, in Poland, and here, for the first time from his leaving Warsaw, he found a good house, good bed, a kind, attentive family, and every comfort which his situation demanded, for want of which he had been obliged to travel when he was unable: but it was too late; the disorder proved an inflammation on the lungs, which had been long time seated, and after a few days' suffering terminated his useful life. It was the wish and intention of Thomas Barlow, who was with him, to have had the body embalmed and transported to America by Dantzic, or to bring it away with him; but fate seemed to have decreed otherwise. The Cossacks were in possession of the neighboring country, which they were ravaging with fire and sword, sparing neither age, sex, nor condition, and every moment he expected them, so that his life would have been the sacrifice of his remaining any longer, and the mountains of snow rendered it impossible to bring away the body with him, as it was with the utmost danger and difficulty that he and his servant escaped.

"This circumstance adds double poignancy to our anguish, especially to my poor sister's : it harrows up her soul to think his precious remains lie buried in such a distant, savage land, and that in a few months there will be an impassable distance between her and them. It would be a melancholy consolation to her if they were deposited at Kalorama, or indeed in any part of the country he loved so well, and in whose service he expired. I hope his countrymen will do justice to his worth and his virtues, and that his memory will live forever. There probably never was a death which created such an universal sensation, or one more lamented by all classes of society, than Mr. Barlow's. He may justly be considered as another of (Napoleon's) victims. From the consciousness of this, and the desire of the Government to conceal as much and as long as possible the disasters of this fatal campaign, which has filled every family with mourning and desolation, or from some political motive with regard to England (which seems most probable), may be imputed the extraordinary circumstance of Mr. B.'s death not having been mentioned in any of the papers here ; hence it is hardly known out of Paris, and even many in it to whom notices have been sent, doubt it.

"The Americans all wear mourning, with the exception of W——, and have sent an address to my sister, signed by every one but him."

News of the death of her minister did not reach the United States until the succeeding March. The *Connecticut Courant* (Hartford) announced the sad news in its issue for March 9, 1813, as follows : "The schooner Thetis has arrived at Philadelphia. Captain Bolton has despatches for Government, announcing the death of Mr. Barlow, our minister at the court of France. He died on the road between Dresden and Paris of a fever brought on by the fatigues of his journey to and from Wilna."

Mr. Madison, in his second inaugural, thus referred to the deceased minister: " The sudden death of the distinguished citizen who represented the United States in France, without any special arrangements by him for such a conclusion, has kept us without the expected sequel to his last communications: nor has the French Government taken any measures for bringing the depending negotiations to a conclusion through its representative in the United States."

The Republican journals received the news of his death with every expression of regret, and published formal eulogiums on his life and character ; the Federalists merely announced the fact of his death. In France, the poet's demise excited, perhaps, a more general feeling of regret than in his own country.

On the receipt of the news in Paris, the Americans resident there called a public meeting, at which resolutions of sorrow at the untimely decease of the statesman, as well as formal eulogiums on his talents and worth, were passed. A letter of condolence was also voted and sent to Mrs. Barlow, who all through the terrible journey had been waiting and suffering in Paris, and was now bearing as best she might the bitter sorrows of widowhood. The letter of condolence is rather a tame affair, but that of Mrs. Barlow in reply, for brevity, simplicity, and a mournful eloquence, has rarely been excelled. This is the letter :

" GENTLEMEN :—With sentiments of grateful acknowledgment I receive the assurances of esteem and regard which my resident countrymen in Paris bore my dear departed husband. He left his peaceful retreat with no other motive than a desire to be useful to his country. To that ardent desire he sacrificed his life, and devoted me to unceasing sorrow. Yet it will be most soothing to my afflicted heart to know that my countrymen do him justice, and will permit his memory to live in their remembrance. RUTH BARLOW."

His death was referred to in terms of sorrow and regret by the leading French journals, and at the annual
meeting of the Society for the Encouragement of National
Industry, with which Barlow had been identified, held
in the succeeding March, the Duke de Nemours delivered a glowing eulogium on his life and character, which
was reported in full in the Paris *Mercury* for the 18th
of April, 1813. The same year Oelsners published at
Paris a sketch of his life and writings in quarto form, accompanied by one canto of the " Columbiad," translated
into French heroic verse. If the reader is curious to
know what action the American republic took toward
perpetuating the memory of her martyred servant the
answer is—Nothing: she accepted his services, but left his
bones to moulder, unmarked, on the bleak Polish wastes
where he fell. Wifely love, however, supplied the omission and erected a monument above his grave, to which
a French savant contributed an elegant Latin epitaph,
and which his friend, Helen Marie Williams, dedicated
in these lines—

> " When o'er the Polish desert's trackless way
> Relentless Winter rules with savage sway,
> When the shrill polar storms, as wild they blow,
> Seem to repeat some plaint of mortal woe,
> Far in the cheerless space the traveller's eye
> Shall this recording pillar long descry,
> And give the sod a tear where Barlow lies—
> He who was simply great and nobly wise.
> Here, led by patriot zeal, he met his doom,
> And found amid the frozen wastes a tomb.
> Far from his native soil the poet fell,
> Far from that western world he sang so well,
> Nor she, so long beloved, nor she was nigh
> To catch the dying look, the parting sigh ;
> She who, the hopeless anguish to beguile,
> In fond memorial rears this funeral pile,
> Whose widowed bosom on Columbia's shore
> Shall mourn the moments that return no more,
> While bending o'er the wide Atlantic wave
> Sad fancy hovers on the distant grave."

Late in the autumn of 1813 Mrs. Barlow and her sister, accompanied by Thomas Barlow and the young French lady he had married, returned to America, and took up their residence at Kalorama. Here, in quiet and seclusion, the bereaved lady spent the remaining years of her eventful life, and died in 1818, greatly revered for her amiable character and deeds of charity. The old seat of Kalorama still remains intact, although the capital city in its onward march is fast approaching its gates. In the south-west corner of the grounds, on the banks of a little rivulet shaded by fine old forest trees, stands the ruinous brick tomb in which her remains, with those of the Senator and the Judge, her brothers, and others of her family repose. Two marble slabs, set into the brickwork on either side of the door, bear these inscriptions:

" *Sacred to the repose of the dead and the meditation of the living.*

JOEL BARLOW.

Patriot, Poet, Statesman, and Philosopher, lies buried in Zarniwica, in Poland, where he died 24th December, 1812, Æt. 58 years and 9 months.

RUTH BALDWIN BARLOW,
His wife, died 29th May, 1818, Æt. 62 years.

ABRAHAM BALDWIN,
Her brother, died a Senator in Congress from Georgia, 4th March, 1807, Æt. 52 years.

'His memory needs no marble;
His country is his monument,
Her Constitution his greatest work.'

GEORGE BOMFORD,
Colonel of the Ordnance of the United States, died 25th March, 1848, Æt. 66 years.

HENRY BALDWIN BOMFORD,
His son, Sept. 9th. 1845.

HENRY BALDWIN,
Associate Justice of the Supreme Court of the United
States, died April 21st, 1844, Æt. 64 years." *

---

* The writer visited Kalorama in February, 1881.   He is informed that the
tomb has since been removed.

CHAPTER X.

PERSONAL.

THE critic, after a careful analysis of the character of Joel Barlow, would probably rank him, first, as philanthropist; second, as statesman; third, as philosopher; and fourth, as poet. His philanthropy crops out in every line of his writings, in every act of his life. His letters to Washington, to the citizens of the United States, to Monroe, while abroad on the French mission, and his Fourth of July oration at Washington, give evidence of broad and liberal statesmanship. His philosophical turn was most apparent in his private letters and intercourse with familiar friends. As a poet he was certainly respectable. His "Hasty-Pudding" would be an addition to any literature, and in all his poems are passages that show the inspiration of the true poet. It is as the pioneer of American poetry, however, that he is worthy of the highest honor. He was not a voluminous writer, the following being, it is believed, a complete list of his published works :

I. "The Prospect of Peace," a political composition, delivered in Yale College at the examination of the candidates for the degree of Bachelor of Arts, July 23, 1778. 12mo, pp. 12. New Haven, 1778.

II. "Elegy on the late Titus Hosmer." 8vo. Hartford, 1780.

III. "A Poem spoken at Yale College," 1781.

IV. Imitation of the Psalms of David, translated by Dr. Isaac Watts, corrected and enlarged by Joel Barlow. To which is added a collection of hymns. The whole applied to the state of the Christian Church and religion in general. 12mo, pp. 384. Index and tables. Glasgow, 1786.

V. "An Oration delivered at the North Church, Hartford, at the meeting of the Connecticut Society of the Cincinnati, July 4, 1787, in commemoration of the Independence of the United States." Quarto, pp. 20. Hartford, 1787.

VI. "The Vision of Columbus," a poem in nine books, 12mo, pp. 264. London, 1787.

VII. "A Letter to the National Convention of France on the defence of the Constitution of 1791, and the extent of the amendment which ought to be made." 8vo, pp. 70. London, 1792.

VIII. "Advice to the Privileged Orders in the several States of Europe. Resulting from the necessity and propriety of a general revolution in the principles of Governments." 12mo, pp. 128 and 88. London, 1792.

IX. "The Conspiracy of Kings, a poem addressed to the inhabitants of Europe from another quarter of the Globe." 4to, pp. 20. London, 1792.

X. Preface and Notes to the fifth edition of Trumbull's "McFingall." London, 1792.

XI. "The Anarchiad," a satirical, political poem written by Barlow, Trumbull, Alsop, Humphreys, and Hopkins; first published in a New Haven newspaper from 1786 to 1793.

XII. "A Letter addressed to the people of Piedmont on the advantages of the French Revolution, and the necessity of adopting its principles in Italy. Translated from the French by the author." 12mo, pp. 45. New York, 1793.

XIII. "Letter from Paris to the citizens of the United States on the subject of the fallacy heretofore pursued by their Government relative to the commercial intercourse with England and France." 8vo, pp. 100. London, 1800.

XIV. "View of the Public Debt, Receipts and Expenditures of the United States." 8vo, pp. 67. London, 1800.

XV. Second Letter to his fellow-citizens of the United States on certain political measures proposed to their consideration. 8vo, pp. 40. New York, 1801.

XVI. "The Columbiad," a poem. 4to, pp. 470. Portrait and ten splendid steel plates. Philadelphia, 1807. The same with an index. Royal 8vo. London, 1809.

XVII. Letter to Henry Gregoire, Count of Capri and Member of the Institute of France, in reply to his letter on the "Columbiad." 8vo, pp. 14. Washington, 1802.

XVIII. "The Hasty-Pudding," a poem in three cantos, written in Chambèry, in Savoy, January, 1793. 8vo, pp. 22.

XIX. The excellency of the British Constitution, etc., consisting of certain extracts from the writings of Joel Barlow. 8vo, pp. 8. London (no date).

XX. "Ruins of Empire," translated from the French of Volney.

XXI. Proposition for a National Academy.*

" In private life," says one of his contemporaries, " Mr. Barlow was highly esteemed for his amiable temperament and many social excellences. His manners were generally grave and dignified, and he possessed but little facility for general conversation : but with his intimate friends he was easy and familiar, and upon topics which deeply interested him he conversed with much animation." Another writer thus refers to his domestic relations :

" The affection of Mr. Barlow for his lovely wife was unusually strong, and on her part it was fully reciprocated. She cheerfully in early life cast in her lot with his ' for better or for worse '—and sometimes the *worse,* so far as their pecuniary prospects were concerned, seemed to be in the ascendant. In their darkest days—

---

* Dates as given do not in all cases refer to the first edition.

and some of them were very dark—Barlow ever found light and encouragement at home in the smiles, sympathy, and counsel of his prudent, faithful wife. No matter how black and portentous the cloud that brooded over them might be, she always contrived to give it a silver lining, and his subsequent success in life he always attributed more to her influence over him than to anything else.'' The above was written without knowledge of the letters to his wife which have been spread, many of them, before the reader. In point of fact the mutual love, trust, and confidence between the happily mated pair has not been strongly enough stated. "Never did two souls love as we have loved," the husband wrote at forty-five; indeed, the fervor and devotion seen in their letters has not been equalled since those of Abelard and Heloise, and amid all the intrigue and gallantry of the society in which a large part of their married life was spent, not a doubt or a suspicion of one another's constancy is apparent. They had a pretty custom of observing every anniversary of their wedding day; and the husband further commemorated it by anniversary verses. Four only of these little tributes have been preserved, but they will serve to show the character of the rest. The first was written at Chambèry, Jan. 26, 1793, and is as follows:

> "Blest Hymen, hail that memorable day
> Whose twelfth return my constant bosom warms,
> Whose morning rose with promised pleasure gay,
> Whose faithful evening gave me Delia's charms—
> Those charms that still, with ever new delight,
> Assuage and feed the flames of young desire,
> Whose magic powers can temper and unite
> The husband's friendship with the lover's fire.
>
> "Say, gentle god, if e'er thy torch before
> Illum'ed the altar for so pure a pair?
> If e'er approached thy consecrated bower
> A swain so grateful, so divine a fair?
>
> "Love, the delusive Power who often flies
> Submissive souls that yield to thy decree,

Charmed with our lasting flame, approves the ties,
    Folds his white wings, and shares his throne with thee.

" United Sovereigns ! hear my fervent prayer,
    Extend through life your undivided sway,
In love and union bless your suppliant pair
    With many a sweet return of this delightful day."

Another was inscribed, "To my wife, on the anniversary of our wedding, 26th January, 1800."

" If nineteen years of marriage ties
    Can make me love so strong,
Pray tell how high the flame will rise
    When nourished twice as long.

" For nourishment, like what you give,
    So sweet, so wholesome too,
Will bid the torch forever live,
    And live alone for you."

In 1801 :

" My foolish rhymes on wedding days
    I thought would make you vain,
Or Love would sicken of his lays
    And ask them back again.

" But little prospect now appears
    That aught our souls can sever,
Since after Hymen's twenty years
    I love you more than ever."

For 1802 :

" If seven long years of laboring life
Old Jacob served to gain a wife,
She doubtless must have been the best,
The rarest beauty of the East—
For sure the sire of Jews had strove
To have his pennyworth even in love.
But thrice seven suns have passed the line
Since I have laboring been for mine,
And I'm expert at bargains too—
A Yankee blade, though not a Jew—
Which proves, unless I judge amiss,
My wife is thrice as good as his.
One thing I *certainly* can tell,
I always love her thrice as well."

However dignified and severe the poet may have appeared to strangers, there was a rich fund of humor and satire in his composition. Many passages in his letters might be cited in proof of this. The following is one of his epigrams, found among his papers:

> " The ruffian of England with equal remorse
> Cuts the head from his king and the tail from his horse;
> The Frenchman, more polished, lets nature prevail,
> Lets the king wear his head and the horse wear his tail."

On another occasion, while returning from England, Mrs. Barlow and Fulton being at Paris, he imagines the following poetical dialogue " between Wife and Toot."

> *Wife.*—Ah, where's my dear Hubby, whom Fate, in its malice,
> Snatched away long ago.
> *Toot.*—   Now, I'll bet he's at Calais.
> *Wife.*—I'll bet he's not, though. But, Tooty, my dear,
> Suppose him at Calais, when think he'll be here?
> *Toot.*—Be here! let us count. This is Thursday you say,
> His passport and baggage will take the whole day;
> Then other vexations fall in by the hundred—
> Surrounded, examined, palavered, and plundered.
> But he'll set off to-morrow, and then, I divine,
> We shall have him next Sunday between us to dine;
> For he'll whirl along rapidly through the relays,
> Cheek by'jowl with Machere, and in Parker's post-chaise.
> *Wife.*—All that's but a fancy. I'll bet what you dare
> He's not here on Sunday, nor is he now there.
> *Toot.*—I'll hold you ten guineas, and sixpence to boot.
> *Wife.*—Done.
> *Toot.*—   Done, here's my hand for't.
> *Hub.*—   I'll go halves with Toot.

Unlike some great men, he was punctilious in small things. Neatness of apparel, attention to the amenities of life he insisted upon. Withal, he was a sturdy Republican, with a deep hatred for everything tending to degrade the man, and especially for the acquisition of great estates with the consequent creation of a horde of flunkeys and dependents. His interest in the industrial progress of his country was very great; new varieties of seeds, improved agricultural implements, new methods of farming, improved breeds of sheep and cattle, the newest machines in manufacturing, were topics that engaged much of his thought. In one of his first letters to Mrs. Madison he sends a root of the sugar beet, then unknown in this country. He was interested, with other gentlemen in Redding, in a mill for the kiln-drying of corn for export to the West Indies. He aided his brother, Aaron Barlow, in building a foundry in Weston, and he was interested with Alexander Wolcott in a large manufactory of woollen, and perhaps cotton, goods in Middletown, improved machinery for which he secured while abroad. He was also engaged with the latter gentleman in the importation of merino sheep into America.

But no description, however skilfully done, can give the reader so vivid an idea of his character as does a letter written by him to his wife while he was absent in Algiers, in mortal danger from the plague, and which was to be delivered her only in case of his death.

It is a unique production in its way; some of its expressions, coming from a youthful Benedict, might be deemed extravagant, but after fifteen years of married life were creditable to both husband and wife. The following is the letter:

ALGIERS, *8th July*, 1796.

To MRS. BARLOW IN PARIS :

"*My dearest Life, and only Love:*—I run no risk of alarming your extreme sensibility by writing this letter, since it is not my intention that it shall come into your hands unless and until, through some other channel, you shall have been informed of the event which it anticipates as possible. For our happy union to be dissolved by death, is indeed at every moment possible; but at this time there is an uncommon degree of danger that you may lose a life which I know you value more than you do your own. I say I *know* this, because I have long been taught, from our perfect sympathy of affection, to

judge your heart by mine ; and I can say solemnly and
truly, as far as I know myself, that I have no other value
for my own life than as a means of continuing a conjugal
union with the best of women—the wife of my soul—my
first, my last, my only love.

"I have told you in my current letters that the plague
is raging with considerable violence in this place. I
must tell you in this, if it should be your fortune to see
it, that a pressing duty of humanity requires me to expose
myself more than other considerations would justify, in
endeavoring to save as many of our unhappy citizens as
possible from falling a sacrifice, and to embark them at
this cruel moment for their country.

"Though they are dying very fast, yet it is possible
my exertions may be the means of saving a number who
otherwise would perish. If this should be the case, and
I should fall instead of *them*, my tender, generous friend
must not upbraid my memory by ever *thinking* I did too
much. But she cannot help it—I know she cannot.
Yet, my dearest love, give me leave, since I must anticipate your affliction, to lay before you some reflections,
which would occur to you at *last*, but which ought to
strike your mind at *first*, to mingle with and assuage
your first emotions of grief.

"You cannot judge, at your distance, of the risk I am
taking, nor of the necessity of taking it ; and I am convinced that, were you in my place, you would do more
than I shall do ; for your kind, intrepid spirit has more
courage than mine, and always had.

"Another consideration : many of these persons have
wives at home as well as I, from whom they have been
much longer separated, under more affecting circumstances,—having been held in a merciless and despond-
ing slavery. If their wives love them as mine does me
(a thing I cannot believe, but have no right to deny)
ask these lately disconsolate, and now joyous, families
whether I have done too much ?

"Since I write this as if it were the last poor demon-
stration of my affection to my lovely friend, I have much
to say; and it is with difficulty that I can steal an hour
from the fatigue of business to devote to the grateful,
painful task. But tell me (you cannot tell me), where
shall I begin? where shall I end? how shall I put an
eternal period to a correspondence which has given me
so much comfort? with what expression of regret shall
I take leave of my happiness? with what words of tenderness, of gratitude, of counsel, of consolation, shall I
pay you for what I am robbing you of,—the husband
whom you cherish, the friend who is all your own?

"But I am giving vent to more weakness than I intended. This, my dear, is a letter of *business*, not of love,
and I wonder I cannot enter upon it, and keep to my
subject.

"Enclosed is my last will, made in conformity to the
one I left in the hands of Dr. Hopkins of Hartford, as
you may remember. The greater part of our property
now lying in Paris, I thought proper to renew this instrument, that you might enter immediately upon the settlement of your affairs, without waiting to send to America
for the other paper.

"You will likewise find enclosed a schedule of our property, debts, and demands, with explanations, as nearly
just as I can make it from memory in the absence of my
papers. If the French Republic is consolidated and her
funds rise to par, or near it, as I believe they will do
soon after the war, the effects noted in this schedule may
amount to a capital of about $120,000, besides paying my
debts;—which sum, vested in the American funds, or
mortgages equally solid, would produce something more
than $7000 a year perpetual income.

"If the French should fund their debt anew at one half
its nominal value (which is possible), so that the part of
your property now vested in those funds should diminish
in proportion, still, taking the whole together, it will not

make a difference of more than one third; and the annual income may still be near $5000. Events unforeseen by me may, however, reduce it considerably lower. But whatever the value may be of what I leave, it is bequeathed simply and wholly to you.

" Perhaps some of my relations may think it strange that I have not mentioned them in this final disposition of my effects, especially if they should prove to be as considerable as I hope they may. But, my dearest love, I will tell you my reasons, and I hope you will approve them. For if I can excuse myself to *you* in a point in which your generous delicacy would be more likely to question the propriety of my conduct than in most others, I am sure my arguments will be convincing to those whose objections may arise from their interest.

" *First.* In a view of justice and equity, whatever we possess at this moment is a joint property between ourselves, and ought to remain to the survivor. When you gave me your blessed self you know I was destitute of every other possession, as of every other enjoyment. I was rich only in the fund of your affectionate economy, and the sweet consolation of your society. In our various struggles and disappointments, while trying to obtain a moderate competency for the quiet enjoyment of what we used to call the remainder of our lives, I have often been rendered happy by misfortunes; for the heaviest we have met with were turned into blessings by the opportunities they gave me to discover new virtues in you, who taught me how to bear them.

" I have often told you since the year 1791, the period of our deepest difficulties (and even during that period), that I had never been so easy and contented before. And I have certainly been happier in you during the. latter years of our union than I was in the former years;—not that I have loved you more ardently, or more exclusively, for that was impossible; but I have loved you *better;* my heart has been more full of your excellence, and less agitated with objects of ambition, which used to devour me too much.

" I recall these things to your mind to convince you of my full belief, that the acquisition of the competency which we seem at last to have secured is owing more to your energy than my own; I mean the energy of your virtues, which gave me consolation, and even happiness, under circumstances wherein, if I had been alone, or with a partner no better than myself, I should have sunk.

" These fruits of our joint exertions you expected to enjoy *with me;* else I know you would not have wished for them. But if by my death you are to be deprived of the greater part of the comfort you expected, it would surely be unjust and cruel to deprive you of the remainder, or any portion of it, by giving even a part of this property to others. It is yours in the truest sense in which property can be considered ; and I should have no right, if I were disposed, to take it from you.

" *Secondly.* Of *my* relations, I have some thirty or forty, nephews and nieces and their children, the greater part of whom I have never seen, and from whom I have had no news for seven or eight years ; among them there may be some necessitous ones who would be proper objects of particular legacies, yet it would be impossible for me at this moment to know which they are. It was my intention, and still is, if I live to go to America, to make discriminations among them according to their wants, and to give them such relief as might be in my power, without waiting to do it by legacy. Now, my lovely wife, if this task, and the means of performing it, should devolve on you, I need not recommend it; our *joint* liberality would have been less extensive, and less grateful to the receivers, than *yours* will be alone.

" *Your own* relations in the same degrees of affinity are few in number. I hope I need not tell you that in my affections I know no difference between yours and mine. I include them all in the same recommendation, without any other distinction than what may arise from their wants and your ability to do them good.

"If Colonel B—— and his wife (or either of them being left by the other) should be in a situation otherwise than comfortable, I wish my generous friend to remedy it so far as may be in her power. We may have had more powerful friends than they, but never any more sincere. *He* has the most frank and loyal spirit in the world; and *she* is possessed of many amiable and almost heroic virtues.

"Mary ——, poor girl! you know her worth, her virtues, and her talents; and I am sure you will not fail to keep yourself informed of her circumstances. She has friends, or at least *had* them, more able than you will be to yield her assistance in case of need. But they may forsake her for reasons which, to your enlightened and benevolent mind, would rather be an additional inducement to contribute to her happiness.

"Excuse me, my dearest life, for my being so particular on a subject which, considering to whom it is addressed, may appear superfluous; but I do it rather to show that I agree with you in these sentiments, than to pretend that they originate on my part. With this view I must pursue them a little farther.

"One of the principal gratifications in which I intended, and still intend to indulge myself, if I should live to enjoy with you the means of doing it, is to succor the unfortunate of every description as far as possible,—to encourage merit where I find it,—and try to create it where it does not exist. This has long been a favorite project with me; but having been always destitute of the means of carrying it into effect to any considerable degree, I have not conversed with you upon it as much as I wish I had. Though I can say nothing that will be new to you on the pleasure of employing one's attention and resources in this way, yet some useful hints might be given on the means of multiplying good actions from small resources; for I would not confine my pleasure to the simple duties of *charity,* in the beggar's sense of the word.

"*First.* Much may be done by advising with poor persons,—contriving for them,—and pointing out the objects on which they can employ their own industry.

"*Secondly.* Many persons and families, in a crisis of difficulty, might be extricated, and set up in the world, by little loans of money, for which they might give good security, and refund within a year; and the same fund might then go to relieve a second, and a third; and thus a dozen families might be set on the independent footing of their own industry, in the course of a dozen years, by the help of fifty dollars, and the owner lose nothing but the interest. Some judgment would be necessary in these operations, as well as care and attention, in finding out the proper objects. How many of these are to be found in prisons,—thrown in and confined for years, for small debts, which their industry and their liberty would enable them to discharge in a short time!

"Imprisonment for debt still exists as a stain upon our country, as most others. France indeed has set us the example of abolishing it; but I am apprehensive she will relapse from this, as I see she is inclined to do from many other good things which she began in her magnanimous struggle for the renovation of society.

"*Thirdly.* With your benevolence, your character, and connections, you may put in motion a much greater fund of charity than you will yourself possess. It is by searching out the objects of distress, or misfortune, and recommending them to their wealthy neighbors in such a manner as to excite their attention. I have often remarked to you (I forget whether you agree with me in it or not) that there is more goodness at the bottom of the human heart than the world will generally allow. Men are as often hindered from doing a generous thing by an *indolence,* either of thought or action, as by a selfish principle.

If they knew what the action was, when and where it was to be done, and how to do it, their obstacles would be overcome. In this manner one may bring the resources of others into contribution, and with such a grace as to obtain the thanks both of the givers and receivers.

"*Fourthly.* The *example* of one beneficent person, like yourself, in a neighborhood or a town, would go a great way. It would doubtless be imitated by others, extend far, and benefit thousands whom you might never hear of.

" I certainly hope to escape from this place, and return to your beloved arms. No man has stronger inducements to wish to live than I have. I have no quarrel with the world; it has used me as well as could be expected. I have valuable friends in every country where I have put my foot, not excepting this abominable sink of wickedness, pestilence, and folly,—the city of Algiers. I have a pretty extensive and dear-bought knowledge of mankind; a most valuable collection of books; a pure and undivided taste for domestic tranquillity; the social intercourse of friends; study; and the exercise of charity. I have a moderate but sufficient income; perfect health ; an unimpaired constitution ; and to give the relish to all enjoyments, and smooth away the asperities that might arise from unforeseen calamities, I have the wife that my youth chose, and my advancing age has cherished,—the pattern of excellence,—the example of every virtue,— from whom all my joys have risen, in whom all my hopes are centred.

" I will use every precaution for my safety, as well for your sake as mine. But if you should see me no more, my dearest friend, you will not forget I loved you. As you have valued my love, and as you believe this letter is written with an intention to promote your happiness at a time when it will be forever out of my power to contribute to it in any other way, I beg you will kindly receive the last advice I can give you, with which I am going to close our endearing intercourse. . . . Submitting with patience to a destiny that is unavoidable, let your tenderness for me soon cease to agitate that lovely bosom ; banish it to the house of darkness and dust with the object that can no longer be benefited by it, and transfer your affections to some worthy person who shall supply my place in the relation I have borne to you. It is for the living, not the dead, to be rendered happy by the sweetness of your temper, the purity of your heart, your exalted sentiments, your cultivated spirit, your undivided love. Happy man of your choice! should he know and prize the treasure of such a wife! O treat her tenderly, my dear sir ; she is used to nothing but kindness, unbounded love and confidence. She is all that any reasonable man can desire. She is more than I have merited, or perhaps than you can merit. My re-signing her to your charge, though but the result of un-controllable necessity, is done with a degree of cheer-fulness,—a cheerfulness inspired by the hope that her happiness will be the object of your care, and the long continued fruit of your affection.

" Farewell, my wife ; and though I am not used to subscribe my letters addressed to you, your familiarity with my writing having always rendered it unnecessary, yet it seems proper that the last characters which this hand shall trace for your perusal should compose the name of your most faithful, most affectionate, and most grateful husband."

JOEL BARLOW.

Here ends our record of the life of one who was a poet, philosopher, patriot, and martyr. Singularly enough, we believe the present volume to be the only work of a histori-cal character in which the talents and public services of Joel Barlow have received recognition. In the many and bulky volumes devoted to American history he is almost entirely ignored.

To this statement there is, however, one exception.

On page 399 of Vol. II. of McMaster's " History of the People of the United States," we find this passage :

" This Barlow is memorable as the only one of our countrymen who has been guilty of the folly of attempting to produce an American epic poem. But a better title to immortality is the infamous part he bore in enticing innocent Frenchmen to buy and settle the lands of the Scioto Company on the Ohio. Towards America Barlow felt the same contempt which any man who admires poetry must feel toward the scribbler who defiled the English language by writing the ' Columbiad ' ; and, when he heard that John Adams was chosen President he poured out his thoughts on the position in a letter to Abraham Baldwin, a brother-in-law and a Member of Congress. The letter abounded in obscure passages, but the one selected by the prosecutors of Lyon contained an expression of surprise that the answer of the House to the President's speech of April 5, 1797, had not been an order to send him to a madhouse."

In his account of the founding of Gallipolis and the wrongs of the French emigrants Mr. McMaster is equally violent and unjust. To Barlow's biographer these attacks did not seem worthy of notice, since their bitterness and evident animus destroyed their effect. They are inserted here as curious instances of the survival in our day of the campaign literature of 1799–1800, and in proof of the proposition advanced in our preface, that it is simply impossible for the historian of Federal proclivities and environment to do justice to the great leaders of Republicanism in America.

INDEX.